DAVID LOADES

THE FIGHTING TUDORS

❖

The National Archives

First published in 2009 by

The National Archives
Kew, Richmond
Surrey, TW9 4DU, UK

www.nationalarchives.gov.uk

The National Archives brings together
the Public Record Office,
Historical Manuscripts Commission,
Office of Public Sector Information
and Her Majesty's Stationery Office.

A catalogue card for this book is available
from the British Library.

ISBN 978 1 905615 52 0

JACKET ILLUSTRATIONS:
top Meeting at the Field of Cloth of Gold,
by Friedrich Bouterwerk, 1845,
after Hans Holbein the Elder
(AKG-images / Erich Lessing);
bottom Elizabeth I, the Armada Portrait,
c. 1588, attributed to George Gower
(© The Gallery Collection/Corbis)

DESIGN BY Ken Wilson | point 918

PRINTED IN MALTA BY Gutenberg

CONTENTS

❖

PREFACE

ONE ASPECT of the Tudor achievement has been little remarked
upon: the Tudors converted the governing elite from a military and
clerical base to a civilian and secular one. Medieval kings were (or had
to pretend to be) soldiers, and they governed largely through nobles
who shared the same culture. By the end of Elizabeth's reign, England
was run by lawyers and civil servants. Not only was the military culture
purely ornamental, but the lineage-based concept of honour which it
had supported was obsolete as well. The rise of the gentleman and of
the secular administrator at the expense of the prelate and the noble has
been well recorded, but the role of warfare in bringing this about has
not. The aim of this study is to examine the way in which each of the
Tudors in turn made use of conflict, not only in the service of their
own image, but to detach the arts of fighting from the government of
the country. The result was both a political and social revolution.

INTRODUCTION

❖

THE FACE OF
KINGSHIP

OF THE 118 YEARS during which the Tudors reigned over England, 1485–1603, approximately 28 were spent officially at war. In addition to this there were various undeclared conflicts, such as that in France in 1562–3, perpetual simmering unrest in Ireland, and endemic raiding and counter raiding along the border with Scotland. This study is about these conflicts and their interplay with the images of successive Tudor monarchs; in examining these themes, the changing role of the monarch within the political framework is revealed, from the prudent Henry VII to the warring Elizabeth I, who civilized the government of her country.

In all major conflicts the Crown was a party, although in the case of the border raids it exercised no direct control. Renaissance monarchy was highly personal, so the profile of the king or queen in wartime was directly relevant to the effectiveness of his or her civilian government. The Tudors also faced an additional challenge in that they inherited an aristocracy that was accustomed to violence—indeed it actively embraced violence in its code of honour. Edward IV, the last long-serving monarch before the Tudor dynasty, had circumvented this problem by employing his nobility on their own terms, and casting himself as the 'Lord of lords', a device that mobilized their honour obligation for his own purposes. This, however, was a fragile compromise, and the Tudors set out to replace it with a more robust concept of public service. Henry VIII, under whom the most significant advances were made, did this by magnifying his martial image, hijacking the honour system and using it to create a service mentality that he could use for other purposes. He also quite deliberately patronized an educational philosophy that sought to replace lineage with virtue as the criterion of honour.

Elizabeth, under whom the transformation was completed, deftly turned her gender into a weapon, and became the damsel whom the knight must defend. Unlike her father, her martial imagery was passive, not active, but it was equally significant. She was also able to use the educational changes of Henry's reign to create a new and sophisticated ideal of service, which was essentially civilian and legal in its culture. The consolidation of church and state under the Royal Supremacy turned her into a Godly Prince, to whom obedience was a religious duty, and these two things together relegated the lineage-based theory of honour to the margins of political life. It also made her own lack of a military presence almost irrelevant. In a sense it took a female ruler to replace the *noblesse d'épée* with the *noblesse de robe* in the government of the country, but that indicated a political and social change of revolutionary significance.

This was no less than the civilization of government, which had been for centuries in the hands of men who had seen themselves first and foremost as soldiers. A king who could not lead an army was not a proper king. For example, Edward II and Richard II (who were both deposed) made serious political mistakes, but each also gratuitously weakened himself by failing to acquire the necessary soldierly image. By contrast, Henry IV defeated Owain Glyndwr, and Edward IV won his crown upon the battlefield at Towton.

A king's court was composed of his companions in arms, and his image was that of a warrior. It was by war that his kingdom was created, and by war that it survived — or not.[1] Land holding and the social structure were designed with military priorities in mind. A king divided his realm into great fiefs, each of which was held by a trusted soldier in return for the service of so many knights and men-at-arms. The nobleman then divided his holding into sub-fiefs, each of which was held by a knight who owed his lord military service, along with so many men. Feudalism was never as tidy as this model might suggest, but the principle was generally accepted.[2]

It is important to remember that when Henry VII, the first Tudor king, succeeded to the throne in 1485, the creation of his image was only partly in his own hands. The voice of history was, as he was only too well aware, predominantly the voice of the church. In its chronicles it did its best to soften the harsh realism of feudal government, and over the course of time produced two alternative images of kingship: the lawgiver and the saint. The latter might be no more than an excuse for military failure, as was the case with St Edmund, but it might also be applied to those whose patronage of pious causes was more conspicuous than their successes in battle, as was the case with Edward, known as 'the Confessor'.[3] The lawgiver, on the other hand, was a king whose civilian exploits were thought to have eclipsed his military ones. Alfred and Henry II come into that category, although each was also a successful soldier. By offering these alternative models of kingship, ecclesiastical chroniclers were able to play down the warrior image in the service of more civilized ideals.

There was also an element arising from the monarchs' personal morality and the degree of religious fervour which he exhibited. Ecclesiastical writers had denigrated some monarchs—for example William II, Stephen, John and Edward II—either because they had pursued policies hostile to the church or because of their alleged moral irregularities. On the other hand, kings such as Henry II and Edward I were praised in spite of the promiscuity of the one and the brutality of the other, because they were generous patrons and founders of religious houses.[4]

Apart from the church, the other constituency that played a part in shaping the royal image was the nobility. Here the priorities were different. A nobleman might be pious, but he was not particularly interested in his sovereign as a benefactor of the church. From his point of view a good king was one who listened to the advice of his noblemen, and who shared their essentially military- and lineage-orientated culture.[5] Edward III and Henry V, for example, were approved of because they led their nobles in successful wars, enhancing both their self-esteem and their profit margins.[6] Noble attitudes are rather hard to assess because these men, unlike the churchmen, did not on the whole leave written accounts of their opinions. Such letters as survive, however, particularly from the fifteenth century, derive mainly from that class, and some of the chroniclers who were in their service reflect their attitudes. The opinions of the gentlemen who were also their dependants, naturally tend in the same direction, and formed such public opinion as there was in the period.[7]

The contemporary royal image, however, was not mainly constructed out of written words. Even when they were composed in the vernacular, chronicles were intended for a very limited circulation—sometimes no further than the monastery in which they were written.

Perceptions were visual, and often ephemeral. The ceremonial of the court—the king's *maiestas*—was valuable for the impression that it made upon visitors, and particularly foreign ambassadors, but was not visible to the outside world.[8] The king was seen as he moved from residence to residence, and when he went on pilgrimage, but was most conspicuous on progress. The point of these royal peregrinations had originally been to bring royal justice to the provinces, and to demonstrate that the king's control over his agents was real. He travelled in state with a large entourage, and encouraged loyal displays by 'showing himself' to the people. The queen did the same thing on a smaller scale, particularly if she had a baby son to display, only her 'showings' were more likely to have a specifically pious purpose. Other presentations were more occasional. Coronations were conspicuously visual events, as were royal weddings (usually) and christenings, which were attended by large and appreciative crowds.[9] None of this was particularly martial, except that large escorts of armed retainers were usual when the king went on his travels, but campaigns of course were different. If the king had to take the field against the Welsh or the Scots, or against rebels within his own kingdom, he usually made sure that he moved with the full panoply of war—with 'banners displayed' in the contemporary idiom. Henry V made his return from France in 1420 the subject of a suitably martial parade.

Most of his subjects saw their king very seldom, if at all, and his image depended upon rumour and report. So it was part of the duty of those gentlemen who occasionally attended the court to make favourable report of their royal masters. This naturally meant that the king was to some extent a political construct, and could be seriously damaged by aristocratic disaffection, even of a temporary nature. In order to maintain a soldierly *persona*, the king had to be frequently at war, and constantly victorious—a heavy demand that hardly any king (apart from the short-lived Henry V) could meet. Royal funeral effigies were often clad in armour, and trophies displayed at their tombs, but there was more than a suspicion of role playing about all this. A king in armour at the head of his troops was not necessarily good news for his own security, and there must have been many occasions when an image of peace and prosperity was to be preferred. And yet the martial presentation persisted. Perhaps it was intended to frighten off potential opponents, perhaps it was just deeply engrained in the warrior culture of the nobility. For better or worse, the king was the leader of those who fought.

The warrior image was reinforced from the twelfth century onwards by the rise of tournaments—mock battles designed originally to keep the king's nobles in military practice, and later to project the chivalric values that all aristocrats were supposed to embrace. These were given a legal form by Richard I in 1194.[10] Early tournaments were not the tidy jousts of later practice, but pitched battles involving a number of knights on each side, and ranging across considerable stretches of country. There were few rules, and casualties were often heavy. In short, they were very much like real warfare. The church did not like them, but numerous papal bans were ineffective.[11] It was the invention of chivalry and the rise of the joust that eventually reduced these primitive melees to something like order. Tournaments were an important factor in the creation of the monarch's image, because they were public displays, and the disguisings that accompanied fifteenth-century jousts were as useful in showing off the royal taste and wealth as they were for the prowess of the participants.

Jousts, and chivalry in general, served not only to keep warriors in practice, but also to keep women in their place. Women were not supposed to be soldiers. In the twelfth century, for example, the Empress Matilda found this to her cost. Although in many respects more able than her rival Stephen, she could not be a warrior and was necessarily dependent upon others to lead her armies for her, so Stephen, who was a competent soldier (if little else) emerged victorious—in the short term at least.[12]

Women were supposed to be the objects of chivalric attention, not its practitioners. As the inspirers of heroic deeds they presided at tournaments, and distributed their favours to their chosen knights. Courtly love was a way of rescuing ladies from the undisciplined attentions of courtiers whose manners were those of the military camp, but it also removed them from the real world of politics.[13] So it came about that women could transmit titles of nobility, but not hold them. They could inherit fiefs, but not perform the military service attached to them. A woman was always under tutelage; to her father until she married, and then to her husband. Queens were particularly vulnerable in this respect, being in such conspicuous positions. They were supposed to enhance the royal honour of their husbands, by bearing his children, interceding for the victims of his wrath, and patronizing charitable causes. There was a feminine side to kingship, and that was the queen's job.[14] One of the ways in which she did this was by presiding at her lord's war games, providing an alternative focus for loyalty that did not challenge him, and by distributing favours on his behalf.

The supportive role of the queen, and the exemplary nature of her piety, was usually taken more or less for granted. Of the early consorts, only Eleanor of Aquitaine, who brought Henry II a very substantial inheritance, emerges as anything of a power in her own right. Later queens were usually trophies of foreign policy, and that was particularly true of Catherine de Valois, the bride of Henry V, who brought her back 'with triumph' from France in 1420. Catherine would probably have received no more attention than her predecessors if it had not been for her second marriage, to Owain ap Tudor, and her resulting place in the subsequent Tudor genealogy.[15] Margaret of Anjou, the consort of Henry VI, was also the by-product of foreign policy, although in her case it was a failed policy that left her in the political firing line from the early days of her marriage. Although she bore Henry a son in 1453, circumstances soon thrust her into the less traditional roles of politician and quasi-warrior, which brought down upon her the disapprobation of the image-makers. Edward IV's marriage to Elizabeth Woodville divided opinion, but that affected the King's image rather than hers. On the one hand were those who regarded it as a romantic, if quixotic, gesture, and consequently saw the Queen as some kind of chivalric heroine. On the other hand were those (including many of the Council) who saw it as a catastrophic political blunder, and blamed the factionalism that affected Edward's later days on her malign influence.[16] Objectively they were probably both wrong, but she was of (relatively) humble birth, and she did have a lot of relations for whom the King was expected to provide. Anne Neville, briefly the Queen of Richard III, is known mainly as the tragic victim of Shakespeare's plays. She predeceased Richard in March 1485, and it was subsequently rumoured that he had poisoned her in order to marry his niece, Elizabeth of York.

As long as the king was effective and plausible in a military role, this division of labour—the kingly warrior, the queenly supporter—worked well enough. However, when the king was not effective, as was the case with Henry VI after 1453, the queen faced a real dilemma. Margaret was forced to assume a role of political leadership that suited her personally but was quite alien to her proper role. Her image became that of an unnatural termagant—the image that Shakespeare perpetuated in his cycle of history plays. In a sense Henry VI changed places with his wife, assuming the image of a pious and gentle victim, and it was this unnatural reversal that did so much to undermine the Lancastrian cause, leading to Henry's deposition in 1460.[17]

❖

In order to understand the Tudors better, it is necessary to look back to the fourteenth century. The reign of Edward III, who in 1327 restored confidence in the monarchy after the catastrophic reign of his father, is remarkable not only for the King's military successes, which made England a major power in Europe, but also for the opportunity this created for the rise of the English soldier. Before Edward's reign a few men had joined the mercenary companies that were by then fighting in the perpetual wars of France and Germany, but soldiering was not a common trade and the English had made no distinctive impact upon it.[18] During the prolonged battle for the French throne that was the Hundred Years War, however, the English bowmen made a unique place for themselves in military mythology when they won a spectacular victory at Crécy in 1346, and repeated the achievement at Poitiers 10 years later.[19] As Petrarch observed, the English were always capable of springing a surprise. The longbow was cheap, relatively easy to manufacture, and once the 'great bow' had been introduced, extremely effective. In the pastoral and upland communities, particularly those bordering on Wales, most youths were brought up to handle the longbow from their childhood, and the conversion of such natural archers into soldiers was relatively easy once the opportunity had been perceived.[20] This represented a challenge to the old order: by the time of Crécy the heavily armed cavalryman had been the key to military success for almost 200 years. Both his mount and his equipment were expensive, and the typical horseman was a knight or seigneur whose superiority on the battlefield reflected his social superiority and chivalric mystique. However, confronted with massed archers armed with the formidable longbow, this cavalry proved vulnerable and tactically inept. Both Edward III and his son, the Black Prince, were somewhat equivocal about the victory at Crécy, trying to claim as much credit as possible for the noble commanders, because otherwise it was a victory for peasants over their natural superiors, and the implications of that were uncomfortable to contemplate.

The experience of victory, and the plunder that often went with it, was alluring to ordinary men, and many of them, when their retained service was over, joined one or other of the 'free companies' that afflicted France in the later 1350s. It was a good time to be a mercenary, and the English archer found himself much in demand.[21] However, after the treaty of Brétigny in 1360 the political tide turned against the English. By the time of the truce of Bruges in 1375 only Calais and the coastal strip of Gascony were left of the extensive English conquests. Edward III died in 1377. He had reigned for 50 years and left two distinct images: for about half his reign he was a triumphantly successful soldier, but towards the end of his life he fell (reputedly) into dotage, thus compromising his image, which became that of a doddering old man under the influence of his mistress, Alice Perrers.[22]

Henry V (r.1413–22) was an immensely significant military monarch: the chivalric hero who conquered France. His position was open to challenge because of the circumstances of his father's accession —or as some would put it, usurpation—and Henry was anxious to 'busy giddy minds with foreign wars'.[23] He became legendary for his remarkable victory against the odds at Agincourt, where the English bowman, in eclipse since 1360, was once again the hero of the hour. The triumph proved to be short lived, because although Henry secured the recovery of most of the territories surrendered at Bruges, and indeed his own claim to the French succession by the treaty of Troyes in 1420, he died in 1422.

Another reason for Henry's fame was that alone, it would appear, amongst the medieval kings of England, he understood the significance of sea power.[24] While England was linked, first to Normandy and then to the Angevin Empire, the Channel was principally an obstacle to communications. Successive kings did own a few sailing ships, which they used as transports, but a 'Navy Royal', when it was needed, was raised by calling upon the ship service of port towns such as the Cinq Ports, or by mobilizing the resources of the feudal nobility.[25] Although Edward III won sea battles at Sluys in 1340 and against the Castilians 10 years later, he neither saw himself, nor was seen by others, as a sea king. Henry V was different, partly because throughout his father's reign an unofficial war had been waged at sea through the medium of large-scale piracy, to which all governments turned a blind eye. In 1403 a force of French and Bretons attacked and burned Plymouth. Dartmouth and Bristol retaliated, taking 80 prizes.[26] None of these operations owed anything directly to royal initiative, and insofar as there was an image of the sea fighter, it belonged to the individual captain or nobleman who commanded on the spot. The system of mobilization was similarly decentralized, and although such limited operations were frequent, the impression given is one of constant confusion.[27] By 1410 the Prince of Wales, as he then was, decided to get a grip on this situation. When the young Henry took control of the Council that year, his father owned two ships. By the time that Henry V succeeded to the throne in 1413 that number had increased to six, and to thirty-seven four years later. This increase was directly related to the resumption of open hostilities with France in 1415, and reflects a deliberate determination to secure control of the sea. In this he was completely successful; so successful that his fleet never had to fight a sea battle. For about five years Henry was a sea king, and his great flagship the *Grace Dieu* displaced 1,000 tons, making her the largest ship ever to have been constructed in an English yard.[28]

Unfortunately this extension of the royal image was of short duration. Henry died in 1422, but even before that he had begun to dispose of his navy. Wooden-built cogs and balingers deteriorated fast, whether in service or not, and since they were not fundamentally different in design from merchant ships, could be readily sold off.[29] Over the next 20 years or so the fleet went into terminal decline. The *Grace Dieu* was laid up, and destroyed by fire in 1439. In 1450 the office of Clerk (or Keeper) of the Ships was discontinued. English piracy, effectively suppressed by Henry V, revived strongly. Insofar as there were 'sea lords' in the middle of the fifteenth century, they were noblemen such as the Earl of Warwick, who waged his own battles in the Channel and whose private fleet played a significant part in the overthrowing of Henry VI in 1461.

Henry VI (r.1422–61, 1470–71) proved unable to sustain his father's military momentum, losing Normandy in 1450 and Gascony in 1453, bringing an ignominious end to Henry V's triumph. Nothing could have been further from the image of a victorious king than the sick and deranged Henry of 1453. Years later Henry VII decided that there was only one way to make a virtue out of such meek submissiveness, and sought to have his putative kinsman canonized. In that he was unsuccessful, but popular opinion had got in ahead of him, attributing various miracles to the royal remains.[30] By contrast, and in spite of the brevity of his success, the warrior image of Henry V, and of the English bowman, lived on. It may have been some consolation during the protracted domestic struggles known as the Wars of the Roses, to remember that there had been a time when the English had put the fear of God into the French, instead of into each other. It was in this sad humiliation that the 'Agincourt myth' celebrating Henry V was born. Henry was the last of the great warrior kings of medieval England, and it was, significantly, to his image that Henry VIII in due course wished to appeal.

Edward IV (r.1461–70, 1471–83) was a fine specimen of late medieval kingship. Tall and handsome, he had no difficulty in fulfilling the warrior stereotype, and he had just enough military success to give it credibility. Although he did not joust himself, he made sure that enough of these courtly festivities were provided to keep abreast of the latest Burgundian fashions. By the mid-fifteenth century the joust *à outrance* (with sharpened weapons) was becoming rare, and as far as we know all Edward's tournaments were jousts *à plaisance*, and fought with rebated (that is blunted) weapons.[31] Edward IV reinvented Edward III's Order of the Garter, in imitation of the Golden Fleece, and built a magnificent new chapel for the knights at Windsor. He was also a great practitioner of the arts of courtly love. His own marriage to Elizabeth Woodville had a suitable air of romantic mystery about it, and he ran a series of mistresses, culminating in Elizabeth (Jane) Shore just a few months before his death. Edward IV adhered closely to the chivalric image that tradition and culture had by then created for a king. Even his piety was conventional, so that the monastic chronicles, such as that of Croyland, commented favourably upon his exploits and censured his failings only briefly.[32]

Edward also conformed to the royal stereotype in other ways. He conferred extensive powers on a handful of trusted nobles, in much the same way as his Angevin forebears had done. His brother Richard, Duke of Gloucester exercised a vice-regal power in the north, and William, Lord Hastings ruled much of the Midlands in the same fashion.[33] This worked well as long as Edward himself was alive and in control, but as a system of government its limitations were ruthlessly exposed when the same nobles fell out among themselves after his death. His heir was bastardized and deposed within weeks of his accession by that same brother whom Edward had trusted so highly. The Yorkist affinity was split right down the middle. Edward IV had endeavoured to lead his nobility from the front, setting an example as the *preux chevalier,* and had thereby enhanced rather than diminished their power. Like their French or Burgundian counterparts, English nobles were immensely proud of their ancestry, and the (often mythical) deeds of their forebears,[34] so that the distinctiveness of those who were armigerous was carefully preserved.

Although there were still some baronies of remote provenance, by the reign of Edward IV it was accepted that only the king could turn a gentleman into a knight, or a knight into a nobleman.[35] At the same time, it was alleged that only God could create a gentleman, and it was not until 1483 that this perception was undermined by the creation of the College of Heralds. Thereafter the College was responsible for conferring coats of arms, and in theory deciding who had, or had not, the appropriate ancestry. In practice this soon became a transparent fiction, and the College sold new coats of arms for cash, but although this undermined the military pretensions of the gentry, it was to take over a century of remorseless royal pressure to eliminate the centuries-old perception that a gentleman's first service to his lord was in arms.[36] At the end of the fifteenth century military imagery was still an aristocratic preserve, and it was shared by the whole nobility of lineage, from the king down to the humblest gentleman. In England it was the only distinction that they did share, because no one was exempt from taxation, and only the nobility by title enjoyed the privilege of trial by their peers. Every other offender, irrespective of rank, was tried by the ordinary courts, and a gentleman, or even a knight, was subjected to the due process of the assizes, along with ordinary folk. So the image of the *nobilitas minor* did not depend upon any kind of privileged status, but only upon his coat of arms—in other words upon his presumed military function.

Edward IV was not exactly a sea king, but during the crisis of 1469–70 he did manage to seize control of Warwick's fleet, before his catastrophic miscalculation of the situation enforced his precipitate flight to the Low Countries in October 1470.[37] After his return and his decisive victory at Tewkesbury, Edward continued to deploy warships, but they were still not his own, and the importance of creating a fleet was scarcely learned. In 1474 he was forced to pay 11,000 crowns (about £4,000) in compensation to Basque merchants whose ships had been plundered by English pirates, and in 1476, when Brittany was crucial to his foreign policy, the similar claims of Breton merchants amounted to over 50,000 crowns.[38] It was not until 1480 that he revived the office of Clerk of the King's Ships, and even then Thomas Rogers was given custody of only half a dozen small ships. Instead the image that Edward created for himself was that of the sun in splendour, which was more appropriate to the magnificent disguisings of the Anglo-Burgundian tournament than to any military prowess, and the image that the chroniclers recorded was that of the strenuous knight, potent both in bed and on the field of battle.

It was Edward's good fortune that his eldest daughter was to marry Henry VII. Because although Henry derived his claim to the throne (such as it was) from the other side of the dynastic blanket, he was quite shrewd enough to see that Elizabeth of York was a political asset, and the prompt birth of Prince Arthur an even greater one. It was not in his interest to diminish his father-in-law, let alone to deny that he had been a rightful king. Instead he was able to concentrate upon destroying the reputation of Richard III, who had intruded himself between them.

The image of Richard III (r.1483–5) was created almost entirely by his enemies, and needs to be viewed with caution.[39] We do not know how he would have chosen to represent himself. His claim was dressed in legal clothes that required him to represent Edward V—his nephew and the elder of the 'Princes in the Tower'—as base born, but few really believed that and the reason why so many supported him in his coup was because of his impressive track record, both in government and on the field of battle. He was, reliable evidence suggests, not in any way deformed, and if he suffered from anything it was paranoia rather than a lust for power. Yet he has entered historical mythology as 'crook-backed Dick', the evil schemer and archetypical wicked uncle. This, of course, made him an easy act to follow, and it was made easier by the fact that much of it originated during Richard's own reign. The personal tragedies that he suffered in the deaths of his wife in 1485, and only son during 1484 were unsympathetically represented as Divine judgements, and his position was so weakened that several of the nobles who mobilized ostensibly in his support in 1485 changed sides upon the field of battle, thus ensuring his defeat and death.[40] Evidence suggests that, given the opportunity, Richard would have been just as competent as his brother; instead of which he emerged with one of the worst images of any English monarch.

❖

Although some kings, and even some queens, chose their own images and fostered them with care, most had them imposed by circumstances. Richard II's most enduring image is probably that of the refined young man represented on the Wilton diptych, but it was also influenced by the dubious privilege of being represented on the stage by William Shakespeare. Henry IV made what use he could of traditional royal iconography, but was trapped in a permanent insecurity by the circumstances of his accession.

One last factor should be taken into account: sometimes shifting historical perspectives, and the agendas of chroniclers, brought about changes. John, for instance, who was reviled as a tyrant, and notable chiefly for having been forced to concede the Great Charter, was lauded by John Foxe in the sixteenth century for having attempted to stand up to an overweening papacy.[41] Foxe chose rather to denounce the monastic chroniclers who had promoted his evil reputation. Edward I wished to be known as the arbiter of Scotland, but is nowadays (and for many years) better commemorated as the man who subdued the Welsh. His son Edward II, by contrast, has one of the least satisfactory of memorials—a failed soldier, run by favourites and eventually deposed by his wife's lovers—what could be more ignominious? Only in his case no John Foxe came to the rescue.

CHAPTER ONE

HENRY VII

❖

THE
PRUDENT
KING

HENRY TUDOR (r.1485–1509) was no warrior hero, and is best known for his more cautious characteristics, but his battles to seat himself on the English throne and to vanquish other contenders ensured that his military reputation was established from the outset. He then worked hard to build up the national defences, ensure loyalty to the crown and improve his financial reserves.

Henry had virtually no hereditary claim to the English throne. In fact he would have had a better claim to the throne of France through his maternal grandmother, if it had not been for the Salic law which limited the succession to males. His mother, Margaret Beaufort, was the granddaughter of John Beaufort, Marquis of Dorset and Somerset, who was the son of John of Gaunt (in turn the son of Edward III) by his third marriage to Katherine Swynford. This would have consti-tuted a claim of a sort, if it had not been for the fact that John had been born before his parents were married. Although their subsequent union had legitimated him for most practical purposes, it had been specifically decreed by Henry IV that this did not extend to any claim to the Crown.[1] Margaret had been married in 1455 to Edmund Tudor, Earl of Richmond, who was the son of Owain ap Tudor and Catherine de Valois, the widow of Henry V. Edmund had died, probably at Carmarthen, in November 1456, leaving his wife pregnant, and their son Henry was born on 27 January 1457.[2]

For the first three or four years of his life young Henry of Richmond lived, more or less peacefully, with his mother at Pembroke Castle, under the notional protection of his uncle Jasper Tudor, Earl of Pembroke. However, Jasper was loyal to the House of Lancaster, and in September 1461 Pembroke Castle surrendered to William, Lord Herbert, a follower of Edward IV, the Yorkist King. At the age of about five, Henry was therefore parted from his mother and brought up as William's ward, destined to marry with his daughter, Maud, and given an education suitable to the boy's intended status in life. Not very much is known about this process, except that his tutors thought well of his ability. He was, presumably, well read in the stories of chivalry that were part of every nobleman's upbringing, but of instruction in the martial arts we hear nothing, and it seems reasonably certain that in spite of his rank, he was not brought up to be a warrior. However the fortunes of politics relieved Lord Herbert of his ward when Henry VI was briefly restored in 1471, and it seems to have been in the company of his uncle that Henry first visited London as a 14-year-old during that readeption.[3] When Edward recovered the throne after a few months, Jasper brought his young charge back to Wales, and it was from Tenby on 2 June 1471 that they sailed to take refuge in Brittany—an exile that was to last another 14 years.

Although the Tudors' landfall in the duchy was largely an accident, they were hospitably received by Duke Francis II, and Henry's education appears to have been completed over the next few years.[4] Again we know next to nothing about the process. There is no suggestion that he showed any particular proficiency in arms, and nothing in his later life suggests that he was either skilled or interested in military matters. What he did acquire was a very thorough grasp of the French language, and a keen awareness of the fragile state of Franco-Breton relations.

At the beginning of 1483 Henry's prospects in England appeared to be minimal. Edward IV was only 40 years old, and had two healthy sons to succeed him. Then quite suddenly the political landscape changed. On 9 April 1483 Edward died, and on 25 June his eldest son, Edward V, was declared a bastard and deposed by his uncle, Richard of Glouces-ter.[5] This action split the Yorkist party irretrievably, and when the Duke of Buckingham rose in rebellion against Richard in the autumn of that year, it was in the name of Henry of Richmond that he acted. On 10 October 1483, and fortified with 10,000 crowns from the Duke of Brittany, Henry set off to join him. He had in theory 5,000 men and 15 ships, but only his own ship got anywhere near the south coast, and that was met with such a frosty reception that he backed off with nothing achieved. Buckingham was captured and beheaded soon after.[6]

What this escapade did, however, was to establish Henry of Richmond as a serious pretender, and not only did the remains of the Lancastrian party begin to rally to him, but disaffected Yorkists also sought him out. In December he entered into an agreement with the widowed Queen Elizabeth to marry Edward's eldest daughter. Meanwhile Richard III began to make serious efforts to extract his 'traitor' from Brittany, and by offering support against the looming threat of France entered into a conspiracy with certain Breton nobles to spring Henry from under the nose of their own Duke.[7] Warned in time, Henry escaped into France, and when Francis discovered what had happened, he was highly indignant with his own men, allowing the rest of the English exiles to withdraw, in spite of the fact that this involved surrendering significant political leverage. No sooner had he arrived at Montargis, where the French court was then situated, than Henry received a significant boost to his pretensions, because John de Vere, the Earl of Oxford, who had been imprisoned for 10 years at Hammes, escaped and joined him, with a retinue of experienced Lancastrian soldiers.[8] Henry began to style himself the rightful King of England, and his following grew in size and strength. Some came over from England to join him, including Thomas Grey, the Marquis of Dorset (Edward IV's stepson); others were already in Paris, perhaps as students at the university, and these included Richard Fox, who was to prove one of Henry's most loyal servants. Henry began to petition Charles VIII of France for aid in the 'recovery of his kingdom', and the latter scented a real advantage against his old rival. Richard III became seriously apprehensive, and the death, first of his heir in April 1484 and then of the Queen a year later, cast a further blight over his regime.

By the summer of 1485 Henry's image was that of a king in exile. Meanwhile the bards of his remote homeland were building an image of their own. The idea that one day, somehow, a king of Welsh lineage would rule again in Britain had never completely died out, and now that day seemed to be impending. The fact that Henry Tudor was no more than one quarter Welsh by blood was not allowed to impede the growth of the myth of the *mab darogan*, or son of prophecy—the one who was to come to rule in splendour.[9] The origin of this prophecy was traced (of course) to Merlin, but its resurrection in 1485 probably owed more to hard-headed gentlemen of Lancastrian sympathies than it did to ancient memories. When Charles VIII's regent, Anne of

Beaujeu, decided in the early summer of that year to offer somewhat grudging and limited backing to the English pretender, the seeds of further support were already sown and growing in Wales. We do not know what the French thought of Henry's prospects, and their actual support melted away before the venture began because circumstances in Brittany had changed. In the event all that Anne did was allow him to recruit mercenaries with borrowed money. Nevertheless the Lancastrian exiles had proved strong enough to break the siege of Hammes in the Calais Pale, and that was an ominous portent for Richard's military control.[10] When Henry finally left the Seine on 1 August 1485, he had with him no more than 2,000 French troops, so that the outcome of his venture was bound to depend upon his reception—and it was no accident that he headed for Milford Haven, at the western extremity of Wales.

In spite of the extent to which fortune had favoured him over the previous 18 months, it must have seemed to any objective observer that Henry had embarked on a desperate gamble. He might have been the Son of Prophecy, and persuaded many Englishmen to overlook the bar on his hereditary claim to the throne, but he was a man of 28, with no military training or experience, pitted against one of the most successful and resourceful generals that England could show. As he advanced through Wales men rallied to him, including the formidable Rhys ap Thomas, but still when he emerged into the English lowlands he had no more than about 5,000 men, less than half the size of the force that Richard could muster against him. Such odds, however, were deceptive. Not only were his own deficiencies as a commander made good by the presence of John de Vere and Rhys ap Thomas, but the King's host was riven with dissension. So worried was Richard about the reliability of Thomas Stanley that he held his son, Lord Strange, as a hostage, and Stanley was not his only anxiety.

The battle that followed at Bosworth Field on 22 August 1485 was variously and confusingly reported,[11] and it is not clear that Thomas Stanley played any part on either side, but what does seem clear is that Richard's rash courage undid him, and that a significant part of his army did not engage. What is also clear is that the King was defeated and killed in the battle. The story of his crown being discovered under a hawthorn bush and presented to the victor is probably apocryphal— but it symbolizes the outcome clearly enough. Henry was present on

the field throughout the battle, and that must have required considerable courage, but no one at the time or since has commented upon
either his generalship or his skill in arms. The victory upon which the
fate of England depended was won by a novice who had neither the
standing nor the image of a soldier.[12] Nevertheless it was the victory
that mattered. At a time when many still believed that the will of God
was revealed on the battlefield, His verdict could not have been clearer.
Judgement had stalked Richard since the deposition (and probably
murder) of his brother's lawful heir. His son had died, his wife had died,
his nobles had deserted him and finally he had also been killed. It did
not require much effort or ingenuity on Henry's part to represent himself as the agent of the Divine purpose. His title was promptly endorsed
by parliament, by the papacy and by his neighbouring rulers, but it
rested in practice on the judgement of battle.

BOSWORTH FIELD

THIS BATTAILE *was fought at Bosworth in Leycestershire, the xxii day of
August, the whole conflict endured little above two houres. King Richard
as the fame went, might have scaped and gotten sauveguard by flyyng: For when
they which were next about his person sawe and perceyved at the first ioyning
of the battaile the Souldiers faintly and nothyng courageously to set on their
enemies, and not only that, but also that some withdrewe themselves privily out
of the prease and departed. They began to suspect fraude, and to smell treason,
and not only exhorted but determinately advised him to save himself by flight:
and when the losse of the battaile was imminent and apparent, they brought to
him a swift and light horse to convey him away. He which was not ignoraunt of
the grudge and ill will that the common people bare towarde him, castyng away
all hope of fortunate successe and happy chaunce to come, aunswered (as men
say) that on that day he would make and ende of all battayles, or else there
finishe his life…When the Erle [of Richmond] had thus obteyned victory, and
slaine his mortal enemy, he kneeled down & rendred to almighty God his
heartie thanks…*

[*Grafton's Chronicle, or History of England*, edition 1809, Vol II, p.155]

Henry represented himself as the lawful King. He was studiously vague
about how that came about, but was careful to date his accession from
the day before the battle.[13] Logically he should have denounced
Edward IV as well as Richard III as a usurper, but since he was about to

marry Edward's daughter and heir—Elizabeth of York—that would not have been sensible. In fact Edward's title was glossed over by the vilification of Richard, and when the marriage took place in January 1486, the event was hailed as the reconciliation of the rivalries of York and Lancaster. What was not of course said was that if Edward IV had been a lawful ruler, then Elizabeth had a claim superior to that of her husband. There was no Salic law in England—but she had not led a victorious army in battle.[14]

It was not to be expected that Henry's seizure of the crown would go unopposed, and in April 1486 the Stafford brothers and Viscount Lovel rose in rebellion. The uprising was quickly put down, and Lovel fled to Flanders, where he was joined early in 1487 by the Earl of Lincoln.[15] The latter was John de la Pole, the eldest son of Elizabeth, Edward IV's sister by the Duke of Suffolk. He was also Richard III's designated heir. At first the Earl of Lincoln made no sign of wishing to exploit his opportunity, but in 1487 he endorsed the pretensions of Lambert Simnel, a youth who was being set up to impersonate Edward, Earl of Warwick, the son of George, Duke of Clarence and Edward IV's nephew. With the support of Margaret of Burgundy, and accompanied by Lincoln and Lovel, Simnel proceeded to Ireland, where he was recognized as King Edward VI, in spite of the fact that the real Earl of Warwick was held in the Tower by Henry.[16]

Warwick had in fact a superior hereditary claim to Richard, which the latter had dismissed on a technicality, and in terms of Yorkist legitimacy was second only to Elizabeth. So, given the custom of preferring males to females, Simnel constituted a real threat. He landed at Furness in Lancashire on 4 June 1487, accompanied by a more impressive force than that which Henry had led out of Wales. However, he attracted few supporters, and the King was better served than Richard had been. When the two armies met at Stoke on 16 June, Henry won a hard fought but decisive victory. Simnel was captured and the Earl of Lincoln died on the field. Because the King had commanded in person, although no commentary speaks of his prowess, his image as a victorious war leader was significantly enhanced.[17] Stoke was in fact the last battle at which Henry was to appear, but thereafter his reputation was established.

Meanwhile the King had taken other steps, which probably appear more important in retrospect than they did at the time. With his crown he had inherited three or four small ships, and a clerk named Thomas Rogers, whom he reappointed on the 14 November 1485.[18] He quickly decided to add to this very minimal naval establishment. There is no record of the decision, but at some point before 15 April 1487 he instructed Sir Richard Guildford and Sir Reginald Bray to build for him two large warships. The first of these was to be of 600 tons, and 'like unto the Colombe of France'. It was built at Reding Creek, near Smalhithe on the river Rother, and was subsequently named the *Regent*.[19] Where Sir Reginald Bray built his ship is not known, but it was probably at Portsmouth or Southampton, where she is known to have been fitting out in August 1488. She was called the *Sovereign*. Only piecemeal accounts survive, so we do not know how much either of these ships cost, but we do know that they were carracks on the Portuguese model, and were built for fighting. The *Regent* (which was the larger) was equipped with no fewer than 225 serpentines, which were light guns of forged iron intended for anti-personnel use. The *Sovereign* carried 141 serpentines, mounted in the castles and the waist of the ship.[20] There is no suggestion of a gun deck, or of gun-ports, and serpentines would have been useless against the structure of an enemy ship, but these were the first, as well as the largest custom-built warships to be laid down in England.

The reason why Henry decided to deploy scarce resources in this fashion when he had no intention of fighting a foreign war is a matter for speculation, especially as he gave away one of his smaller ships at the same time. It seems that his intention was to make a power statement, and to register his presence on the international scene as a 'sea king'. He clearly did not intend to create a standing navy, but by placing his smaller ships in the care of trusted officials, and by paying bounties to shipbuilders to encourage them to build larger vessels that would then be available for royal service, he did bring into existence what might be called a 'shadow navy'.[21] Moreover he was able to do this without calling upon the resources of his nobility as his predecessors had done, with somewhat unsatisfactory results.

Henry's naval policy was never stated, and can only be reconstructed from what he did. A few years later, in 1495, he caused a dock to be excavated at Portsmouth, and partly fortified the harbour, thus creating an embryonic naval base. Docks had been created before, and were usually temporary holes in the foreshore where particular ships could be careened and repaired, but this one was intended to be permanent, and cost £193.0s.6d.[22] In 1497 he also built two more small warships, the *Sweepstake* and the *Mary Fortune*. These cost £120 and £110 respectively, and their armament is unknown. They carried powder and shot, but that may well have been for handguns. As Michael Oppenheim observed, 'the royal navy, although small, was large enough for any purely fighting work it was likely to be called upon to perform under a king who had no projects of territorial aggrandisement'.[23] The problem of piracy was not seriously addressed, and indeed seems to have been less during this reign than either before or after, perhaps because there was no war to act as a 'cover'. Henry hired other ships as he needed them. When a force was sent to Brittany under Lord Willoughby in 1490 it was carried and escorted by 18 ships, but of these only three belonged to the King.[24] As a display of naval force this was quite sufficient to secure control of the Channel.

In October 1492 Henry made the gesture that was expected of an English king by leading an invasion force into France and laying siege to Boulogne. He led this force in person, but there is no suggestion that the French commanders quailed in consequence. Henry's image as a warrior was strictly for domestic consumption, and he responded quickly and positively to suggestions for peace. By the treaty of Étaples in early November he accepted a French indemnity of 745,000 crowns, and abandoned Brittany to its fate.[25] This subsidy more than covered the costs of mounting the expedition, and if it dented his reputation, he clearly did not care. Although the union of France and Brittany spelled potential maritime danger to England, such a threat did not emerge during this reign, when French ambitions were focused mainly on northern Italy, and first Charles VIII and then Louis XII were anxious to maintain good relations with their northern neighbour.

AN INVASION OF FRANCE, 1492

WHILE THE COMMISSIONERS *were thus consulting on the Marches of France, the king of England... was arrived at Calice, where he prepared all things necessary for such a journey. And from thence he removed in four battailes near to the town of Boleyn, and there pitched his tents before the towne, in a place mete and convenient, and determined to give a great assault to the towne. In which fortress was such a garrison of warlike Souldiers, that valiauntly defended the towne, and the same so replenished with artillery and municions, that the losse of the Englishemen assaulting the towne, should be greater dammage to the realme of England than the conquering and gainyng of the same should be gaine or profit. Howbeit the king dayly shot, rased and defaced the walles of the said towne: But when every man was prest and redie to geve the assault, a sodaine rumor rose in the armie, that a peace was by the commissioners taken and concluded, which brute, as it was pleasaunt and delectable to the Frenche men, so it was to the English nation bitter sowre and dolorous, because they were prest and redye at all tymes to set on theyr enemyes...*

[*Grafton's Chronicle*, pp.189-90]

Only towards Scotland did Henry display a more bellicose face, and that was in response to the welcome that James IV extended to Perkin Warbeck in 1495. Warbeck was another pretender, claiming in this case to be Richard, the younger son of Edward IV, who had supposedly escaped the clutches of Richard III, and whose hand had been strengthened by the recognition that had been accorded him by the Duchess Margaret, the aunt of the real prince.[26] In September 1496 James translated his welcome into action, and crossed the border with a small force. It quickly transpired that Warbeck had no support in northern England, and the Scottish incursion turned into a destructive border raid of the sort that was only too familiar. The Earl of Surrey was sent north to respond in kind, and Henry decided to use the occasion as an excuse to get some money out of parliament. The main result of this tactic was the Cornish rebellion of 1497, which suggests that the men of the far southwest were very far from being overawed by the King's reputation as a warrior. It was not so much Henry as his local agents who allowed the rebels to advance as far as Blackheath in a somewhat unrealistic display of strength.[27] Loyal forces under Lord Daubeny defeated them completely on 22 June, and the King, with his domestic image intact, was able to turn his attention back to the north. In spite of the disappointment of the previous year, James had not given up on Warbeck, and was locked into a tit-for-tat with the Earl of Surrey. In July 1497 he invaded again, this time with a larger force, and laid siege to Norham Castle. Surrey duly responded, supported by the Earl of Westmorland and half a dozen border barons, but his campaign is shrouded in mystery. Estimates of the size of his force vary from 8,000 to 20,000, and his objective is no clearer.[28] He seems to have operated exclusively within a dozen miles of Berwick, destroying villages and taking minor forts. He raised the siege of Norham, but seems to have been under instructions not to bring James to battle. Another version declares that James would only fight on his own terms. In the event nothing decisive happened.

What did happen, however, was that Henry deployed his fleet to the north. The *Regent* sailed for Berwick towards the end of July 1497, and was followed by the *Sweepstake* and the *Mary Fortune*, both brand new at the time. Another 10 hired ships completed the squadron.[29] This force was commanded by Lord Willoughby, and its main purpose seems to have been to intimidate and to convince the Scots of the seriousness of the King's intentions. It also carried powder and other munitions, and possibly some reinforcements, but in spite of its formidable nature it appears to have done no actual fighting. At one point the Admiral was in the Firth of Forth, which was well to the north of where the action was taking place. It may be that this was part of the intimidation, or perhaps some additional operation was planned and then countermanded.

There is an element of shadow-boxing about the whole campaign, because even before the fleet was sent north, Henry had issued instructions to Richard Fox, the Bishop of Durham, to commence peace negotiations.[30] These were ongoing throughout, and probably explain the reluctance of either side to engage in a decisive battle—or one that could have been decisive. It would have been typical of Henry to use a warlike image in order to secure a satisfactory peace—it was, after all, what he had done in France five years earlier. In this case his real objective was to secure the ejection of Warbeck from Scotland, and since that was achieved early in July, while the warlike posturings were still in their early stages, it is not surprising that the campaigning on both sides became little more than an exchange of gestures. A truce was signed at Ayton in September 1497, which became a full peace in January 1502, when James agreed to marry Henry's daughter Margaret as soon as she was old enough—an event that came about in August 1503, when the bride was a few weeks short of her 13th birthday.[31] Warbeck turned up in Cornwall early in September 1497, at the same time as the truce, but presented only a shadow of a threat. Captured by rapidly mobilized local forces, he confessed his true name and origin, and was consigned to the Tower. He was to be executed two years later, along with the

Earl of Warwick, for a shadowy and possibly fictitious attempt to escape from custody.

Henry was now as secure as he was ever likely to be. With Warbeck and Warwick both dead, and Lambert Simnel labouring as a scullion in the royal kitchens, there remained only Edmund, Earl of Suffolk to pose any kind of a threat. Edmund was the younger brother of John de la Pole, and on his brother's death had become the leading Yorkist pretender. He had taken refuge in the Low Countries, where he lived under the protection of the Dowager Duchess Margaret until her death in 1503, and there he remained until he fell victim to Anglo-Habsburg diplomacy. Known as the 'White Rose', he was returned to England by the terms of the treaty of Windsor between Henry and the Archduke Philip in 1506, and was to be lodged in the Tower until Henry VIII found it expedient to have him executed in 1513.[32]

By 1499 Henry VII had three sons—the eldest of whom, Arthur, was committed in marriage to Catherine, the daughter of Ferdinand and Isabella of Spain—and was on amicable (or at least peaceful) terms with all his immediate neighbours. '[H]is crown', wrote Pedro de Ayala, 'is ... undisputed and his government strong in all respects'. This did not make him loved, the judicious diplomat continued, because he would have liked to employ more foreigners in his service, and govern in the French fashion, but he could not do so because of the 'diabolical' jealousy of the English. 'He likes to be much spoken of, and to be highly appreciated by the whole world', but he lacked the stature for such adulation. The Queen, he added sardonically, is beloved because she is powerless.[33] In spite of such weaknesses, the image that Henry presented to the world was one of power and success. But it depended little on any warlike qualities, and it seems that the King was radically estranged from the military culture that still prevailed among his nobility. Although they were essential ornaments of his court, and he liked to keep them where his eye could be on them, he trusted relatively few nobles, and those of ancient lineage least of all. Apart from his uncle Jasper (who died in 1495) and his kinsman by marriage, Thomas Howard, Earl of Surrey, he preferred to be served by lesser men, who were more obviously dependent upon himself, such as Sir Reginald Bray, or by clergy like John Morton and Richard Fox.[34]

One of the problems with establishing an image for Henry is that so much of it is retrospective. Most notably the miserly, avaricious king, who alienated his subjects by his greed, was created largely by the imagination of Francis Bacon in the early seventeenth century. To his contemporaries he certainly became acquisitive in later life, and this was condemned as a fault, but it was not the dominant characteristic that shaped their memories of his reign. The historian Polydore Vergil was both contemporary and retrospective. He came to England in 1506, and knew Henry personally, but wrote the relevant part of the *Anglica Historia* after the King's death, probably in 1512–13.[35] His account is by far the fullest and most specific in its description of the first Tudor monarch, but it does not necessarily express how he was perceived by his own subjects, particularly in the earlier part of his reign, of which Vergil had no first hand knowledge. He did, however, give us the only detailed description of Henry's physical appearance, characteristics and attitudes in later life:

THE CHARACTER OF HENRY VII

HIS FIGURE WAS SLIM *but well built and strong; in height he was above the average. Extremely attractive in appearance, his face was cheer- ful, especially when he was speaking. He had small blue eyes: a few poor black stained teeth. His hair was thin and white; his complexion sallow. He was distinguished, wise, and prudent in character; and his spirit was so brave and resolute, that never, even in moments of greatest danger did it desert him... He was most successful in war, although by nature he preferred peace to war. Above all he cherished justice... But in his later days all these virtues were obscured by avarice, from which he suffered, as we have shown above. This is surely a bad enough vice in a private individual, whom it constantly tortures: but in a monarch it is, indeed, the worst form of all vices, since it hurts everyone...*

[Polydore Vergil, *Anglica Historia*, ed. D. Hay, 1950, pp. 142–6.]

Henry had, we are told, a most excellent and retentive memory, more typical of a scholar than of a governor. He was shrewd and prudent in his conduct of public affairs 'so that no one dared to get the better of him through deceit and guile'. He was fortunate in war, although averse to waging it, and there is no suggestion that he ever sought glory on the field of battle.[36] Above all, he was a lover of justice, and that meant the exemplary punishment of violent crime, so that his subjects were able to conduct their lives in peace 'far removed from the assaults and evil doings of scoundrels'; assaults that he implied had ruined more than enough fortunes over the previous 30 years. He was, Vergil admitted, avaricious towards the end, but that did not prevent him from keeping splendid hospitality. 'He well knew how to maintain his royal majesty and all that appertains to kingship at every time and in every place'. This last observation can be supported from his household accounts, and is not at all consistent with the image of the miser.

It may well be that this somewhat schizophrenic picture of Henry's attitude to money was derived from two different aspects of his public policy. On the one hand he was well aware of the need to maintain the *maiestas* of his court, both to impress his own subjects and to compete with his neighbours. He employed gunners and maintained a lavish artillery train (which he had no intention of using) for the same purpose.[37] On the other hand he used fiscal penalties to keep order among the aristocracy, particularly bonds and recognisances for obedience and good behaviour. There were a great many ways in which a subject could become indebted to the Crown, and the intense scrutiny and rigorous enforcement of these payments by the King's Council Learned in the Law after 1500 certainly caused widespread resentment.[38]

One of the commonest, and politically the most important of these offences, related to illicit retaining. It had for centuries been the normal practice of nobles and major gentlemen to maintain large households of servants, who could be transformed into armed retinues at short notice. These retinues then formed the core of the companies with which their leaders served the king in war. The armies that had fought in the Hundred Years War had largely been raised by this means. When the country began to descend into civil strife after 1450, such bands were continued, partly for protection and partly to carry out their lords' coercive or aggressive intentions. Many lords also sought to extend their influence by issuing contracts of retainer to tenants and others outside their normal households in a system known as 'bastard feudalism'.[39] A lord acting in this manner would then have three levels of power. At the centre would be his normal household servants; and then beyond them his contracted retainers, who sometimes had written terms, but very often not; and then beyond them again his 'well willers', who were inclined to support him when the circumstances required but were not bound to do so. In the case of a major lord, such as the Earl of Warwick, these connections could form a substantial private army, the political influence of which might be significant.

Successive kings had been well aware of the danger that this practice posed to domestic peace, and as long before as 1399 retaining outside the household had been forbidden by statute. However, the fact that this statute had been repeated in 1401, 1406, 1411, 1429 and 1468 indicates that it was not effective.[40] The main problem had been that Henry IV, Henry VI and Edward IV each had an interest in applying it selectively, to curb the activities of potential opponents without restricting those of their supporters. Down to 1453 there had also been the need to recruit armies to fight in France. As the war became increasingly defensive and unsuccessful it became correspondingly difficult to recruit such armies, and the retinues of those lords who were still willing to serve became proportionately more important. So the statutes were selectively applied, which made them worse than useless. It is hard to see Edward IV using any such restraint against his brother Richard, who was effectively his Vice-Regent in the north. By 1485 the self-image of the lord was still as bound up with the size of his retinue as it was with other aspects of his warlike prowess, and this constituted a serious problem for a king who had no intention of waging war if he could possibly avoid it. So using the dispensing power of the Crown, Henry developed a system of licences. In other words he formalized the existing selective application of the statutes, but he did so very carefully and favoured only those who were prominent in his service. To this system he then gave legal form and substance by an additional statute of liveries in 1504.[41]

This Act, *De Retentionibus Illicitis*, started off by pointing out that 'little or nothing is or hath been done for the punishment' of offenders against the earlier statutes. This time it was going to be different. For every oath, badge or livery issued the penalty was 100*s.* a month, and the same to the party receiving it. A person buying or wearing an unauthorized livery was to be subject to a fine of 40*s.* a day, and imprisonment at the discretion of the King's judges. Informants against offenders were to be rewarded at the King's pleasure, and any contracts issued in breach of the statute were to be null and of no effect.[42] The only parties exempt from these penalties were those licensed under the King's hand or by Privy Seal to do the King service in the wars 'or otherwise at his commandment', and abbots or priors of monasteries who were permitted to issue liveries to their tenants, 'according as it hath been used or accustomed'. The act was to apply from the feast of Pentecost (26 May 1504) for the rest of the King's natural life.

Prosecutions under the act do not seem to have been numerous. A few came before the Council and a few before the Court of King's Bench, but reading between the lines of the accounts suggests that quite a few offenders who stood in danger of prosecution in fact compounded their penalties without undergoing the indignity of standing trial.[43] The Earl of Oxford seems to have been one such. The only significant exception was George Neville, Lord Abergavenny, who was made an example of in 1507. Neville was certainly a major offender, and was fined a mammoth £10,000. Most of this was later remitted, but the signal was clear enough. Any peer with military pretensions had better suppress them, or at any rate not attempt to go in for unlicensed retaining. Force, as far as Henry was concerned, was a state monopoly, and containing these private retinues was a part of his basic duty to preserve the peace of the realm.[44] Written licences were also an effective way of distinguishing legitimate from illegitimate activity. One of the problems during the Civil Wars was that private lords had 'raised their powers', ostensibly in the service of the Crown, and had then employed them for their own purposes of private warfare or coercion. Anyone attempting similar action after 1504 could be challenged to produce his licence, and the challenger could be sure of effective royal support. 'He cherished justice above all things', as Polydore Vergil reported, and his image was that of a stern unbending judge, prudent and wise but not at all charismatic.[45]

Henry VII's foreign policy was that of diplomacy rather than war, because its mainspring was dynastic and domestic security. The only reason why he had signed the treaty of Redon with Brittany in 1489 was to protect Breton independence, and to prevent the consolidation of French naval power in the Channel. This was in England's interests and had nothing to do with the years of exile he had spent in the duchy. Similarly his protracted negotiations with Ferdinand and Isabella were designed to secure the recognition of an ancient royal family, and to seal that recognition with a marriage alliance.[46] The first phase of his foreign policy came to an end with the treaty of Étaples, in which he conceded defeat over the Breton issue, a concession that his friendship with Ferdinand enabled him to make without any fear of dire consequences. The second phase, from 1492 until about 1503, followed on naturally, and was again dictated by his relations with the Spanish King, whose main concern at this time was to check French plans for

expansion into Italy. It was this consideration that brought Henry into
the Holy League in 1496, although no war resulted, or was expected
to. In this phase he was also preoccupied with Scotland, for reasons that
we have seen, and that did lead to war—or at least the nearest thing to a
foreign war that the King was ever to wage—but ended again with peace
and a marriage alliance. By contrast the third phase was discontinuous
because it was shaped by the random factor of death, particularly the
deaths of Queen Elizabeth in August 1503 and Isabella of Castile in
November 1504.[47] Prince Arthur had died soon after his wedding in
1502, and that led indirectly to the death of his mother (in childbirth in
an attempt to strengthen the succession), but did not in itself disrupt
relations with Ferdinand. It was Isabella's death that did that, by setting
the King of Aragon at odds with his son-in-law Philip of Burgundy
over the Castilian succession.[48] Henry had no desire to fall out with the
master of the Low Countries, and entered into an agreement with Philip
in 1506 that effectively ended his special relationship with Ferdinand,
although it did not lead to any breakdown of diplomatic relations.

This phase was also partly shaped by the fact that both Kings were
now widowers, and could deploy themselves on the marriage market.
When Philip died unexpectedly towards the end of 1506 there was
some talk that Henry might marry his widow, Juana, in spite of the fact
that she was the sister of his own daughter-in-law, and of unstable
mind. Although mindful of the political advantages of such a union,
Henry backed off.[49] Perhaps he was concerned over reports of Juana's
obsession with her late husband, or perhaps he did not really want to
remarry, but neither this negotiation nor others that were mooted
came to anything. He did go so far as to obtain a very specific description of the charms of the young Queen of Naples, but took no action
upon it.[50] More promising were the discussions, which did actually
take place, for a marriage between his younger daughter, Mary (who
was 10 in 1506) and the six-year-old Charles, Philip and Juana's elder
son, but they also failed. Ferdinand was more positive, and shelved his
long-running battle with France by marrying Louis XII's niece, Ger-
maine de Foix in 1505. Within a few years this had the effect of bringing Louis, Ferdinand, Maximilian, Charles and the Pope together in
the League of Cambrai, which was directed against the Venetians, but
Henry was not invited to join this unusual consensus. During the last
few years of his reign he was able to enjoy the luxury of being

unaligned. His power was secure, he had a son to succeed him, and each of his neighbours for reasons of their own was cultivating his goodwill. This was a far more satisfactory situation from Henry's point of view than to be locked into an alliance that might at any time turn into a pretext for war.

In 1507, aged 50, Henry was an old man and his health was giving cause for concern. No one would now have expected him to be a warrior, and he was profoundly relieved to have manoeuvred himself into a position where that was no longer necessary. As Polydore Vergil put it, 'leagues and confederacies he had with all Christian princes, his mighty power was dreaded everywhere, not only within his realm but without also'. More recently an historian summed up his achievement: 'He was astute, cautious, prudent and patient. He attempted nothing rash or ill-considered, avoided impetuosity, and generally manifested a well-informed and well-balanced mind'.[51]

But he was not a hero, and his greatest admirer never represented him as a soldier.

In one respect however, Henry did conform to traditional norms. His piety, although probably not deeply felt, and certainly not passionately expressed, was impeccably orthodox. This was partly due to his early need for papal recognition, as well as to a lack of intellectual curiosity. His interest in problem solving was strictly practical, and he was no more concerned with abstruse theological problems than he was with political or administrative innovations. The humanist critique of the ecclesiastical establishment, which was reflected in the education that he provided for his sons, seems to have passed him by completely.[52]

'He was', says Polydore, 'the most ardent supporter of our faith, and daily participated with great piety in religious services. To those whom he considered to be worthy priests he often secretly gave alms so that they should pray for his salvation. He was particularly fond of those Franciscan friars whom they call observants for whom he founded many convents, so that with his help their rule should continually flourish in his kingdom.'

To those Lollards who were still to be found in England he was conventionally hostile. Some 70 people were put on trial for this heresy in the course of his reign, but these were tried in the ecclesiastical courts, and only handed over to the secular authorities if they refused to recant. The penalty for such refusal was death, a penalty that only the lay magistrates could inflict. However, most of these heretics were humble folk, and not made of the stuff of martyrs. Only three are known to have been burned during the reign.[53] The King was not normally involved in any of these proceedings, but he did intervene in the case of one priest who was executed at Canterbury in 1498. The circumstances are not clear but Henry apparently exhorted the victim to recant, which he duly did, and the King 'gained great honour' thereby. It was an empty victory because the priest was relapsed and was burned anyway, but it was noted that 'he died as a Christian', an outcome for which the King got the applause. The story is probably authentic, but there is a natural suspicion that it was 'set up' in order to give Henry the credit for a more proactive orthodoxy than he usually displayed.[54]

His good relations with Rome paid dividends in many ways. He was able to allow expressions of mild anti-clericalism in parliament, particularly over the curtailment of benefit of clergy and rights of sanctuary—with which he was in any case in sympathy—without causing offence in the Curia. His episcopal appointments also seem to have been confirmed without any friction, which was a useful asset given his propensity to employ clergy in senior administrative positions, and to reward them with ecclesiastical preferments.[55] He was also able to allow his mother to influence some appointments, and to use others for diplomatic promotions. No doubt the appointment of papal servants, such as Giovanni de Gigli to Worcester and Adriano de Castello to Hereford, were part of the trade-off that made this possible, and oiled the wheels of Anglo-Papal relations. Henry promoted papal festivals and generally made it his business never to be at cross-purposes with the Holy See in his foreign relations. The three successive Popes with whom he had to deal, Innocent VIII, Alexander VI and Julius II, although very different in character, were all equally concerned to check both French and Spanish aggression in Italy, and for that reason found the habitual neutrality of the King of England an asset that they were anxious to preserve. Three times he was granted those special marks of papal favour, the Cap and Sword and the Golden Rose, and he became so confident that his episcopal nominations would be accepted that he took to granting the temporalities ahead of consecration.[56] He even corresponded at length with each Pope in turn about the desirability of a crusade against the Turks, which was always a 'politically correct' topic, although he never had the slightest intention of taking the cross in person.

Perhaps his attitude to religious foundations was prompted by his own genuine piety, perhaps by the rather more heartfelt piety of his Queen, or perhaps by his desire to secure a good 'press' from the church. He founded houses of Spiritual Franciscans at Canterbury, Newcastle and Southampton, and for the Conventuals at Richmond, Greenwich and Newark, he built the Savoy Hospital in London and the magnificent chapel known by his name at Westminster Abbey.[57] This last was not completed in his lifetime, and the splendid tomb in which he lies side-by-side with Elizabeth dates from 1512–19. Although the poor undoubtedly benefited from his generosity, these benefactions give the impression of having been made with one eye on his image as a 'Godly Prince', and in that respect they undoubtedly paid dividends. Henry had no imagination, and was no more capable of finding original ways to express his religious feelings than he was of innovating in his system of government. The idea that he created a 'new monarchy' is still highly controversial.[58] What he did with great success was to make the old monarchy work effectively, and he did this by prudence, by attention to detail and by a few changes of emphasis. Unlike Edward IV, or his own son, Henry VIII, he created virtually no new peerages outside his own family. Thomas Stanley, Earl of Derby and Edward Courtenay, Earl of Devon, both in October 1485, were the only ones. There were quite a few restorations of those who had forfeited for the Lancastrian cause—Thomas Grey, Marquis of Dorset, Edward Stafford, Duke of Buckingham, Thomas Howard, Earl of Surrey and John de Vere, Earl of Oxford—all within the first few months of the reign. The remainder were his own kindred; his uncle Jasper as Duke of Bedford and his sons Arthur and Henry as Dukes of Cornwall and York. None of these, with the exception of Jasper, were conspicuous in government. Henry preferred to work through the Commissions of the Peace, and took steps to restore their credibility by statute in 1489.[59] Proclamations of intent were to be made at sessions to be held four times a year, and no Justice was to wear the livery of any other Lord, save the King only.

By the middle of his reign he was powerful and effective, but exciting he was not, and never had been. The creation of a positive image for him was therefore no easy task. He built up his power, even in the early years, by being shrewd and careful. Flamboyant gestures were alien to his nature, and although he took steps to ensure that England's defences, both military and naval, were in good order, the victories that he won were all political. It is perhaps not surprising that the avarice of his later years was exaggerated after his death in order to give his glamorous son a flying start. It must be remembered, however, that Henry VIII was what his father had made him, and that the splendid athleticism that made him such a dashing figure in the tiltyard had been acquired under a regime designed by his profoundly non-military father. Perhaps Henry VII was more aware of the military imagery of monarchy than he was willing to acknowledge, or express.

CHAPTER TWO

HENRY VIII

❖

THE
RENAISSANCE
PRINCE

FROM THE AGE OF TEN, Henry VIII (r.1509–47) had been his father's heir, and the sole hope of his dynasty. He had, as we have seen, been most carefully educated, mainly by John Skelton and William Hone, and the Dutch scholar Erasmus was suitably impressed, both when he met him as an eight-year-old child in 1499, and when he corresponded with him seven years later.[1] He was a gifted musician and a competent theologian, but what contemporaries first noticed about him was his magnificent physique. 'His majesty', wrote one observer, 'is the handsomest potentate I ever set eyes on'; 'much handsomer that any sovereign in Christendom', declared another, and with this beauty went a very large and athletic body.[2] As Prince of Wales he had been trained in the martial arts, and although his anxious father had never allowed him to display his skills in public, his yearning to do so was well known. Henry VII had dutifully rather than enthusiastically provided such an entertainment in the summer of 1507. The poet who recorded the event also noted

> Syth our prynce moost comly of stature
> Is desyrous to the moost knightly ure
> Of armes to whiche marcyall aventure
> Is his courage
>
> Notwthstondynge his yonge and tender aege
> He is moost comly of his parsonage
> And as desirous to this ourage
> As prynce may be...[3]

It is therefore not surprising that the new reign was greeted with an upsurge of expectation, which embraced tilts, tournaments and foot combats, as well as plays, dancing and masques. The King, nevertheless, did not immediately leap into the fray. He may have been restrained by his Council, or possibly by Catherine of Aragon, the wife whom he wedded within weeks of his accession, but for the first few months he confined himself to less warlike displays, and to showing off his body in sumptuous robes, in dancing and on the tennis court. It was not until January 1510 that he made his long-awaited debut in the lists, and it may have been significant that by then Catherine was well known to be pregnant.[4] The pregnancy ended in a miscarriage, but once launched, Henry was no longer to be restrained from appearing in public tournaments, and for the next 15 years repeatedly 'exulted in the display of his physical prowess to friend, subjects and visitors from abroad'. It became one of his best-known characteristics.

These tournaments were both more and less than war games. They were less in that they were governed by the strictest rules of engagement, and confined within the lists. Although they might take the form of jousts or of foot combats, the days of sharpened weapons and of free-range battles were past. Challenges were issued and responded to in accordance with established etiquette, and the object was to break lances rather than to unhorse an opponent. There could still be fatalities, but these resulted from accidents rather than from intent.[5] Henry occasionally left his visor up, and endured a number of heavy falls, but his life was never seriously endangered during his active jousting career. Tournaments were more than war games in that they had become by this time carefully structured displays of chivalric virtue, in which the symbolism of the lady's favour assumed increasing importance. They were also occasions for exhibitions of a more theatrical nature. In February 1511, to celebrate the birth of the short-lived Prince Henry, a symbolic challenge was issued by four knights bearing the names of Valiant Desire, Bon Valeur, Joyous Penser and Coeur Loyal—of whom the last was actually the King.[6] The challengers entered the lists in a huge pageant car, made to look like a forest, of green velvet and damask, in the midst of which was a golden castle. The whole pageant was adorned with 'great beasts' of heraldic significance, guarded by wild men or foresters.

When the pageant rested before the Queen, the forenamed

foresters blew their horns, then the device or pageant opened on
all sides, and out issued the foresaid four knights, armed at all
points, every of them [with] a spear in his hand, on horseback...[7]

The tournament shields of all the participants were then presented to
the Queen, and the jousting commenced. Similar spectacles accompanied all the major court tournaments down to the siege of the
Chateau Verte in 1525, which, although not quite Henry's swansong,
marked the end of his regular participation.

These tournaments and the masquings, disguisings and pageantry
that accompanied them, were a regular feature of Henry's magnificence in the early years of his reign, and their impact derived very
largely from the King's personal participation. Courtiers made their
fortunes from their skill in the lists, and the most successful of them all,
Charles Brandon, became Duke of Suffolk and the King's brother-in-
law. Brandon was so a good a jouster that he knew when (and how) to
let the King win without appearing to do so.[8]

In December 1511, Henry VIII joined the Holy League against
Louis XII of France. There was no pressing reason why he should have
done so, except the purely domestic one of wishing to give his bellicose nobles something to do. They had been constrained and frustrated
by Henry VII's policies of peace, and angered by his use of fiscal penalties against them, so there was a good case for allowing them to exercise
their traditional prerogative of serving the King in arms. There was also
the King's desire to emulate Henry V, whose image loomed large in his
mind. This obviously required that he should lead an army to France,
but it also required the command of the seas, and in that respect Henry
was an innovator. He inherited about half a dozen ships from his father,
including the now somewhat elderly *Regent* and *Sovereign*, but these
would not be enough for his purpose, and he decided to build and to
buy, rather than relying upon 'taking up' privately owned vessels.[9]
Within weeks of his accession he had ordered the laying down of two
new warships, and although the *Peter Pomegranate* seems to have been
much like the *Sovereign*, the other, later named the *Mary Rose*, showed
an interesting and original design feature. It was built with a gun deck
carrying (probably) six heavy guns firing through ports cut in the side
of the ship. Ports for loading and unloading were of French origin, and
the Portuguese had used a few big guns on board ships in the Indian

Ocean, but bringing them together in this way was new.[10] It may well have been the King's own idea, because he was deeply interested in both ships and guns and is known to have had a hand in the design of the *Great Galley* a few years later. We do not know where, or by whom, these two ships were built, but it was probably at Portsmouth or Southampton because a warrant survives dated 29 January 1510 authorizing the payment of £2,372 by John Dawtrey, the Receiver of Customs at Southampton to Robert Brygantine, Clerk of the King's Ships, towards the costs of building two such vessels.[11] This would have represented about 40 per cent of the total cost, and if they had been built in the Thames or the Medway the assignment would have been made upon the Port of London.

In 1511 Sir Edward Howard encountered the Scottish rover Andrew Barton, and took his ship, the 120-ton *Lion*, as a prize.[12] It was added to the embryonic Royal Navy, as was the *Mary and John*, rebuilt after a fire, but when Sir Edward was appointed Admiral and issued with his instructions on the 8 April 1512, the King owned no more than eight or nine ships. The remaining nine or ten that made up his fleet on that occasion were 'taken up' in the traditional fashion. Henry, however, was not satisfied. He wanted to be a sea king in a much more active and substantive way than his father, and in the course of 1512 he purchased no fewer than seven ships varying in tonnage from 240 to nearly 1,000, at least three of them from the Genoese. In the same year he also built the *Great Bark* of about 300 tons, and two smaller ships—the *Dragon* and the *Lizard*. Three others were acquired by unknown means, so that by the beginning of the campaigning season in 1513 he had in his own possession about 20 fighting ships, varying in size from 100 tons to 1,000.[13] Howard had his fleet at sea by the end of May 1512, and there were rumours of a great landing in Picardy. However, that was to run far ahead of the game. Howard was intended to secure command of the Channel, without reference to any specific military operation, and did so with some ease because the French fleet, having surrendered the initiative, remained in harbour. For several weeks the English Admiral chased fishing boats, and took what prizes he could from any French merchants who ventured to sally forth. Using his fleet in a free-standing operation of this kind also appears to have been a novelty, although whether the idea was Howard's or the King's is not apparent.

It was not until the middle of August 1512 that anything resembling a naval battle took place. The French fleet was assembling at Brest, and most of the ships were two or three miles from the harbour when the English (whose intelligence was excellent) suddenly appeared to challenge them. The fleets were about equal in size, the French having 22 ships and the English 25, but most of the French made straight for the refuge of Brest, leaving only a handful to sustain the English attack.[14] The result was confusion, as the English seem to have queued up to tackle their opponents, and the only conclusive outcome was the mutual destruction of the *Regent* and the *Cordelière*, which were grappled together when the latter's magazine exploded. The loss of life was appalling, only about 200 of the 1,200 or so men on the two ships escaping.[15]

THE BURNING OF THE *REGENT* AND THE *CORDELIERE*
Wolsey to the Bishop of Worcester, Farnham, 26 August 1512

AND TO ASCERTEYNE *yow of the lamentabyll and sorrowful tydyngs and chance wych hath fortunyd by the see, owr folks, on Tuysday was fortnight, met with 21 gret shyppes of Frawnce, the best with sayle and furnyshyd with artyllery and men that evyr was seyn. And after innumerabyll shotyng of gunnys and long chasyng one another, at the last the Regent most valyently borded the gret caryke of Brest, wherin were 4 lords, 300 gentylmen, 800 solgers and mariners, 400 crossbowmen, 100 guners... with so marvelose nombyr of schot, and other gunys of every sorte. Owr men so valyently acquyt themsylfe that within one ower fight they had utterly vanquished with schot of gonnys and arrows the said caryke, and slayne moste parte of the men within the same. And sodenly as they war yelding themsylf, the caryke was one flamyng fyre, and lyke wyse the Regent within the turning of one hand. She was so ankyrryd and fastyd to the caryke that by no meanys possybyll she mygth for her salfgarde depart from the same and so both in fight within three owrys war burnt, and most parte of the men in them...*

[Alfred Spont, *Letters and Papers relating to the War with France*, 1512–13, NRS 1897, pp.49-50.]

Tactically the advantage remained with the English, and Howard stayed at sea, capturing a number of small ships and raiding the coast at will. The Norman ships that had gone to Brest quietly slipped away, and the French fleet was disbanded in early September. Henry, we are told, was very pleased with his navy's achievement, and granted Sir

Edward Howard the reversion of the office of Lord Admiral of England, then held by the ineffective Earl of Oxford. His initiative in seizing control of the Channel had paid off. There had been no great naval victory, but the French challenge, coming late in the day, had been effectively repulsed. By contrast, the Marquis of Dorset's expedition to Guyenne had been a disaster. The intention had been to support a Spanish invasion of the province, which, if successful, would have resulted in the recovery of a small part of what had once been the English empire. Ferdinand was supposed to be taking the military initiative and providing the logistical back-up for his allies. Neither materialized, and instead the King of Spain used Dorset as a cover for his own seizure of Navarre. Without supplies or proper employment, the English troops fell to plundering and discipline collapsed. Taking advantage of their commander's illness, the English captains then acted unilaterally, and requisitioning a number of merchant ships, brought their whole mutinous force — or what was left of it after dysentery had taken its toll — back to England.[16] Ferdinand feigned great indignation at the desertion, and Henry was left to rue his trusting nature. He had failed to take the lesson of a similar fiasco on a smaller scale in 1511, and had been twice outwitted by his wily colleague.[17] It was partly as a result of this sharp political lesson that in 1513 the King decided to confine his military operations to the north. His search for glory had so far made an unpromising start.

In December 1512 Louis XII brought six Mediterranean galleys round to the Channel and placed the veteran captain Prégent de Bidoux in charge of them. By the beginning of March they were victualled and prepared, although what they were supposed to do remains something of a mystery. A raid on Plymouth or Falmouth was rumoured, but seems to have been frustrated by the weather.[18] Such low-built, shallow draft vessels could not operate in northern waters, especially during the winter. The advantage that they did have was that they were mobile independently of the wind, and each carried a forward firing great gun (a basilisk) that was capable of damaging the stoutest sailing warship. By the middle of March 1513 not only was Prégent mobilized, but 15 or 16 sail of Norman ships were also at sea. This time the French had no intention of being taken by surprise. It was 10 April before Howard was also at sea, and this time he had a much larger fleet than previously — 23 royal ships and 26 that had been hired.[19] It is not clear that all these ships were at sea at the same time, or that all were fighting ships, but he clearly enjoyed numerical superiority. The French blockaded themselves in Brest, and this time the English went in after them. Howard succeeded in landing men at two places, but he lost one ship (wrecked on rocks) in the process, and the attack was a failure. Nevertheless the Admiral was so confident of success that he wrote to the King 'to come thither in person, to have the honour of so high an enterprise'. Henry (whose intelligence of the true situation may have been better) was not tempted, but the suggestion is a significant one.[20] In fact, attacked by Prégent's galleys and chronically short of food, Howard was forced to seek a limited success before he would be compelled to withdraw. He decided to try and take out the galleys, and on 25 April attacked with his rowbarges. It was mere folly. The galleys were backed in between bulwarks full of ordnance, and his rowbarges were simply not up to the job. Through sheer bloody-minded courage he managed to get aboard the leading galley, but was inadequately supported and being thrust back into the sea, was drowned. Demoralized by their loss, and completely out of victuals, the English retreated to face the indignation of their disillusioned monarch.[21]

On 4 May 1513 Edward Howard's brother, Thomas, was made Lord Admiral in his place, and spent the next month trying to re-establish discipline in the fleet, and to re-victual it for further service. That was not likely to be off Brittany, because almost immediately after the debacle of the attack on the galleys, the French fleet disbanded, and Prégent's command was out of action for many weeks because so many of the rowers were sick or injured. The Scots were not yet ready to join them, and in any case the danger from the English fleet was thought to be over. On the English side, Ferdinand had signed a truce with Louis on the 13 April, and the Spanish ships that had been supposed to join Howard simply went home.[22] Most of the hired ships were discharged, and the Admiral's desire to avenge his brother's death remained unrealized.

Towards the middle of June 1513 the King's ships were pulled back from Plymouth to convoy the 30,000 or so men whom the King was leading to Picardy when they crossed from Dover to Calais. The French were not prepared to confront so formidable a force, and as the army advanced across Artois it met with only token resistance. The fore-ward and the rear-ward, commanded by the Earl of Shrewsbury, reached the town of Thérouanne on 22 June and laid siege to it. About a month or so later Henry, leading the 'King's Ward' or core of the army, joined them.

THE KING ADVANCES TO THÉROUANNE, 1513

THE KING *hearing that his enemies approached… set forward his hoste and in good order came to Dornham where is a fayre castell standing in a woode countrie, the Frenchmen were ever lurkyng in the woods vewyng the kings conduite and order as he passed… And when the king came to the ryver he perceyved that many gentlemen made danger to enter the river: Wherfore he alighted down of his horse and without any more abode entred the river, then all other entred and came over… When all this was done, the king on the xxiiii day of August entred into the Citie of Tyrwyn at ix of the clock before noone with great triumph and honour, his person was apparelled in armure gylt and graven his garment and barde purple Velvet full of borders, & in all places traversed with braunches in runnyng work of fine golde… after whom folowed his Henxman with the pieces of armure accustomed. Thus with great glorie this goodly prince entered and took possession of the towne of Tyrwyn…*

[*Grafton's Chronicle*, pp.257, 265.]

Henry had reached Calais on 30 June, and had then spent about three weeks reorganizing the security of the Pale before setting off.[23] Early in August the French decided that they must do something about the siege of Thérouanne, and sent a sizeable force to revictual the fortress. The English, who had good spies, knew all about this intention, whereas the French seem to have been misinformed about the disposition of the besieging army. As a result de Piennes, the French commander, rode into a trap, and his gendarmerie, which had been intended to make a dash for the town, found itself instead confronted with the whole force of the English cavalry at Bomy. Archers and light cannons had also been positioned to take the advancing force in the flank, and the only option open to de Piennes was to get out as quickly as possible before he was totally encircled. Under orders not to risk a major engagement, the French fled and the encounter became known as the battle of the Spurs.[24] The failure of this relief effort, which occurred on 16 August, removed any possibility that the garrison could survive much longer, and on 22 August they asked for a parley. Terms of surrender were agreed. On the following day they left with bag and baggage, and 4,000 of them were allowed to join the main body of the French army. Over the next few days the fortifications of the town were systematically destroyed. Henry staged no ceremonial entry into Thérouanne; with much of the town in ruins there would have been little point, but he was very pleased by his success. Any sense of triumph, however, was rapidly deflated by the news from Scotland.

Ironically, given the King's quest for glory, the most important victory during this war was won in Henry's absence. In May 1513, Louis XII encouraged King James IV of Scotland to invade England. When Henry left for France he made his Queen, Catherine of Aragon, Governor of the Realm, and charged Thomas Howard, the Earl of Surrey, to defend the border with Scotland. On 9 September 1513 James was defeated and killed at Flodden, and his bloodstained hauberk sent to the Queen Catherine.[25] 'This battle' [Flodden], the queen wrote, 'hath been to your grace and all your realm the greatest honour that could be, and more than ye should win the Crown of France, thankes be God for it.' Perhaps; but it was not quite what Henry was looking for.[26]

THE BATTLE OF FLODDEN, 1513

...then the Lorde Admyrall [Thomas Howard] perceyved four great battayles of the Scottes all on foote with long speres lyke Moorish pikes: which Scots furnished them warlike, and bent them to the foreward, which was conducted by the Lorde Admyrall, which perceyving that sent to hys father the Erle of Surrey his Agnus Dei that hong at his brest that in all hast he would ioyne battaile even with the brunt or brest of the vantguarde; for the forewarde alone was not able to encounter the whole battaile of the Scottes, the Erle perceyving well the saying of his sonne, and seeing the Scottes readye to discende the hyll, advaunced himselfe and his people forwarde, and brought them egall in grounde with the forewarde on the left hande, even at the brunt of brest of the same... Then out brast the ordinaunce on both sides with fire, flame and hideous noyse, and the Master Gonner of the Englishe part slew the maister Gonner of Scotlande, so that the Scotishe ordenaunce did no harme to the Englishemen, but the Englishemens artillery shot into the mydst of the kings battaile and slew many personnes, which seeing the king of Scottes and hys noble men made the more haste to come to ioyning, & so all the foure battailes in manner descended the hyll at once. And after that the shot was done which they defended with Pavishes, they came to handstrokes...

Thus through the power of God on Frydaye, being the ix daye of September,

in the yere of our Lorde 1513, was James the fourth king of Scottes slayne at
Bramstone (chiefely by the power of the Erle of Surrey, Lieutenant for king
Henry the eyght, King of England, which then lay at the siege before
Tournay)…

[*Grafton's Chronicle*, pp.274–5.]

The crown of France was well out of Henry's reach, but the English army had hardly been tested as yet, and the question was — what should be its next objective? Logically it should have been Boulogne or Montreuil, both of which were close to Calais and thus strategically significant. However, Henry had been joined at Thérouanne by no less an ally than the Emperor Maximilian, and such places were of no interest to him. Maximilian had tickled Henry's vanity by serving in English colours, and in return he managed to persuade the King to direct his attention to Tournai, which sat on the boundary between France and the Empire. The Emperor had long desired to wrest control of it from the King of France, and this was an opportunity not to be missed, especially as Louis XII appeared to have neither the will nor the means to come to its assistance.[27] Early in September 1513 Henry moved his army against Tournai, and loosely invested it. The town was virtually indefensible, and the civic leaders had little will to resist. Negotiations followed, but the Tournois had very few cards in their hand, and if they wished to protect the town from sack, there seemed little option but to surrender to the Emperor, who was the main interested party. However, a proposal to that effect was dramatically frustrated by a virtual insurrection of the common people, who declared for France and hoisted the flag of St Louis on the town hall.[28] This defiance suited Henry admirably, because what he wanted above all things was a glorious conquest, not a tame surrender — and particularly not to the Emperor. So, having reassured himself that no French army was in the offing, on 16 September he laid Tournai under a full siege, and began to bombard it. He appears to have directed the cannoneers in person, although whether this had any effect on their efficiency is not on record.

The bombardment soon had its effect, and on 18 September 1513 negotiations were resumed. They did not immediately succeed because of the continued divisions within the town, but by 21 September even the most militant had come to the conclusion that there was no alternative to surrender. The question remained — on what terms? Henry now changed his stance. Hitherto the option had been surrender to the Emperor; now the alternative was offered, surrender to Henry as King of France. This seems to have confused the citizens, as well it might, but a truce was quickly agreed while the final terms of surrender were worked out. These were completed by 23 September, and involved accepting Henry as their sovereign, and paying him a large indemnity; in return for which all the commercial privileges of the town were confirmed.[29] Citizens who could not accept this change of condition were to be allowed to leave, with their possessions. Henry made his ceremonial entry into Tournai on Sunday 25 September, riding a magnificent courser and clad in richly decorated armour. He was accompanied by the English nobility in their finest regalia, henchmen carrying the King's weapons, and heralds in their colourful uniforms.[30] Of the Emperor there was no sign — this was to be an English triumph. So Henry got what he craved most, a victory that could be made to look glorious. He remained in Tournai until 13 October, feasting, jousting and generally showing off, and then handed over the mundane task of administering his conquest to Sir Edward Poynings, an experienced administrator and soldier, who became the Governor.

Henry had now got all that he could reasonably expect to get from the war, and although bellicose preparations were again being made early in 1514, the papacy was pressing the belligerents to settle. It had ostensibly been on the Pope's behalf that Henry had gone to war in 1512, and Leo X, Julius's successor, in gratitude sent him a Sword and Cap of Maintenance in May 1514, with a broad hint that it was time to bring hostilities to a close.[31] There was no further fighting. In July the fleet was laid up, and early in August a treaty was signed. Nothing was said about Henry's claim to the French throne, but Tournai was to remain in English hands (for the time being), and Louis was to pay Henry the arrears of his pension, which went back to the treaty of Étaples in 1492. Mary, Henry's sister, who had been betrothed to the young Charles of Ghent, the Emperor's grandson, was now transferred in marriage to the elderly Louis — a clause that she is said to have accepted only on the understanding that she could have her own choice next time around.[32] Meanwhile the King had taken a step of revolutionary significance, because instead of disposing of his war fleet when peace was signed, as had been the invariable practice in the past, he inventoried 13 of them, and having removed their ordnance, placed them on a care and maintenance basis. The vast *Henry Grâce à Dieu*, which had been launched only a matter of months before, had an inventory that ran to 14 pages.[33] He also kept some half dozen smaller ships in commission, and the hired ships, about 30 in number, were returned to their owners. This action transformed the navy from an event into an institution, because ships needed to be cared for and supervised even when they were out of commission. In 1512 he created the additional office of Clerk Controller and in 1514 added the Keeper of the Storehouses at Erith, which were newly built to cope with the expanded demand for naval supplies that a fleet in being required. There was, for the time being, no departmental infrastructure, and each of the three offices accounted separately: Hopton, the Clerk Controller for the Thames and Medway, Robert Brygandine, the existing Clerk, for Southampton and Portsmouth, and Hopton again for his charge at Erith. The only overall control (apart from that of the King) was exercised by his Chief Minister, Thomas Wolsey.[34]

From this time onwards the navy featured regularly among the business of the King's Council. New ships continued to be built or acquired during the ensuing peace. The *Great Elizabeth* was purchased from Lübeck before the end of 1514, and the *Great Galley* of 800 tons was built during the following year. In 1517 the *Mary Gloria* of 300 tons was added, and in 1518 what should probably be classed as the first royal yacht, the *Katherine Pleasaunce* of 100 tons. New facilities were also constructed, most notably the 'pond' at Erith, adjacent to the storehouses, which was a dock intended to keep some of the great ships, otherwise anchored in the Medway, safe from the winter storms and ice. Later in the century it was to be used as a 'wet store' for masts. By October 1517 about 22 ships were being kept on a care and maintenance basis in the Thames estuary, at a cost of some £700 a year for shipkeepers' wages. These were mariners, about half a dozen to a ship, who were hired to guard the laid-up fleet, and constituted the first regular workforce for which the sea officers were responsible.[35] A few clerks and keepers were also employed at each of the dockyards owned by the Crown—Deptford, Woolwich, Greenwich and Portsmouth—but shipwrights and other workers were hired for those yards when they were needed. It was not until much later, when the burden of work was heavier, that regular gangs were kept on the payroll.

None of this had much to do with the royal image, except that it is probably an indication that Henry did not intend to keep the peace very long. He wanted a navy that could be quickly mobilized whenever the next crisis should arise, and although he continued to be partly reliant upon arming merchantmen, they were getting less convenient with every year that passed. Because of design features for which he was probably responsible himself, warships were becoming specialized craft. The *Henry Grâce à Dieu*, for example, was armed with about a dozen heavy guns, firing through ports; other smaller ships built at this time followed the same line.[36] Merchantmen could not be converted by changing their structure to insert ports, so they became less useful. The political situation was also unstable. Louis XII had died within months of the peace of 1514 — danced to death, it was said, by his young bride, and was succeeded by Francis of Angoulême, who became Francis I. Francis was young and warlike, altogether too like Henry VIII for comfort, and the chances of emulation leading to hostilities were high. Also in 1516 Ferdinand of Spain died, to be succeeded by his young grandson Charles of Ghent, who became Charles I. Charles was a Netherlander and was not welcomed in Spain, so there was likely to be a period of unrest in that country that might easily tempt her neighbours to intervene.[37] Nevertheless war did not immediately follow, and the King of England decided to try a different tactic to enhance his prestige and reputation in Europe. Instead of being the Warrior, he would become the Peacemaker—the ally of the Pope—and would earn the gratitude of a Christendom torn with strife in the face of the advancing Ottoman infidel. He might even go on crusade himself. Since he was still without a son, and the succession in England was uncertain, there were certainly advantages in keeping himself out of harm's way.

The initiative for this departure came from the Pope, who in 1517 set up a conference of cardinals and ambassadors to work out plans for a universal peace in Christendom as the prelude to an attempt to recover Constantinople.[38] The programme so devised was then circulated to heads of state for comment. The responses were conventional enough, but Leo X took them for encouragement, and solemnly proclaimed a five-year truce on 6 March 1518. This was the easy bit as there was no war currently going on in Europe, and legates went out to whip up support for the crusade. Lorenzo Campeggio was sent to England, and Henry seized the opportunity to get Wolsey raised to legatine status as his partner. On 29 July Campeggio made his solemn entry into London, greeted by orations, hymns and salvos of artillery. Five days later the legates were received by the King at Greenwich, where they announced the calling of a crusade. The King, we are told, replied in elegant Latin, but, as Wolsey undoubtedly knew, Campeggio's mission had already been overtaken by events.[39] Henry, having tried war and hostile diplomacy in his dealings with France, had now decided to try his own peace offensive, and effectively hijacked the papal initiative. On 2 October the representatives of France and England signed a new treaty of peace and alliance, replacing that of 1514, which had theoretically expired with the death of Louis XII. This treaty was different, however, in the sense that it was not intended to be limited to the original signatories, but was rather a universal declaration of non-aggression to which more than 20 other powers were invited to accede.[40] Elaborate procedures were put in place whereby the signatories would come to the aid of anyone suffering aggression, but the real guarantee would be the combined force of England and France. In a sense it was the papal plan without the crusade—Henry, in spite of his elegant Latin, had nothing but contempt for the proposed crusade. A new diplomatic principle had been born, that of collective security.

Over the next few weeks, all the relevant powers signed the treaty of London, as it came to be called, and the Pope had little choice but to endorse it, chagrined though he undoubtedly was by the way in which his own plan had been sidelined. To secure French compliance, Wolsey had sold Tournai back to Francis for 600,000 crowns, and negotiated a marriage between Henry's infant daughter, Mary, and the even younger dauphin. These clauses formed the core of the treaty. Contrary to what has sometimes been claimed, however, its wider pretensions were also intended seriously. A ban was included on the hiring of Swiss mercenaries, for instance, and Venice and Urbino (both recent trouble spots) were included among the participants.[41] The prestige of Henry VIII and Wolsey soared in consequence. Henry had been punching above his weight since he first decided to take on the French in 1511, but then he had been part of an alliance and the limitations of his financial and military resources did not matter very much. Now he was not only the ostensible initiator of a pan-European peace treaty, but also with France an equal guarantor of its success. The King, in his own eyes at least, bestrode the world of European diplomacy like a colossus. Unfortunately his triumph was short-lived, because on 12 January 1519 the Emperor Maximilian died without a designated successor, and an imperial election was required. There were two obvious candidates: Charles I of Spain, who was Maximilian's grandson, and Francis I of France, of whom it was already being said that he 'goeth about covertly and layeth many baits to attain the Empire'.[42] It says a great deal for Henry's *hubris* that he believed that he could enter these lists on equal terms, and when in February he received an ambiguous letter from Leo X, talking about a third candidate, he leapt to the conclusion that he would receive papal support. In fact it is likely that the Pope was referring to the Elector Frederick of Saxony, with whom he was already in negotiation, but Henry needed no second bidding. Neither of his main rivals took his candidature very seriously, and Frederick declined to enter the competition. When the election was held on 12 June 1519, Charles, whose capacity for bribery was unrivalled thanks to the backing of the Fuggers (the Augsburg bankers), ran out a clear winner, and that was bad news for the peace of Europe.[43]

The new Emperor not only held the Habsburg family lands in Austria by a variety of titles, and most of the Low Countries as Duke of Burgundy, he was also King of Spain and master of Spain's growing empire in the New World. France now had Charles's lands on three frontiers, and could easily become surrounded. It was very likely, therefore, that Francis would attempt to break this encirclement by renewing the war in Northern Italy. It also meant that Henry's value as an ally was suddenly increased. For the time being, the alliance with France held. According to the terms of the treaty of London, there should have been a meeting between the two rulers in the course of 1519, but manoeuvrings over the imperial election ruled that out and it was January 1520 before Wolsey was empowered to go ahead with the preparations. Meanwhile Henry (or perhaps Wolsey) conceived the idea of a 'summit conference' involving all three leaders, probably with the intention of offering mediation over the potential flashpoint in Northern Italy.[44] Before the end of 1519 an invitation was issued to Charles V (as he now was) to come to England. Charles, who was intending to return from Spain anyway, accepted the idea of a visit, but not of a summit, and planned to come to England in May, significantly just before Henry's planned meeting with Francis, which was by then fixed for June.[45] He clearly hoped to derail the Anglo-French alliance, and thus deter Francis from considering any military options in Italy. Wolsey, meanwhile, was bearing in mind that it never did England any good to fall out with the master of the Low Countries, and contemplating the possibility of being constrained to support France in an armed confrontation with distaste.

At the end of the first decade of his reign, Henry's image had thus undergone a transformation. Having started as *gloriosus*, he then became *miles gloriosus*, but the warrior image had proved disappointing. Renewing the Hundred Years War was wickedly expensive in financial terms, and the legacy that his father had left him (some £300,000 or £400,000) had disappeared as if by magic.[46] He had also had his ego dented by becoming ensnared in the bewildering instability of European politics, being twice betrayed by Ferdinand and once inveigled by Maximilian. What he had gained were 'ungracious dogholes', and then only temporarily. Only against the lesser power of Scotland had he secured an unequivocal victory, and that had not been achieved in person. Here was no Agincourt, or even a passable resemblance to Francis's great victory at Marignano in 1515. So although his magnificence was undimmed, and his tournaments continued with their pseudo-military displays, his international image became that of the peacemaker, and was heralded by an equally vainglorious and competitive display. The high diplomacy was no less accompanied by pageants, banquets and revels than the making of war had been.

There were, however, other ways of displaying his manhood than by fighting wars, or even brokering high profile peace treaties, and they involved the little matter of sexuality. We do not know whether Henry had any sexual experience prior to his marriage to Catherine in June 1509. Given his 'beauty', which everyone commented upon, and his general athleticism, common sense would suggest that he had—but there is no proof. Catherine nevertheless became pregnant within weeks of her marriage, and the fact that the child was stillborn was irrelevant. She became pregnant again, almost as soon as physiology would permit, and the short-lived Prince Henry was born on New Year's Day 1511.[47] In spite of, or perhaps because of, his strenuous regime of physical exercise, there is no suggestion that Henry did not do his duty as a husband. Catherine accompanied him everywhere, took part in all his feasts and revels, and was shown off to visitors like the trophy that in a sense she was. There were rumours of affairs, both at home and in France, but they cannot be substantiated, and when he returned from Tournai he made haste ahead of his army to lay the keys of the town at her feet.

In addition to being decorative, however, Catherine was a diplomat and something of a shrew. She is alleged to have complained bitterly over her husband's purely notional relationship with a married sister of the Duke of Buckingham, an episode that cannot be dated but that seems to have occurred before 1514. In 1512 they also had a falling out over her father's behaviour in respect of Guyenne (see p.45), and there were rumours that their marriage had suffered.[48] It may have been so, but by the summer of 1514 Catherine was pregnant again. By that time, however, (and the events may not have been unconnected) Henry had taken a real mistress, whether to teach his wife a lesson or because he was genuinely smitten is not known. This was Elizabeth Blount, a kinswoman of William Blount, Lord Mountjoy, Catherine's Chamberlain from May 1512, who entered the Queen's service through that connection at Michaelmas in the same year. At that time Elizabeth was about 13, pretty and accomplished in the courtly arts — including flirtation.[49] Exactly when the King became interested in her is not known, but she is alleged to have 'caught his eye' during the New Year celebrations of 1514, when she may have been as much as 15. When they began to sleep together is not known either, but if it was as early as the summer of 1514 she must have possessed more contraceptive knowledge than any well brought up damsel was supposed to have. It was late in 1518 before she finally fell pregnant, and bore the King a healthy son at some time in 1519. This was the only bastard that he ever acknowledged, since Mary Boleyn, who occupied the wrong side of the royal bed for about four years after 1519, bore him no children. Either Henry's virility had gone into a steep decline, or Mary was more than usually careful, because it was in the King's interest to claim as many bastards as he reasonably could.[50] Catherine might complain bitterly in private, but she had only herself to blame for having failed to produce a male heir to the throne. The Queen herself had suffered another miscarriage in 1514, but had then at last succeeded in bearing a child that lived and flourished. Unfortunately it happened to be a girl. Briefly the couple were encouraged, and persisted with intercourse, but Catherine's only subsequent pregnancy in 1518 ended in the familiar disappointment.[51] By 1520 there is no reason to doubt the King's continued virility, but he had precious little to show for it, and his image as a sexual predator was, and is, exaggerated. At courtly love he was a famous adept, but when it came to actual procreation he played in the second division. Catherine seems to have passed an early menopause at the age of about 37 or 38, worn out, perhaps, by failed pregnancies, and that was to leave Henry with a formidable problem.

The King's original military posturings had come mainly in the tilt-yard, but there was also a technological side to his ambition. He was chagrined to discover that, in spite of his father's efforts to build up an artillery capacity, most of the gunners in his service in 1512 were Flemish, and that most of guns that the English used to such effect, particularly at sea, came from Mechelen. There were already gun foundries in the Kentish Weald, but they seem to have been producing only cast-iron falcons, which were small, had a low muzzle velocity, and could not equal the cannon available abroad.[52] Consequently in 1511 Henry established a new forge at Hounsditch, near London, with the aim of making England self-sufficient in the production of guns. However the Hounsditch foundry seems to have produced only bronze guns, and although these were an improvement on the falcons, they tended to buckle and warp in use, which made them less than ideal for prolonged service. It was to this class that the famous 'twelve apostles' deployed in 1513 belonged.[53] We know that Henry attended test firings, and that he was particularly interested in the manufacture of big guns, but for the time being his ambition was not well rewarded. At the other end of the scale, Henry VII had mobilized 1,000 arquebusiers for his abortive Scottish campaign in 1497, although we do not know where either they or their weapons came from. The arquebus (an early form of musket) had been in use in the professional wars of Italy for some years, but this was their first appearance in England. Again Henry VIII aimed to develop this armament, but it would be several years before his ambition was realized, except on a small scale. It was archers who carried the day at Flodden, and bows and arrows were still carried, along with arquebuses, on the *Mary Rose* in 1545.[54]

At first, Henry seems to have been relaxed about the claims of lineage, except where it directly touched his own position. He created William Courtenay Earl of Devon in 1511, the son of that Edward who had been attainted in 1504, and a member of a family whose earldom went back to the mid-fourteenth century. Similarly Thomas Grey was recognized as Marquis of Dorset in the same year, and Margaret Pole as Countess of Salisbury in 1513. Margaret was the daughter of George

(Edward IV's brother), who had held the earldom of Salisbury in addition to the dukedom of Clarence.[55] Unlike his father, Henry had no need to 'adjust' the peerage immediately after his accession, and his creations during the first few years of his reign were similar in number. Initially, the King was not at all reluctant to recognize the merits of a commander who had married into the Plantagenet royal family. It was only when anxiety about his own lack of an heir, coupled with Wolsey's insistent advice about the need to strengthen the central government, began to take over his mind in about 1520 that this attitude began to change.

In spite of his well-founded fears of the practice of retaining, the King also made extensive use of noble retinues in his first French war. Apart from the 2,000 or so members of the royal household, the whole of the large army that he led to Tournai had been raised by Commissions of Array directed to members of the nobility. His own men included many non-combatants, such as cooks, servants and musicians, so about 98 per cent of the fighting force had been recruited by means of the Commissions, and as many nobles as wished were able to discharge what they saw as their primary service.[56] They were able to display their banners and coat armour on the field of battle, and to lead companies adorned with their badges. Not for a generation had such an opportunity presented itself, and the processes of reward duly followed. Thomas Howard, Earl of Surrey was elevated to Duke of Norfolk, the rank that his father had forfeited by being on the wrong side at Bosworth, and Charles Brandon, Viscount Lisle and the King's Standard Bearer, became Duke of Suffolk.[57] To accompany the image of a fighting king, the image of the fighting nobleman was suitably refurbished. The King's search for glory swept the aristocracy along with it.

CHAPTER THREE

HENRY VIII

❖

POVERTY AND
PREOCCUPATION

HENRY REMAINED UNEASY as a peacemaker. He had allowed himself to be persuaded by Wolsey into adopting that role in 1518, and the result had been a great success. However, there is no reason to suppose that he was as distressed as his minister by the war clouds that followed Charles's election in 1519. His meeting with the Emperor in May 1520 had been intended to keep his options open, because, although he continued to profess the warmest friendship for the King of France, suspicion of his intentions was never far below the surface.

The omens for the great meeting between the two monarchs, scheduled to take place on the borders of the Calais Pale in June, were not particularly good. Nevertheless, the Field of Cloth of Gold was one of the great showpiece events of the century.[1] Confronted by a monarch whose resources, both in men and money, were far greater than his own, Henry was determined not to be outshone. His suit, and that of the Queen who was to accompany him, numbered together over 5,000 persons, 'the flower of the nation, male and female'. The equipping and decking out of such a multitude cost thousands of pounds, and tailors, seamstresses and bootmakers had been kept busy for months. Many rolls of sarsenet, satin, cloth of gold and velvet were supplied and consumed. Hundreds of tents and pavilions were sent over to Calais; plate, cutlery, glass, and tons of food both for men and horses. Six thousand men were employed on the preparation of the English quarters—masons, carpenters, glaziers and other craftsmen—many of them local, but many also from England and from nearby Flanders.[2] These latter had to be accommodated either in Guînes or else in Calais, an unusual (and no doubt unwelcome) extension of the normal duties of the royal harbingers. Guînes Castle was completely refurbished, and

alongside it was built a summer palace—a magnificent pavilion with
brick foundations and wooden and canvas superstructure. Many of the
timbers required were too long to fit on any transport ship, and had to
be floated down to Calais, whence they were laboriously hauled overland by teams of horses. Inside the pavilion was a complete set of public
spaces; banqueting hall, chapel, presence chamber and privy chamber,
with offices like the kitchen, cellar and pantry. Only the bedrooms were
missing, because it was not intended that the King should lodge there
—this creation was simply for the entertainments.[3] Clustered around it
were the tents and pavilions that housed the rest of the English company, most of whom were living on the site.

The exact spot where the Kings were due to meet had been identified by an Anglo-French Commission, and lay in a shallow dip of land
half way between Guînes and Ardres. Another sumptuous pavilion was
then set up to accommodate their encounters, and the valley filled
with the lists and galleries to house the chivalric entertainments that
would follow their meeting.[4] All these preparations were Wolsey's
achievement, and provide an eloquent testimony to his immense
energy and to his eye for detail. While he was worrying about the supplies of timber, and the workmen's wages, he also had to concern himself with the price of grain, and the availability of sufficient game birds
for the royal tables. From February onwards innumerable servants and
agents were busied about these affairs, but the controlling brain and
hand behind it all was that of the cardinal. Never was a royal reputation
in safer hands, even down to the armorial displays, the Tudor roses and
the royal beasts, which adorned the great pavilion and had to be graded
very carefully to fit with the importance of the persons concerned, as
well as the King's *amour propre*.

When the Emperor left England at the end of May, he had almost
literally to jostle his way through the flocks of grandees, courtiers and
their wives and ladies, who were gathering to cross to France. Henry
mobilized nearly all his great ships for this enormous display of power
and chivalry. Some were set to 'scour the seas' in anticipation of his
crossing; others were to do duty as transports. The King himself
appears to have travelled in his royal yacht, the *Katherine Pleasaunce*, but
the *Henry Grâce à Dieu,* the *Mary Rose* and the *Great Bark* were all
among the fleet on duty.[5] On 1 June 1520 Calais was in pandemonium
for the reception of this great throng, while Francis moved to Ardres,

where his own equally lavish preparations were now completed. On 3 June Wolsey visited him there, and at the same time his own envoys waited on Henry at Calais. No pains had been spared to make this meeting a success, but the one thing that was lacking, and which no servant could supply, was genuine good will between the principals.

On the 7 June 1520, Corpus Christi Day, and surrounded by the strictest protocol, the two monarchs met at the arranged spot. There was much embracing, and professions of undying love; so far, so good. The next few days were filled with feasting, dancing and archery competitions. Francis visited Guînes and dined with Queen Catherine; Henry visited Ardres and dined with Queen Claude. Catherine's sun had not quite set, but her role in these celebrations was largely formal. The *belle dame* among the English ladies, and the one who led the dance with decorative zest, was the king's sister, Mary, the 24-year-old Duchess of Suffolk.[6] Henry's current mistress, Mary Boleyn, was also present among the Queen's ladies, although not marked by any distinction. Her younger sister, Anne, was in the entourage of Queen Claude; and as Sir Thomas was also present, the Field must have served as something of a Boleyn family reunion.[7] Challenges for the jousts were then issued in the names of both Kings and a galaxy of nobles, led on the English side by the Duke of Suffolk and on the French side by the Duke of Vendôme. Henry and Francis both took part, but it was carefully arranged that they should not joust against each other, and the score sheets that survive for the combats make it very difficult (no doubt intentionally), to decide who 'won'. Many gracious words were exchanged, and not a few hard knocks, but in these aristocratic pastimes emulation was kept on a tight rein. More fur flew in the 'beauty competition' between the two sets of ladies than in the lists, and there the French were usually accorded the victory—but then the reporters were also French![8] There were also more plebeian sports, in which the Kings nevertheless took part: archery (in which the English excelled) and wrestling (at which the Bretons proved rather more skilled than the Cornish). The latter almost caused a diplomatic incident when Henry challenged his opposite number to a bout, and was comprehensively thrown, an incident that, we are told, left the English King 'bitter and heavy hearted'. Henry's desire (and need) to appear physically invincible was an important part of his image, and he found this reverse hard to bear.

THE FIELD OF CLOTH OF GOLD, 1520

THURSDAIE *the viii daie of June being Corpus Christi daie the king of England and the Frenche king mett in a valley called the goulden dale which dale lyeth in the mid waie betwixt Guines and Ardre in which Ardre the frenche king laie during the triumph. In the said dale the king had his pavilion of cloth of gould… the kings grace was accompanied with five hundred horsemen and three thousand footemen. In like wyse the French king was accompanied with a great company of horsemen and footemen: at the tyme of the meeting of theis ii renowned Princes there was proclamaciouns made on both parties by the heraults and officers of arms that everie companye should stand still the king of England with his companie on the one side of the dale, and the French king on thother side in likewise: then proclamacioun made paine of death that every companie should stand still till the two kings did ride downe the valley and in the bottom they mett where ever of them embrased other on horsebacke in great amytie…*

[Bodleian MS Ashmole 1116]

The celebrations went on for nearly a fortnight, coming to a conclusion on 23 June. Serious politics had been sedulously avoided, and at the end both sides were able to take part in an open-air mass, celebrated by Wolsey, at which the theme was peace. The two Kings vowed to build a chapel on the spot dedicated to Our Lady of Peace, and went their separate ways. A great deal of money and energy had been expended but it was (and is) uncertain what had been achieved. Two ancient enemies had been brought together in peaceful competition rather than in war, and Henry's image had been greatly enhanced. The general impression that the English were a collection of barbarians had been definitively dispelled, and Wolsey's reputation as an organizer ascended to new heights. Nevertheless old animosities continued to lurk close to the surface, and as one astute Venetian observer noted 'These sovereigns are not at peace … they hate each other cordially.'[9] Within a fortnight, Henry was riding to Gravelines for an unheralded meeting with Charles and the Archduchess Margaret. Then, and during the return visit that Charles and Margaret paid to Calais a few days later, serious politics was discussed, and a mutually satisfactory conclusion reached. The entertainment was splendid, but nothing on the scale of the Field of Cloth of Gold. When he returned to England in mid-July, Henry went off hunting in the West Country, and Wolsey went on pilgrimage to Walsingham. Both no doubt felt that they had done good work over the previous month.

Henry in fact had more cause to be satisfied than did the Emperor, who had gained little more than the reaffirmation of existing treaties. Charles was convinced that it would only be a matter of time before Francis broke the peace, and he was anxious for a firm alliance with England in anticipation. But in the summer of 1520 Henry was not to be drawn. He may have disliked Francis intensely, but he took his duties as a peacekeeper seriously. The trouble was that the situation he was trying to preserve was inherently unstable, and by the end of 1520 the anticipated French aggression had begun on a small scale. Charles was crowned King of the Romans at Aachen on 23 October 1520, and Francis responded by niggling at the frontier. Then between February and April 1521 he intervened in the *comuneros* revolt in Castile, captured Spanish Navarre and launched a vicarious attack upon the Duchy of Luxembourg.[10] On 29 May Charles signed an alliance with the Pope, and open war erupted between France and the Empire. On receiving this news, Henry was personally inclined to side with the Emperor, but Wolsey appears to have persuaded him first to offer his mediation. A complex and somewhat bogus negotiation followed, in the course of which Wolsey went to Calais on 2 August 1521, ostensibly for a mediation meeting, but really to sign a new agreement with Charles. This was duly done on 13 August, providing for a declaration of war by England in the event of the existing struggle not having ended by November. England was then bound to launch a small naval campaign against France in 1522, and to join in a full-scale joint invasion in May 1523.[11] However, it was only when it was clear that mediation had failed and that the war would continue, that this treaty was ratified on 24 November. It was not made public, and Francis appears to have been unaware of it.

Within a month the fleet was being mobilized, but the war effort in 1522 was half-hearted, partly because of the need to keep an eye on Scotland. The Duke of Albany had gone there from France with the express intention of stirring up trouble for England, and in September made an abortive attempt to lead a force across the border.[12] Troops needed to be kept in readiness to withstand such an incursion, if it should come in earnest. The fleet was at sea by the end of May, but its objectives remained strictly limited, not least because of the usual difficulties over victualling. On 1 July the Lord Admiral, the Earl of Surrey, attacked and partly destroyed the town of Morlaix, but was unable to proceed with a planned attack on Brest because his provisions had still not arrived.[13] Shortly after, the fleet returned to Portsmouth, and the Earl was redeployed to lead an Army Royal of 15,000 men into France from Calais—presumably passing the Chapel of Peace on the way. However, the Emperor's forces, with which they were supposed to collaborate, were nowhere to be seen, and after wasting a great deal of time and money the army returned to Calais on 16 October and was disbanded. Meanwhile the fleet remained at sea, some ships being designated in August to 'keep the Narrow Sea', some to go westward to lay off the coast of Brittany, and some to go north to stiffen precautions against the Scots. This disposition, which was almost entirely defensive, seems to have lasted until mid-October, and once the army was safely back from France, the fleet returned to its winter quarters. Only a few of the smaller ships were left in commission as an early version of the Winter Guard.[14]

MORLAIX
The Earl of Surrey to Wolsey, 3 July 1522

P LEASETH IT YOUR GRACE *to be advertised that at this time I have advertised the King's grace of the taking of Morlaix, with the circumstances of much part of that hath been done since my coming hither, whereof I do forebear to write to your grace because I know the same shall come to your hands. I trust of this time your grace hath caused more victuals to be sent after us, which shall be very welcome for we have need thereof… Great pity it were to see this well willed company, for lack of victual to leave undone that which we bere be in mind to essay, and what danger it shall be, with so little victual, to put ourselves so far from the coast of England upon the coats of enemies I report me unto your grace, notwithstanding undoubtedly as soon as we shall have wind to depart hence and draw beyond the Trade [Brest] we shall not fail to do so, and shall not return as long as we have any beer left, though in our return we should drink water… Scribbled in the Mary Rose within the haven of Morlaix…*

[TNA SP 1/25, f.22. Loades and Knighton, *Letters from the Mary Rose*, pp.92–3.]

Meanwhile Charles, more visible than his army, had visited England again on his way to Santander. He arrived at Dover on the 28 May and spent over a month at Greenwich and Windsor, indulging in a round of hunting, banquets, tournaments and pageants. He also conducted some urgent discussions with Henry, as a result of which the latter issued a belated declaration of war against France—just a week or two before the attack on Morlaix.[15] Realizing that it would be futile to attempt to persuade the King to launch a major campaign that season, and probably knowing (although not admitting) that his own forces would default on his obligation, Charles concentrated his energies successfully on a detailed plan for a combined assault the following year, a result that was then embodied in a further treaty. He left for Spain on 6 July, highly satisfied with the results of his visit. He would have been less pleased had he witnessed the sluggishness with which the English prepared for the joint operation to which they were committed, but he was only to see the result. The one important thing Henry did do in 1522 was to issue a General Proscription for the conduct of musters. Statistics from nearly 30 counties returned a total of 128,250 able men, classified by wealth and by the weapons they were expected to produce.[16] This great effort was denounced in some quarters as a mere pretext to carry out a subsidy assessment, 'to obtain new assessments by subterfuge under the pretext of holding musters'. However, there seems to be little doubt that it was intended for the purpose alleged, and gave the King an exceptionally thorough insight into the manpower resources of his kingdom. The information returned varied a little from county to county, and included mariners as well as soldiers, but it was an imperfect guide to the wealth of individuals, and would have been less useful for taxation than the special commissions that were later issued for that purpose.

In one respect, however, the returns are interesting as well as informative, because one of the questions asked was to whom the individuals named 'belonged'.[17] This naturally suggests a census of noble and gentry retinues, but the question was seldom answered and it would seem that tenurial relationships no longer translated readily into military dependency. The time was coming, perhaps had already come, when a nobleman or a gentleman mobilizing forces for the King's service would depend less on his own 'well-willers' and more on the muster lists in general for his recruitment. It is also fairly clear from the returns that those who provided the harness and weapons were not necessarily the men who would be expected to use them.[18] The concept was beginning to emerge of a pool of able men, who would be fit to serve the King if called upon, irrespective of whether they had the resources to arm themselves or not. The militia was supposed to be a home defence force, exempt from service overseas, but the King's commissioners were now moving to a position where they would ignore that limitation in putting their companies together.

In spite of his freshly renewed treaty obligations, Henry showed no enthusiasm in preparing for a new campaign in 1523. The fleet was mobilized by the end of April, but for the time being efforts continued to be focused on Scotland. A squadron patrolled the east coast to prevent troops arriving from France, and the Scots briefly blockaded the Humber. On 11 June there was a skirmish at sea that resulted in the death of the English Vice-Admiral, Sir Henry Sherbourne, and at least seven ships were intercepted on their way to Leith.[19] In June and again in September Lord Dacre and the Marquis of Dorset led raids on Kelso and Jedburgh, and on 21 September the Duke of Albany returned again from France with 3,000 soldiers, using the western route to evade the English blockade. It seemed that serious action was imminent, but the border lairds were unenthusiastic and the season was getting late. Nothing happened. Sir William Fitzwilliam, as Vice-Admiral, was patrolling the Channel in June and July, but nothing much is known of his activities, beyond a raid on the small town of Tréport early in August.[20] It looked as though another season would pass without serious fighting. However, by the end of June a major change had taken place, which was a direct result of the crisis that had arisen within France. When the wife of Charles, Duke of Bourbon and Constable of France had died in the spring of 1521, Francis I had tried to claim her inheritance, in spite of the custom that should have allowed the Duke to retain possession during his own life. By the end of 1522 Bourbon's sense of grievance had grown to the point where he was plotting rebellion and negotiating with the Emperor. At first Henry had been wary of him, perhaps unconvinced of his ability to achieve anything significant. However in June the King underwent a change of heart, and offered terms to the Constable, which resulted at the end of July in a three-cornered treaty between Bourbon, Henry and Charles, committing all three to a joint invasion of France.[21] By the end of August the Duke of Suffolk was ready to go with upwards of 10,000 men, and a few days later, on 6 September 1523, Bourbon signed a secret clause with Henry alone, agreeing to recognize the latter as King of France.

Suffolk had been commissioned to raise his army as soon as the original agreement with Bourbon had been signed, on 24 July 1523, and seems to have used a mixture of traditional and more modern methods. Some 1,700 men were raised from his own lordships in North Wales, and others from among his dependants elsewhere, but the majority seem to have been 'taken up' by his agents in the counties. About 1,000 were volunteers, who agreed to serve without pay in return for a share of the plunder, which perhaps gives some indication of what sort of campaign it was expected to be.[22] When Suffolk reached Calais on 24 August, 1,600 men from the garrison also joined his force. The campaign was supposed to be a joint effort between Henry, Charles and Margaret of Austria, with Henry providing the main force, Margaret the artillery and Charles some troops and money. However, while Henry and Margaret both delivered on their promises, Charles did not. Distracted by a revolt in Gelderland, his Netherlands contingent never arrived, and of the 100,000 ducats (£33,000) which he was supposed to contribute, only 48,000 was actually delivered.[23] Indeed the Netherlands end of the operation had already disintegrated before Suffolk arrived. There were also strategic disagreements, because whereas Henry wanted to capture Boulogne, the Emperor was insistent that the priority must be to link up with Bourbon, who was supposed to be advancing from his base in east-central France. A meeting of 7 September resolved these disagreements in the Emperor's favour. It was agreed that the English would strike south by way of Doullens and cross the Somme at Corbie. Suffolk might, or might not, meet Bourbon, but at least his campaign would be a major distraction in the latter's favour. The final instructions issued to the English commander about 20 September envisaged such a link, but by that time there were serious doubts, not only about Bourbon's intentions, but also about his capability.[24] How many other nobles would be with him? Were his dependants fully supporting his action? Bourbon was finally proclaimed a traitor by Francis on 16 September, and by that time the threat from him had largely evaporated. By the end of October he was no longer a factor, and the Duke of Suffolk, already well south of Corbie, was left in a very exposed position.

To add to his difficulties, there was plague in the camp. This had first appeared as early as 10 September, but had been kept in check by regular movement. However, by the end of October it was a serious problem.

Suffolk would have liked a decisive battle, but the French would not co-operate, defending strong points but otherwise withdrawing in front of him. He had advanced rapidly to the Somme, meeting only sporadic resistance and bypassing the defended places, but his captains were itching for a fight, particularly fellow courtiers such as Lord Leonard Grey, whose service had hitherto been mostly in the lists. They were disappointed because most towns surrendered on demand, and were sworn to Henry as King of France, a submissiveness that they were soon to regret.[25] Francis was concentrating his defences north of Paris, and hoping that sickness and the appalling weather would do his work for him. Nor was he disappointed. In the absence of any meaningful support from the Emperor, and of any support at all from Bourbon, Suffolk hesitated, and when news that a German incursion had been defeated reached him on 1 November, he began to retreat.

Henry was in two minds what to do, and considered sending his army into winter quarters. He continued to send money and reinforcements, but his instructions were contradictory and confusion prevailed in the English Council of War. Suffolk was keen to advance again, and the King did not want to lose the advantages gained by his success, but even Margaret's co-operation, which had hitherto been staunch, was now in doubt. Eventually the weather made up his mind for him, because 11 November was one of the coldest days of the century. Men and horses were literally freezing to death and the demoralized army became mutinous.[26] An advance on Guise was aborted and the Council of War decided to abandon the campaign. The German and Netherlandish contingents were disbanded and the English withdrew to Calais. Once there the army seems to have disintegrated, and to have come home in dribs and drabs as shipping offered. In spite of having been reasonably well paid, the soldiers were in a sorry state, and excited the compassion and charity of their fellow countrymen, which was by no means usual in the case of a returning army. To what extent this collapse may have been Suffolk's fault is not clear. In any case it did his favour at court no harm, because although Henry was reportedly very cross at the abandonment of the campaign, and no doubt equally cross with the failure to maintain discipline towards the end, by 10 March the Duke was back in the tilting ring, and in high fettle. Jousting was more in his line than commanding armies.

It is difficult to say what effect the campaign of 1523 had on Henry's

fighting image. He had honourably discharged his treaty obligations, at
a huge cost to his treasury. The campaigns of 1522 and 1523 had cost in
excess of £400,000, some £352,000 of which had been raised by
forced loans. After a bitter row a similar sum was voted by parliament in
1523, well short of the £800,000 for which Wolsey had asked, and
which was really needed.[27] Wolsey's credibility suffered a heavy blow,
and the King's own reputation suffered—a fact of which he may not at
once have been aware. By the end of 1523 he was hard up, thoroughly
disillusioned with the Emperor, and no nearer obtaining his objective
of glory on the battlefields of France. This last blow was cushioned by
the fact that he had not commanded in person, but it was his honour
that was at stake, and he knew that perfectly well. The only persons
who gained were Suffolk, whose reputation survived intact, and
courtiers such as Lord Grey and Sir Richard Wingfield, who had done
good service both on the field and in Council. Suffolk's incursion has
been described as 'the last campaign of the Hundred Years War', and in
so far as it was fought for honour and for the Crown of France, that is
accurate, but in terms of both its objectives it was futile.[28] A tournament would have been just as effective, and much cheaper.

At first none of this was realized. Henry spent Christmas comforting
himself with talk of renewing the attack, now that a way had been
found into 'the bowels of France', and of resurrecting the challenge of
the Duke of Bourbon. However by the spring his belligerence had
cooled—perhaps in the face of dawning financial reality—and he
changed his tune. He was still prepared to attack, but only if the
Emperor and Bourbon were already in the field. It seems that he was
still yearning for a fight, but Wolsey and circumstances combined to
restrain him. The Pope was urging peace, and the cardinal found it
expedient to agree with him. The Duke of Bourbon was stirring again,
and diplomatic contact was established with him, but his appeals for
financial assistance fell on deaf ears, because there was simply no
money to send.[29] For a while it seemed that that was an error of judgement, because at the end of July the Constable invaded France from
Italy and laid siege to Marseilles. Henry became briefly animated and
spoke of launching his army again into France, but fortunately for
Wolsey the moment passed. In early September, Bourbon's effort collapsed, and he retreated hastily into Italy. The King had not mobilized
—even the fleet does not seem to have left port—and there was now no

cause for him to do so. England remained officially at war with France, but during 1524 no sword was drawn in anger, and Henry confined himself to making threatening noises from the sidelines.

He had not abandoned his ambitions, but for the moment circumstances made any realization of them impossible. Then circumstances dramatically changed, because on 14 February 1525 Charles V inflicted a crushing defeat on the French outside the walls of Pavia in northern Italy. The French army was destroyed and Francis himself was captured.[30] Nothing appeared to stand between the Emperor and the total conquest of France. All Henry's acquisitive instincts were revived by this news; not since the victories of Henry V had such an opportunity presented itself, and the Great Enterprise became again the first item on his agenda. Within a month troops were being mustered, commissions issued, and on 21 March another levy was demanded, hopefully known as the Amicable Grant.[31] An embassy was despatched post-haste to Spain to coordinate a new invasion, optimistically including the Duke of Bourbon, who had also been animated by the news of Pavia. Henry was not greedy. He would be prepared to settle for the acquisition of Normandy and Picardy, plus Boulogne and a few other towns. He was prepared to lead an army of 20,000 men in person, and he was prepared to set out straight away.[32] Alas for ambition! Charles was not interested in furthering Henry's schemes. He had won his victory, and was anxious for peace. If the King of England wanted to conquer part of France, let him get on and do it, but he should not look to the Emperor for cooperation. Henry had insulted Charles by reprimanding his ambassador before the Council, but that was a trivial matter compared to the Emperor's poverty. Henry had blithely promised 150,000 crowns towards the cost of a joint enterprise, but that was small beer, and in any case (as he soon realized) beyond his means, because the Amicable Grant was a fiasco. The taxpayers simply went on strike; even an otherwise loyal nobility refused to pay their assessments, and there were protests and rumours of insurrection.[33] Whatever the King might think, the war was bitterly unpopular, and confronted with this concerted opposition, Henry retreated. He feigned ingenuously to know nothing of the demand, and Wolsey loyally took the blame. In a manner that was typical of him, the King then convinced himself that his chancellor was indeed to blame, and the seeds of doubt were sown between them; but it was obvious that Henry was not going to get his war. His hostility towards the Emperor festered. Charles had not only spurned his plans — he owed him a great deal of money.

Wolsey began to look for a way out, and picked up a peace negotiation that had been mooted before the news of Pavia had upset everyone's equilibrium. Negotiations were resumed on 22 June 1525 with Louise of Savoy, acting as Regent during her son's captivity, and peace was signed at the More, one of Wolsey's residences in Hertfordshire, on the 30 August.³⁴ In January 1526 Francis, utterly weary of his situation, signed the treaty of Madrid with the Emperor, making sweeping concessions in order to recover his freedom. He had no intention of adhering to the treaty, and Charles probably suspected as much, but he too was anxious for a way out of the stalemate. Within months Francis had put together the League of Cognac with the papacy and Venice for the express purpose of curbing the Emperor's overwhelming power. Wolsey had been an active participant in the formation of this league, but England did not join because Henry was anxious to preserve his status as a potential mediator.³⁵ In other words he was attempting to redeem his European reputation by returning to the position of 1518. He feigned great indignation when Charles repudiated his treaty obligation to marry his daughter Mary in the wake of the treaty of the More, but this was an expected rebuff and did not substantially change his position. He wanted to be the arbiter of Europe, but after the accidental sack of Rome in 1527, Charles was not prepared to play his game, and in January 1528 he played his last card, and joined the League of Cognac. This was a purely platonic commitment, and did not result in any fighting. Indeed, both Wolsey and the King became so immersed in Henry's matrimonial troubles that they almost missed the negotiations that finally led to the peace of Cambrai in the summer of 1529.³⁶ Thanks to his tangle with the canon law, the arbiter of Europe had become a virtual bystander.

Meanwhile a significant domestic development had taken place, again involving Wolsey. Edward Stafford, the Duke of Buckingham, had a remote claim to the throne going back to Anne, a granddaughter of Edward III, who had married Edmund, Earl of Stafford, and in 1519 the Venetian envoy, Sebastian Guistanini, believed that he might become King if Henry died without a male heir. Edward never hinted at any such ambition, but he was inordinately proud of his ancestry, and sometimes let slip that he regarded the Tudors as mere parvenus.³⁷

He also pursued, with what can only be described as obtuse persistence, his claim to the hereditary High Constableship of England. This office had been in abeyance since the mid-fifteenth century, when it had been withheld from Edward's great grandfather, Humphrey Stafford, by Henry VI. Humphrey had been allowed to petition for it, but his suit had not been granted. This may have been because of an (untested) belief that the High Constable had the power to arrest the monarch, if he should be guilty of misconduct. Henry VIII in any case turned a deaf ear to the Duke's complaints, which did not sweeten the latter's temper. Buckingham was a powerful man, well connected by marriage, with a large following in the Marches of Wales, and a strong castle at Thornbury. In other words he was just the kind of old-fashioned peer whom Cardinal Wolsey regarded with the greatest suspicion.[38] Buckingham was a member of the King's Council, but was not much consulted and by 1520 was seriously out of favour.

All this rankled and he began to make indiscreet complaints, not only about the cardinal but also about the King. At the same time he fell out seriously with some of his own servants, who in revenge disclosed this information to the Council. Henry took fright, and although Buckingham had not actually done anything treasonable he had probably 'imagined' the King's death, and that was sufficient. He was arrested, tried and executed, and his affinity made not the slightest attempt to save him—perhaps he had offended many of them as well. This taught Henry a number of salutary lessons, which he absorbed under Wolsey's tutelage. Men with Buckingham's pride of ancestry were men with dangerous pretensions, who needed to be kept under control. Although it had not been tested in this case, a better supported man in a similar position could easily have raised a private army, as his grandfathers might have done during the civil wars. Peers should be first and foremost instruments and servants of the King, and should not be able to claim any wealth or power that did not derive directly from him.[39]

This change of priorities was amply reflected in the numerous creations that were made between 1525 and 1530. His own illegitimate son, for example, as Duke of Richmond; his young nephew Henry Brandon as Earl of Lincoln; George Hastings as Earl of Huntingdon and Thomas Boleyn as Earl of Wiltshire. Henry was never reluctant to create new peers, and in that he differed both from his father and from his two daughters, but the conditions became increasingly strict. Soldiers might still be elevated, as was the case with John Dudley who was created Viscount Lisle in 1542, but the great majority were either civil servants or the kindred of his various Queens. Edward Seymour became Earl of Hertford in 1537 and William Parr, Earl of Essex in 1543. Meanwhile Henry's Council and parliament increased the workload of the Commission of the Peace, and of the various other commissions, such as Sewers, which discharged their unglamorous duties with increasing diligence. By the last decade of his reign, Henry had gone a long way towards separating the essentially civilian processes of government, both from the military aspects of the state and from the role of the peerage, which became increasingly focused on the court.

Scotland had not been included in the treaty of the More, but in January 1526 a three-year truce was signed, and the following summer was the first since 1521 that saw no military preparations in the north. This did not alter the culture of border raiding, which observed its own rules, but it did mean that the northern levies were not officially mobilized, and that the garrison of Berwick remained on a peacetime footing. That garrison, and its larger equivalent at Calais, were the only standing troops maintained by the English Crown, and the only places in English service where professional captains could obtain the relevant training and experience. Otherwise, whenever the King needed an army, even for small-scale service such as the borders, it had to be mobilized specially; which is why it became normal for aspiring soldiers to take service with the Holy Roman Emperor (or occasionally the King of France) and to return to England only when employment was offered.[40] It also meant that, in spite of the campaigns of 1522 and 1523, there were comparatively few experienced soldiers in England.

The navy was rather different, thanks to the changes that Henry had made in 1514. During the period of non-active war between September 1524 and March 1525, 21 of the King's ships spent various periods of time at Portsmouth, which meant that they were still in commission, although the nature of the record makes it impossible to trace the deployment of individual vessels. Between 1525 and 1530 there were 15 ships, mostly small, in and out of Woolwich and Deptford, 'keeping the Narrow Seas'—indicating a regular system of Channel patrols.[41] Piracy and the uneasy nature of the peace would more than justify such a precaution. Three medium-sized ships, the *Minion*, the *Sweepstake* and the *Swallow*, are known to have been based in the Thames at this time, and in 1527 the expenses of repairing them feature in the accounts of Thomas Jermyn, the Clerk of the Ships.[42] Ships continued to be victualled and manned for unspecified service, probably the pursuit of pirates, and in November 1526 a survey of the navy was conducted. This may well be incomplete, but it lists 21 ships under various headings. Five were classed as 'good for the wars'; a further seven described as 'fit for merchant voyages ... if they might be set on work'; and a further four were unserviceable and in need of rebuilding.[43] This suggests not only a policy of 'leasing out' to merchant companies, but also a regular pattern of inspection and maintenance. Seasonal patrols were maintained in the Channel as well as the North Sea and the western approaches, and the captains were sometimes issued with specific instructions. For instance William Gonson, commanding in the Channel in March 1527, was instructed to protect Low Countries' merchants from French pirates, and to endeavour to keep the peace between French and Imperial warships. Quite a lot of Gonson's activities can be reconstructed from his reports, and it seems that England's control of the Narrow Seas was by no means a fiction, even when large warships were not deployed.[44] The records over the next few years are patchy, but in August 1530 the *Minion* and the *Mary Guildford* were despatched to Bordeaux to fetch wine for the royal tables, and Thomas Spert, the Clerk Controller, and William Gonson were busy 'rigging and trimming' both at Portsmouth and in the Thames. In August 1532 the King ordered his ships of war to remain at sea, and sent the necessary money and victuals.[45] There was no war in 1532, or serious danger of war, so these ships were clearly on routine business. Even if there was no apparent danger, Henry's navy made sure that he would not be taken by surprise.

When Thomas Wolsey fell from grace in 1529, for reasons quite unconnected with military affairs, any overall control of the navy lapsed. In fact this seems to have made remarkably little difference, and the three officers of the 'sea causes' carried on as before. A new dock had been excavated at Portsmouth in 1528, explicitly for the repair of the great ships such as the *Henry Grâce à Dieu* and the *Mary Rose*, and it appears that over the next few years inspection and maintenance was on an annual basis. This did not mean that every ship was refurbished every year, but that they were taken on an annual rotation.[46] Nevertheless the momentum seems to have declined, and only three ships were added to the fleet between 1530 and 1535, one of which was promptly lost to Scottish pirates (or to Scotsmen who were deemed to be pirates).[47]

It was not until about 1533 that Thomas Cromwell, by then the King's Secretary and Chief Minister, took the overall control that Wolsey had enjoyed. As Henry struck out into unknown waters with his second marriage and repudiation of papal authority, there were inevitably rumours of war, and these were fanned assiduously by the Imperial ambassador, Eustace Chapuys. Chapuys was a strong supporter of Catherine of Aragon, and anxious to keep alive a belief that the Emperor would intervene on her behalf. Charles had no intention of doing any such thing, but it was not in his interests to let that be known. In August 1533 Cromwell reminded himself that the navy needed attention, and in November Chapuys reported that Henry had ordered the fleet to be mobilized. 'This shows they are beginning to be afraid', he added hopefully.[48] This mobilization probably related to nothing more unusual than the regular departure of the Winter Guard, because November would have been a very eccentric time of the year to have assembled a war fleet.

In the autumn of 1536 some ships were sent out against a series of linked rebellions in Lincolnshire and the northern counties known as the Pilgrimage of Grace, but the Pilgrims were not seafarers and no outsider attempted to come to their aid. Apart from landing some guns at Hull, the navy seems to have seen no action. Although politically important, militarily the Pilgrimage was something of a non-event. At the height of the revolt, the rebels mustered 30,000 men at Doncaster, far more than the hastily assembled southern levies that the Duke of Norfolk led against them, but their leaders were divided and had no desire to fight against the King.[49] They demanded the restoration of Princess Mary, but that had already been done (up to a point), and there was no way that the King was going to sacrifice his leading advisers to this kind of popular agitation. So the great demonstration was wound down by negotiation, and there was no fighting. Although some minor peers, such as Lord Hussey and Lord Darcy, did join the Pilgrimage, the Great Lords, whose support they had expected—the Earls of Northumberland, Derby and Shrewsbury—remained aloof. They were well aware of their shaky position in Henry's scheme of things, and had no desire to arouse further suspicion, so they threw their considerable weight behind the Duke of Norfolk, and that contributed significantly to the relatively peaceful ending of the crisis.

There was action at sea, but it had nothing to do with the Pilgrimage and was confined to the smaller ships. In 1536 Chapuys hopefully declared that it would take 18 months to get the great ships ready for the seas. Cromwell had already got that message. He had ordered a full survey in April 1534, and between then and the end of 1536 had caused the *Mary Rose* and several other vessels to be substantially rebuilt.[50] It was probably as a result of that work that Chapuys reported as he did, deliberately misconstruing the situation. In April 1537 a general mobilization was ordered, but that seems to have been no more than a 'test run' to ascertain the state of the repaired ships, and the only sea fighting of the year was undertaken by a squadron under the Vice-Admiral, Sir John Dudley, which scoured the coast from the Downs to the Severn, taking a number of pirate ships that then became the subject of protracted diplomatic wrangles. Cromwell was walking a tightrope between doing too little and doing too much in connection with naval deployment, and it became necessary to reassure the Regent of the Netherlands that these warships were at sea as much for the security of her own merchants as of those of England.[51] 1538 saw no major change in this situation, but in another respect it was ominous, because there were clear signs that peace was about to break out between the Emperor and the King of France, and that the conflict upon which Henry had depended for his security was about to come to an end. There was nothing that he could do about it, and on 12 January 1539 Charles and Francis signed the treaty of Toledo, each agreeing to make no new alliance with England without the other's consent. The Pope rejoiced, and it looked as though the long delayed crusade was imminent.

Over the previous 25 years, Henry's image had fluctuated, but had always been more than life-sized. In 1513 and 1523 he had been the Warrior; in 1518 and 1527 the Peacemaker; and from 1533 to 1539 the Schismatic. This last image was not of his choosing, but he embraced it with the same panache as the others. A combination of the urgent desire for a legitimate son and lust for Anne Boleyn caused him to repudiate his wife, Catherine of Aragon, who was no longer capable of bearing children.[52] There were precedents for such action, notably the case of Charles VIII of France, and in other circumstances he might have achieved his wish without problems. However the Emperor

Charles V was Catherine's nephew, and was on bad terms with the King in any case, so his opposition was to be expected. Then the sack of Rome in 1527 left Pope Clement VII (who was no hero) at the mercy of the Emperor, and effectively frustrated any annulment that he might have been prepared to offer.[53] After five years of futile diplomacy, and the sacrifice of Cardinal Wolsey, Henry decided to impose his own solution. In 1533 he married Anne Boleyn and prohibited appeals to Rome. On 7 September of that year Anne was delivered of a daughter, named Elizabeth. In 1534 a willing parliament declared him to be Supreme Head (under Christ and in earth) of the Church of England. He thus became a national leader in a sense that neither he, nor any of his predecessors, had ever been before. There was opposition, both principled (from John Fisher and Thomas More) and instinctive (from the Pilgrimage of Grace), but Henry enjoyed majority support among both his nobles and his people, and dealt with resistance ruthlessly.[54] In 1536, he executed his second Queen on trumped up charges of adultery, and began to dissolve the English and Irish monasteries. Then, 11 days after Anne Boleyn was executed Henry married one of her ladies-in-waiting, Jane Seymour. Never had a King acted in such a high-handed way—and the English loved him for it!

None of this had anything to do with fighting, except in a purely metaphorical sense, but it transformed the King's image. Kings had won battles before, they had been great jousters and even (supposedly) great lovers, but no King had ever led a victorious charge against the universal church. It was this that made his Englishness so important. Although he was Welsh by name, and about a twelfth part Welsh by blood, Henry was overwhelmingly English, and saw himself as such. The church that he set out to purify in his own way was the ancient Church of England, uncontaminated by Roman innovations and pretensions. As he settled into his role as Supreme Head, this became a great source of personal satisfaction. Although it may have started out as political expedient, the English church rapidly became an ideological commitment to him. He had (of course) been quite right to reject such a bogus jurisdiction as that of Rome, and all the convenient money-making fictions that had gone along with it. He was not tempted by the doctrines of Martin Luther. Luther was a heretic and—what was almost equally bad—a German. Luther had also had the temerity to accuse him of matrimonial fraud, so although he negotiated with the alliance of German Lutheran princes known as the Schmalkaldic League in 1539, he never had any intention of signing the confession of Augsburg.[55] Henry was a pure Old Catholic, uncontaminated by heresy.

In many ways his most significant move, apart from the declaration of his Supremacy, was his authorization of the English Bible. Ignoring the input of the Lutheran William Tyndale, for whose death he had been responsible, the King convinced himself that the inestimable benefits of reading God's word ought no longer to be open only to learned clerics. Everyone should have access, directly or indirectly, to the Word of Life. The Great Bible was published in 1539, a year that also saw the passage in May of the Act of Six Articles.[56] This Act is usually seen as part of a reaction against the evangelical advances that had occurred under the influence of Thomas Cromwell and Thomas Cranmer, but was in fact no more than a reaffirmation of the King's idiosyncratic theological position.[57] By 1540 Henry had twice rejected opportunities to renegotiate his relations with the Holy See, and had established what he considered to be the correct balance between secular and ecclesiastical authority. He never rejected the apostolic succession, or claimed to exercise the *potestas ordinis* in his own person, but he believed that it was his duty to appoint suitable bishops, and to exercise the *potestas jurisdictionis*. He had invested the image of the Christian Prince with a new and national meaning.

As he grew older, and no longer appeared in the lists, his image changed. His body was now corpulent, and stricken with the arthritis that resulted from many heavy falls in the hunting field and the tournament. He was still a magnificent and imposing figure, but he could no longer hunt all day and dance all night. He had lived life to the full, but it had caught up with him. It was many years since he had last fought a war, and although in principle he still claimed to be King of France, he no longer expected to be able to realize that claim. However, the death of Catherine of Aragon in 1536 had eased tensions with the Emperor, and when Cardinal Reginald Pole had come north with ideas for invoking his assistance for the Pilgrimage of Grace, Charles sent him away with discouraging words. The basic fact of England's strategic position in the never-ending conflicts between the Emperor and the King of France had not changed, and although it might appear that the treaty of Toledo had altered that situation, in fact both parties continued to treat the King of England with kid gloves. As it became apparent during 1540 that the international situation had not been transformed, Henry began to hanker for a renewal of the Imperial alliance, and Charles was prepared to respond. Could the King of England again hold the balance of power?

CHAPTER FOUR

HENRY VIII

❖

YOUTH
REVIVED

THE BIRTH of Henry's longed-for son, the future Edward VI, on 12
October 1537 was met with great rejoicing. But the court was soon
thrown into mourning when the Queen died 12 days later. Although
he grieved for Jane deeply and sincerely, Henry knew that a second son
would be a very useful addition to his dynastic armoury. Consequently,
within days of her death the Council sent instructions to the English
ambassadors in France and the Low Countries to begin the search for a
new consort.

Over the next two years, Henry seriously considered nine women,
glanced at several others, and commissioned five portraits from his
court painter, Hans Holbein.[1] The first favourite was Mary of Guise,
but in June 1538 she was spirited off to wed James V of Scotland, a
rebuff that briefly annoyed the King very much. Then his eye lit on an
attractive 16-year-old widow, Christina, daughter of Christian II of
Denmark, and briefly married to Francesco Sforza, Duke of Milan.
Christina was Charles V's niece, and also had a claim to her late husband's duchy, but the lady herself was reluctant, allegedly claiming
(with reference to the fate of Anne Boleyn) that she would sooner
keep her head on her shoulders.[2] Negotiations went back and forth;
other French princesses were considered. Then on 17 December 1538,
Pope Paul III finally promulgated the Bull of excommunication against
Henry that had been prepared over three years earlier. Reginald Pole
came north again to coordinate action against England, and on 12 January 1539 the peace of Toledo was signed.

These events concentrated English minds in various ways. Firstly,
they led to negotiations with the Schmalkaldic League for a possible
anti-Imperial alliance; secondly, a proposal was canvassed for a marriage

between Henry and Anne, the daughter of the Duke of Cleves (who was Catholic but an opponent of the Emperor); and thirdly, defensive preparations were put in hand against a possible combined Franco-Imperial attack.[3]

The King mobilized his navy, but for some unknown reason did not add to his stock of warships. Instead he decided to fortify the south coast, and chose 25 sites in England where such fortifications should be built. These were mainly commanding harbours, vulnerable stretches of coastline or river estuaries—places such as Deal, Sandwich and Hurst Point. They were intended to mount artillery, and took the form of concentric rings of low stone bastions, a distinctively English development from the renaissance French style.[4] Most of these 25 were actually built, and were paid for by profits from the dissolution of the monasteries. This process had been going on since 1536, and most of the houses had either been suppressed or had surrendered by the summer of 1539. The Court of Augmentations received upwards of £100,000 from that source during the course of that year, in addition to the £90,000 that accrued from the rapid sale of some of the property.[5] The building programme was pressed ahead at breakneck speed, and the defences of Calais and Berwick were also strengthened, stone from the dissolved religious houses being often redeployed to these works. Beacons were prepared, and the counties mustered; ditches were dug and ramparts and palisades erected at points deemed vulnerable and not covered by the new forts. The passage of foreign ships was stayed, and munitions were collected.[6] In the event none of these precautions were needed. Within a couple of months the accord reached at Toledo was falling apart, and as early as April Francis reassured Henry that the warlike preparations in which he was visibly indulging were aimed at the Emperor and not at him. Meanwhile the Emperor had again dispatched Reginald Pole with empty words, and it had become apparent that neither of the great powers was about to attack England.

Nevertheless the defensive preparations were carried through to a conclusion. It would do no harm to be ready for the next time the volatile politics of the Continent produced a similar threat, and Henry was not eager to downplay a situation that gave him an unprecedented position as the national leader of a beleaguered isle. The way in which the country rallied behind its King at this time of trial was very gratifying to a ruler who was well aware of the unpopular nature of some of his

recent policies. Had he not just dealt with the so-called 'Exeter conspiracy', which had involved the noble houses of Courtenay and Pole,
and correspondence with the arch-traitor, Reginald Pole?[7] The crisis
of 1539 was good for his image, and good for his self-esteem. It also led
to the solution of his matrimonial problem. Negotiations with Duke
William of Cleves had been going on since March, and did not seem to
be making much progress. Anne, the main focus of the King's attention, was discovered to be pledged to the Duke of Lorraine—or so it
was said. However, Henry sent another mission in July, and this time
real progress was made. By the end of August 1539 Holbein had painted
his flattering portrait of the princess, and returned to England with it.
Unfortunately the King was impressed. On 4 September William sent
his own mission to England, and on 24 September a marriage treaty was
signed, the question of Anne's earlier contract having been by some
means overcome. William's political position was precarious, poised
between the Emperor and the Schmalkaldic League, and he no doubt
was only too pleased to have the King of England for his kinsman.[8]

Sadly, it did not work. Nobody had thought to tell the King that his
intended had received only the most basic of educations, spoke only
German and had all the charisma of a model *hausfrau*. She was also
appallingly innocent, not only of courtly graces but even of the facts of
life. She seems to have been a gentle, self-effacing soul, with a great
anxiety to please, and not the faintest idea how to go about it.[9] For a
number of reasons, including adverse weather conditions, it was January 1540 before Anne reached Dover, and the impatient King, in a fit of
misguided chivalry worthy of his younger self, decided to intercept her
incognito as she passed through Kent. The poor girl had no idea what
was happening, and thought she was going to be abducted, while
Henry was irrationally disappointed with her lack of *savoir faire*. 'I like
her not' he is alleged to have said curtly.[10]

From there it was downhill all the way. The King was committed to
the marriage and could not escape it, but unsurprisingly the wedding
night was a fiasco, as Henry had no urge and Anne had no response. In
order to avoid humiliation, the King blamed his failure to consummate
entirely upon Anne, and began proceedings to annul his marriage on
that ground—which was relatively straightforward. He might have been
gratified by the incredulity with which this news was received in
courtly circles. His reputation was clearly well ahead of his performance,

and that may have been some consolation. Anne accepted his decision with resignation, and possibly some relief, and the marriage was dissolved in June. A generous financial settlement was made, and Anne stayed in England as a kind of 'honorary sister'. She never remarried, and died in 1557.[11]

It used to be alleged that the fall of Thomas Cromwell, the Lord Privy Seal and Henry's Chief Minister since 1533, was partly caused by the failure of the Cleves marriage, for which he had been the principal negotiator. However, it seems unlikely that there was any direct connection, because Cromwell was undermined by his political enemies on the grounds that he was responsible for the evangelical activity within the Church, which was beginning to offend the King's conservative instincts.[12] There may have been an indirect connection, because the leader of those enemies was Thomas Howard, Duke of Norfolk, and by the time that Cromwell was executed on 28 July 1540, Henry had fallen for Norfolk's niece, Catherine, and married her that same day.

The story of his fifth marriage is as calamitous as that of the fourth, although in a quite different way. Catherine was an experienced flirt, who had already had several lovers, a fact that she successfully concealed from the 50-year-old King. She knew everything that Anne had never even dreamed of, and Henry was temporarily revitalized. He rose early, went hunting with zest, and seemed to have recovered much of his lost youth. However, it did not last. His health fluctuated and his sexual prowess even more so. Catherine became bored with a lover who was intermittently impotent, and during the progress of 1541 entertained more than one gentleman of the court in her bed.[13] Given the lack of privacy in the court, it is not surprising that the King found out. As a Howard, Catherine had many enemies who were only too pleased to take advantage of her little weakness. By November 1541 Henry's dream of love and renewed virility were over, and he was shattered. On 13 February 1542 Catherine was executed for treasonable adultery, and her Chief Gentlewoman, Lady Jane Rochford, also went to the block as an accomplice. But vengeance could not take away the sting of humiliation: the King became morose and at times unapproachable. He was now without either a wife or a Chief Minister, and he began to hanker after the only other thing that might make life worth living again — war.

On 10 July 1541, while Henry was on progress in the north and

hoping to persuade James V of Scotland to meet him at York, Charles
V and Francis I resumed hostilities. By the end of the year, as his fifth
marriage was painfully unravelling, Henry was looking for an Imperial
alliance. The logic of this was the same as it had always been; he had an
hereditary claim to the throne of France, and wanted to stay on good
terms with the Low Countries. He was also anxious to insure himself
against the kind of diplomatic isolation that had threatened in 1539,
and perhaps to test the reality of the sanctions to which he should be
subjected as an excommunicate.[14] On both grounds he was reassured.
In June 1542 Henry sent Thomas Thirlby, bishop of the newly created
see of Westminster—who should have been unacceptable to any loyal
son of the Church—to the Emperor to seal a new pact. This committed England to a joint invasion of France in the summer of 1543. Politically the clock had been put back 20 years; sadly the King's body clock
was not equally obliging. Henry's mind, however, went back 30 years,
to those days when James IV of Scotland had taken advantage of his
absence at the siege of Tournai to invade the north of his realm (see
p.48). He was offended by the way in which James V had failed to meet
him at York, and deeply distrustful of the influence of Cardinal David
Beaton, who had been sent back to Scotland precisely to stir up anti-
English sentiment.[15] Perhaps he was still ashamed that the victory at
Flodden had been won while his back was turned, but for whatever
reason, he decided to take the Scots out this time before embarking
upon his promised Continental campaign.

In September 1542 he set this process in motion by ordering his
commissioners in the north to make unreasonable demands of their
opposite numbers. The Scots were taken aback because they were not
looking for a confrontation. They hesitated and prevaricated, and Henry
issued bellicose instructions to the Duke of Norfolk to carry out a dev-
astating raid across the border. By the end of October this had been
done. The raid lasted only six days, but it caused an immense amount
of damage, and it had the desired affect. Although he was a sick man,
James could not ignore such a blatant piece of provocation. He issued
ritual appeals to the Pope and his fellow princes for aid, and in mid-
November launched the expected counter-attack by sending 20,000
men into the Debateable Ground north of Carlisle.[16] In his anger he
had not given sufficient thought to this riposte. His troops were hastily
levied, poorly commanded and poorly equipped. On 23 November

the Scots were effectively ambushed by a smaller but much better equipped English force commanded by Sir Thomas Wharton. The battle of Solway Moss as it was called was no Flodden; in fact it was little more than a skirmish and the casualties were light, but the Scots were put to flight and a large number of lairds and nobles were taken prisoner.

A fortnight later, and for reasons quite unconnected with this defeat, James V died, leaving his crown to his daughter, Mary, who was just a week old. Scotland had lost its King, its field army and a large proportion of its nobility in the space of less than a month.[17] Henry promptly reasserted his ancient claim to suzerainty over the realm, and removed his prisoners to London to play their part in the next round of his diplomacy. Ignoring his claim, on 3 January 1543 the Scottish Council appointed the Earl of Arran, James Hamilton, as Regent during the minority of the young Queen. Hamilton had Cardinal Beaton arrested, but otherwise showed no sign of yielding to the pressure that Henry was now well placed to apply.

Mindful of the fact that he was supposed to be preparing for a major attack on France in the summer, the King then recalled the Duke of Suffolk and the Earl of Hertford to London, and sent John Dudley, Viscount Lisle, to the north as Lieutenant. It was Lisle who had to deal with the fragile government of Regent Arran, and to dissuade Henry from a violent response when one of his agents in Edinburgh was murdered by English renegades.[18] Interestingly, he did this not on any political grounds, but because it was not conducive to the King's honour to wage war on infants. Henry proceeded cautiously, because he had conceived a plan to exploit the situation, which required him to negotiate constructively with the Regent. A marriage between his own son Edward, then aged five, and the young Queen of Scots would in due course (and given good fortune) bring the two realms peacefully together, with England in the dominant position.[19] In April 1543 Lisle, who in the meantime had been appointed Lord Admiral, was recalled for the action against the French, and replaced by Lord Parr of Kendal —a sure sign that the borders had been downgraded as a security risk. At the end of June the French ambassador was given an ultimatum that was effectively a declaration of war. Lisle was ordered to 'go upon' the French with his fleet, and became preoccupied with the defence of Calais. In July the Scots commissioners signed the treaty of Greenwich,

agreeing to the marriage proposal, and on 12 July the King married
Lord Parr's sister, Catherine, Lady Latimer.[20] In the summer of 1543,
Henry's effectiveness seemed to have been fully restored, but there was
no sign of the promised campaign against France. In fact the King had
already decided that Scotland had to take precedence for the time
being, and as early as February had signed a secret agreement with the
Emperor postponing his Continental campaign to 1544. Charles was
not pleased, but accepted the reasoning behind Henry's delay.

Then things began to go wrong. On 6 July 1543 Sir Rhys Mansell,
commanding the fleet as Vice-Admiral, had an inconclusive skirmish
with the French, who were similarly patrolling, and in November
William Woodhouse brought his battered squadron into the Thames.
That damage, however, had been caused by the weather rather than by
enemy action. The Great Ships were not fully deployed, but private
enterprise was encouraged by the issue of letters of marque. This licence
was made general by proclamation on 20 December, which represented
a new policy departure, but the year ended without any major engagement at sea, and with virtually nothing accomplished.[21]

Meanwhile Scotland was in revolt against the treaty of Greenwich.
Within a few days Sir Ralf Sadler in Edinburgh was sending reports of
the opposition, led by Cardinal Beaton and the Earl of Lennox. Henry
offered both troops and money to the Regent, who stalled and prevaricated. Then the Earl of Arran effectively changed sides, reducing the
pro-English party in Scotland to a rump. On 11 December the Scottish
parliament solemnly repudiated the treaty of Greenwich, and all the
advantages of the victory of Solway Moss were annulled. The Auld
Alliance had been revived, and potentially Scotland was a greater menace than it had been while James V was alive. In 1542 the Scots had had
no aggressive intentions, but now they were hostile and standing to
their defence.[22]

Henry was in no mood to listen to talk of his honour. The question
was—how to re-establish his ascendancy in Scotland? By the end of
January 1544 he had decided upon a major punitive expedition, and
nominated the Duke of Suffolk to carry out an 'enterprise' in March
that would deploy 15,000 men and place a further 2,000 in the border
garrisons. On 2 February Suffolk accepted the mission, and asked that
Hertford and Lisle should be joined in commission with him.[23] It was
even rumoured that the King would take the field in person. That was

probably never a part of his intention, and in any case he was reminded that he could no longer neglect his obligation to the Emperor. Consequently within a few weeks he had had second thoughts. He would command personally in France, and the Duke of Suffolk would go with him.

Hertford was appointed to command against Scotland, and this inevitably meant delays. It was 21 March before Lisle set off for Harwich to muster the ships needed for transport and general support. Hertford went post-haste to Newcastle, where the troops were already assembling, and a few ships had gathered. There he stuck for nearly a month, while the fleet from the south was delayed by adverse weather and difficulties over victualling.[24] The possibility of a surprise attack virtually disappeared, but the Scots were in no position to mobilize a response, and seem to have been unaware of the objectives of the impending assault. It was 20 April before Lisle reached the Tyne with the main fleet, which numbered only 68 ships instead of the 160 that had been originally planned. This seems to have been the result of a decision to use fewer and larger transports, rather than any lack of availability. All the ships displaced 100 tons or more, 11 of them were royal warships and the other 57 had been 'taken up' from the east coast ports in the traditional manner.[25] The reason why so many transports were needed was that it had been decided to use an amphibious attack to get directly at Edinburgh, rather than follow the traditional route from Berwick through the Marches. Hertford issued his battle instructions and embarked his men on 28 April 1544, and then spent five days trying to get out of the Tyne. On 2 May they finally succeeded and made an unopposed landing opposite Inchkeith on the Firth of Forth the following day. Leith, about two miles away, was virtually undefended and was comprehensively plundered. The English captains expressed surprise at the wealth of the town, but that probably reflected a misconception about Scottish towns rather than any particular affluence.[26]

INCURSION INTO SCOTLAND, 1544

AND IN A VALLEY, *upon the right hand, near unto the said town* [Leith], *the Scots were assembled to the number of 5000 or 6000 horsemen, besides a good number of footmen to impeach the passage our said army; in which place they had laid their artillery at two straits through which we must needs pass if we minded to achieve our enterprise. And seeming at the first, as though they*

would set upon the Vanguard: when they perceived our men so willing to
encounter with them, namely the Cardinal, who was there present, perceiving
our devotion to see his holiness to be such as we were ready to wet our feet for
that purpose, and to pass a ford which was between us and them: after certain
shot of artillery on both sides: they made a sudden retreat, and leaving their
artillery behind them, fled towards Edinburgh. The first man that fled was the
holy Cardinal [David Beaton] like a valiant champion: and with him the
Governor, the earls of Huntley, Murray and Bothwell, with divers other great
men of the realm. At this passage were two Englishmen hurt with the shot of
their artillery; and two Scottish men slain with our artillery...

[*The late Expedition in Scotland...1544*, in Pollard, *Tudor Tracts*, p.40.]

English warships raided up and down the Forth, taking and destroying
such forts and strong places as they found, without encountering any
serious resistance. By this time the Scots had understood that the main
target of this attack was Edinburgh, and that it was no part of Hertford's
intention to accept a surrender on terms. On 8 May a force of 5,000 or
6,000 Scots, led by Cardinal Beaton in person, attempted to interpose
themselves between the English and their target. They may have been
untrained levies, or their appearance may have been a mere diversion,
but at the first sign of serious battle they scattered and fled. According
to Lord Lisle, reporting the incident the same day, Beaton was the first
to quit, the others rapidly following his example. However, Lisle's main
objective in writing was to mock the 'popish prelate', with his fancy
dress and Frenchified ways, so the reality may have been rather different.[27] Nevertheless no serious obstacle was placed in the way of the
English advance, and later that same day the main gate of Edinburgh
was blown in with a culverin.

There then followed some fierce street fighting, which is glossed
over in the English reports. The town was taken at the cost of some
casualties, and set on fire. But the castle held out, and its guns inflicted
further damage on the assailants. Hertford having neither the time nor
the resources to indulge in a full-scale siege, did not attempt to take it.
The English cavalry raided as far as the gates of Stirling, burning and
destroying everything in their path as Hertford and Lisle reported with
grim satisfaction on the afternoon of 15 May.[28]

The same day they set fire to Leith and retreated, this time going
overland because they rightly expected to meet no resistance. By 18

May 1544 the army was back at Berwick. Meanwhile the fleet, loaded
with captured ordnance and other plunder, also returned by the way it
had come, inflicting more damage on the coastal towns and villages
and making a diversion to sack St Andrews, which was not on its way,
but which was Cardinal Beaton's metropolitical seat. By 18 May the
ships were also back in the Tweed, whence Lisle, with the core of his
fleet, immediately proceeded south to join the musters for the French
campaign, which were by then in full swing. Apart from a couple of
thousand who were redeployed into the border garrisons, the army
also went south in those same ships. The naval account for the expedition, which was presented on 8 June 1544, deemed it to have lasted for
53 days, and to have cost £2,086 for the English ships involved, and a
further £2,018 for the 11 'stranger' ships that had been employed.[29]
The latter were paid off in the northeast, and did not join the rest of the
fleet in the Channel. Apart from causing great anger, and discrediting
both Cardinal Beaton and the Earl of Arran, the impact of this attack
on Scotland was not as great as Henry hoped. It may well have deterred
the Scots from intervening on the French side in the forthcoming war,
but the treaty of Greenwich, by which the King set great store, remained a dead letter.

From a naval point of view, the Scottish war was a mere diversion.
By 1544 the King's fleet numbered between 35 and 40, and none of the
great ships had been sent north. The *Henry Grâce à Dieu* had been
rebuilt in 1540, and since then 10 ships had been added to the fleet by
building or purchase, including the *Galley Subtle* or *Red Galley*, for
which special shipwrights had been imported from Italy.[30] In late May
and early June this whole fleet was mobilized to transport the Army
Royal to Calais, and was commanded by the Lord Admiral in person.
English ships scoured the Channel, but met with no resistance. The
English army numbered somewhere between 38,000 and 50,000 men.
The county musters had been alerted, and it may be that as many as
36,000 of these men had been raised by that means through the Com-
missioners of Array. The notional figures are 3,700 cavalry and 32,000
infantry, together with 2,000 draft horses and 282 wagons, all of which
were contributed *pro rata* by the counties of south and central England.[31]
The logistical effort was immense and, since there was no longer any
Chief Minister, was shared among numerous officials, led by William
Paulet Lord St John, the Master of the Court of Wards and Stephen

Gardiner, the Bishop of Winchester. Although it was intended that the King would be his own Commander-in-Chief, he had under him, and in effective daily control, those two veteran warriors, the Dukes of Norfolk and Suffolk.

Unfortunately this careful preparation had not been matched by a similar coordination of strategy. It seems that the Emperor's idea was always that the English would strike directly south, aiming for Paris, while his own forces advanced from the east, but that was not Henry's intention.[32] He had moved on since 1525, and although he still used the title 'King of France', no longer thought of that as representing a real ambition. He would be quite happy with a part of northern Artois, and was particularly anxious to secure control of Boulogne. When he arrived at Calais therefore, on 14 July 1544, he had no intention of consulting the Emperor, or of working out a joint strategy with his ally. Instead, on 19 July he laid siege to Boulogne and instructed the Duke of Norfolk, with a part of his army, to besiege Montreuil, a little further south.[33] Charles was disgusted at being thus ignored. Henry had twice postponed his campaign against France for reasons of his own, and now that he had actually come he had completely ignored the strategic priorities that they had discussed in drawing up their agreements.

Henry enjoyed the siege of Boulogne immensely, supervising every move and personally placing the artillery. On his orders the fleet bombarded the town, inflicting heavy damage, and on 11 September the castle was undermined and blown up. Whether the King ever placed himself in any danger while he went about these duties is not clear, but he cheered himself up considerably in the process. It was remarked that he was in better health and spirits than he had been for years — presumably since the first flush of his enthusiasm for Catherine Howard. On 14 September he called upon the defenders to capitulate, and after some haggling, and when it was obvious that no relief was on its way, they complied.

On 18 September 1544 Henry entered in triumph, with a display similar to that which he had put on at Tournai some 31 years earlier.[34] It was a costly victory. Even on the most limited computation the campaign had cost £650,000, and if the cost of the preceding musters and the establishment of the garrison is taken into account, well over a million pounds. It was also costly in another sense because the Emperor, feeling no obligation towards his self-absorbed ally, had signed a separate peace with Francis at Crépy on the same day that Henry had entered Boulogne.[35] If the King wanted to defend his conquest, he would now have to do so on his own. Henry spent just a few days at Boulogne, making arrangements for its defence and government, and returned quietly to England on 30 September. While he was still there a situation full of danger developed to the south, because freed from the necessity of confronting the Emperor, the main French field army was now available to tackle the English. The Dauphin moved swiftly to the relief of Montreuil, still being besieged by the Duke of Norfolk, and threatened to cut his supply lines. The King ordered Norfolk to retreat, which he did with great difficulty, getting himself and his troops back to Boulogne before the King left. The bulk of Henry's army returned with him, leaving a large garrison to defend his conquest, and the French decided against trying conclusions with so strongly fortified a town at that late date in the season.

Had the Dauphin but known it, Norfolk and Suffolk, who had re-mained behind, did not share his conviction about the defensibility of Boulogne. Before the King had even reached London on his return journey, they had led their men north to Calais, on the grounds that his plans for the new conquest were impracticable, leaving the garrison much smaller than it should have been.[36] Henry was furious, and ordered them to return, but they were unable to do so because the Dauphin had interposed himself between the English bases. At the same time, their Imperial horsemen had departed, following the Emperor out of the war. Stranded in Calais, the discredited commanders had no option but to return to England with their depleted forces. Abortive peace negotiations followed, but Henry had no intention of surren-dering Boulogne, or the French of settling without it, so all the King did was buy himself a little time. This turned out to be critical, because the Dauphin had no desire to undertake a siege in December weather, and it was not until the new campaigning season in 1545 that Boulogne was seriously threatened again. Meanwhile the town could be re-inforced and supplied by sea, and that is what happened during the winter of 1544–5. Henry, however, faced 1545 in a bleak mood. He had been ill-served by the commanders he had left behind him in France, and now he faced the prospect of having to defend his conquest with-out Imperial support.

King Francis also faced a problem. He could lay siege to Boulogne, but as long as the English held the command of the sea, there was little prospect of taking it. He had to neutralize the English navy if his army was to stand a chance of success, and he did not think that he could achieve that by a straightforward sea battle. He therefore planned to take out the naval base of Portsmouth, thus depriving the English fleet of its principal dockyard and supply centre. Peace with the Emperor had freed the Mediterranean fleet, and 25 galleys were brought round to the Channel—ideal ships for an amphibious assault, or for operating within the enclosed waters of Portsmouth harbour. From early May onwards Claude d'Annebault, the Admiral of France, began assembling his fleet in the estuary of the Seine.[37] It was slow work because the galleys were delayed, but by the end of June he had about 200 ships under his command, everything from small supply vessels to large fighting ships, and the greatest armada assembled anywhere in the course of the sixteenth century.

Meanwhile the English were at sea. By the end of May, finding no-one else to fight, Lisle had taken about 50 prizes, and ably backed by a swarm of privateers had severely disrupted French trade. By June d'Annebault's preparations were common knowledge, and on 24 June Lisle led out a war fleet of some 35 ships with the intention of causing as much disruption as possible. His original intention seems to have been to use captured hulks as fireships, but the weather disrupted these plans. Then Henry decided for some unknown reason that he wished to issue the attack orders himself, and that caused further delay.[38] Before these issues could be resolved, the Mediterranean galleys arrived, and that strengthened d'Annebault's defences considerably, so that when Lisle eventually attacked, on 6 July 1545, he was repulsed. Quite fortuitously, as he retreated and the French began to celebrate, d'Annebault's 100-gun flagship, the *Philippe,* caught fire and burned to the waterline.

This might have been taken as an ill omen, but the French Admiral was undeterred, and got his fleet to sea on 12 July. He made a diversionary raid on the Sussex coast on 18 July and entered the Solent the following day, landing 5,000 men on the Isle of Wight. However Lisle, who had retreated to base after his failure earlier in the month, was waiting for him with about 80 ships. Although d'Annebault had far more, as fighting units the fleets were not ill-matched. Because the French were intending to land, most of their vessels were troop transports, carrying something over 30,000 men. Between 20 and 30 of their other ships were sailing warships, in addition to the 25 galleys. All of Lisle's fleet, with the exception of half a dozen rowbarges and two galleys, were warships, but they varied enormously in size, only about 20 of them displacing more than 400 tons.[39]

A very large sea battle seemed to be impending, but it did not happen. With the English fleet occupying the harbour, the French could not get in, and when Lisle tried to move his ships out to engage, they could not move for lack of wind. This was a situation tailor-made for the French galleys, and they were sent in to use their basilisks on the becalmed English warships. They had not made much progress, however, when a fitful wind sprang up, and the English ships began to emerge. The galleys retreated in some disorder.

What happened thereafter has been overshadowed by the accidental loss of the King's Great Ship, the *Mary Rose*. The *Mary Rose* was old, having been built originally in 1510; but she had been rebuilt in the late 1530s, and her armament greatly enhanced. By 1545 she had formidable firepower, but her original sailing qualities had been lost in the rebuild, and she was possibly a little top-heavy.[40] Although the French later claimed to have sunk her with gunfire, what seems to have happened was that she discharged a broadside, and then her captain, Sir George Carew, brought her about rather too sharply to discharge the other, leaving the original gunports open. In the midst of this manoeuvre she was caught by a sudden gust of wind, and her open gunports submerged. Once the water had begun to enter, her list could not be corrected, and within a few minutes she had sunk like a stone. Because she was at action stations the anti-boarding netting would have been spread across the waist of the ship, effectively trapping most of the crew. Only a handful are known to have survived.[41] This tragedy did not affect d'Annebault, but with the wind having failed again he clearly felt at a disadvantage, encumbered as he was with so many transports. As Lisle made skilful use of the tides and currents to get his ships out of the harbour and into fighting formation, a prolonged stalemate threatened and d'Annebault decided to retreat. On 23 July 1545 he retrieved the men whom he had landed on the Isle of Wight, where they had suffered the indignity of being driven off by the local levies, and moved off in the direction of Selsey Bill.

THE LOSS OF THE *MARY ROSE*

Francois van der Delft, Imperial ambassador to Charles V, 23 July 1545.
Original in cipher.

O N THE FOLLOWING DAY, *Sunday [19th July], whilst the king was
at dinner on the flagship, news came that the French were only five short
leagues away... The English fleet at once set sail to encounter the French, and
on approaching them kept up a cannonade against the galleys, of which five had
entered well into the harbour, whilst the English could not get out for want of
wind... Towards evening, through misfortune and carelessness the ship of Vice
Admiral George Carew foundered, and all hand on board to the number of
about 500 were drowned except about five and twenty or thirty servants, sailors
and the like, who escaped. I made enquiries of one of the survivors, a Fleming,
how the ship perished and he told me that the disaster was caused by their not
having closed the lowest row of gunports on one side of the ship. Having fired
the guns on that side, the ship was turning in order to fire from the other, when
the wind caught her sails so strongly as to heel her over, and plunged her open
gunports beneath the water, which flooded and sank her...*

[*Calendar of State Papers*, Spanish, Vol. VIII, p.190]

All this had been witnessed by the King, who had dined the previous
day on board the *Henry Grâce à Dieu,* having decided to command in
person against this greatest threatened invasion of his reign. The counties had been mustered (again) and about 30,000 troops awaited the
anticipated French incursion. Perhaps he was disappointed at not being
able to try out his new suit of armour, but more likely he was relieved at
not being forced to hazard his now crumbling body in the chances of
battle. As it was he could have all the credit for the victory, without any
of the risk. However, as he was well aware, it was only half a victory
because the ultimate French objective was not to raid Portsmouth but
to recover Boulogne.[42] The town was already under siege, and after
quitting the Solent d'Annebault crossed the Channel and landed 7,000
of his troops to reinforce the besieging army. As though unsure what to
do next, he then returned to the Sussex coast, where his galleys carried
out some rather aimless raiding. At the end of the first week of August,
Lisle came looking for him with 100 ships and intent on battle. He
came up with the French on 10 August near Beachy Head, but after a
perfunctory exchange of gunfire, d'Annebault retreated under cover of
darkness on the night of 10 / 11 August. He returned to the Normandy

coast, and immediately demobilized. The English were baffled by this behaviour until it became known that plague had broken out in the French fleet, and had become so virulent that he had no option but to give up.[43] A enormous and very expensive effort had thus petered out in failure and disappointment. The siege of Boulogne was lifted, and Lisle retained the command of the sea. It was none too soon because plague had also broken out in his own ships, and a rapid downsizing of the navy became an urgent requirement. Only the Winter Guard was left in commission.

This relief came none too soon, because Henry was close to bankruptcy. His relations with the Emperor were at a low ebb, with mutual recriminations flying backwards and forwards, and punitive raiding into Scotland had resulted in defeat for one of the English forces at Anrum Moor near Melrose in February 1545.[44] The King, however, remained in a bullish mood. He was anxious to repair his fences with Charles, but remained adamantly opposed to the suggestions of his Council and advisers that he should trade Boulogne for peace with France. Peace talks were undertaken during the winter of 1545–6, but failed for that reason, and on 17 January 1546 Henry decided to send the Earl of Hertford to take over the Lieutenancy, and to prepare for a major 'enterprise' in the spring.[45]

The Duke of Suffolk having died the previous August, Hertford was the King's most experienced and skilful soldier, so the intention seems to have been serious. The counties were to be mustered once again, with the intention of raising 16,000 men. Plans were put in preparation to raise another 14,000 German, Italian and Spanish cavalry, and to purchase munitions, naval stores and food. Lisle was sent to sea with no fewer than 45 warships, and Hertford crossed to Calais on 23 March. He then set about fortifying the port of Ambleteuse, near Boulogne, to form a base for the spring offensive.[46] Yet within a week, Henry had decided to negotiate instead. Perhaps his agents had reported difficulties in recruiting mercenaries or purchasing supplies; perhaps he was worried about the intentions of the Emperor; or perhaps his energies were flagging for more personal reasons. Anyway, to the huge relief of his Council, by the end of March secret feelers were being put out in the direction of Paris, and Francis, whose constitution and finances were no more robust than Henry's, responded favourably. On 17 April Hertford and Lisle were required to lay aside their warlike roles, and to go and treat with the French on some 'indifferent ground'.[47] Each side struck bargaining poses, but by 15 May terms had been agreed. Boulogne was to remain English for eight years, at the end of which time it could be redeemed for 2 million crowns (about £600,000), and Scotland was more or less bypassed, the English agreeing not to wage further war unless provoked. Since border raiding was endemic, and could always be used as a pretext, this last clause was virtually meaningless. Henry ratified this treaty on 6 June, and Francis on 1 August 1546, the latter recognizing Henry's titles of Defender of the Faith and Supreme Head of the Church of England without a blush.[48] Less than six months before his death, the King had found peace. Scotland, however, remained unfinished business.

By the time of his death, Henry's navy numbered over 50 ships. Between 1545 and 1547 no fewer than 15 vessels were added to the fleet — seven by purchase, seven by building and one as a prize.[49] At the same time the Admiralty (as it is now proper to call it) had been completely reorganized. This came about partly in imitation of the Ordnance Office, and partly because the long-serving keeper of the Erith store-house (and unofficial Treasurer of the Navy), William Gonson, died in 1544. Gonson's position had been anomalous, and it was unsatisfactory to have the Clerk Controller, John Osborne, doubling as Captain of Portsmouth and a royal agent in the Low Countries. Early in 1545, therefore, a new body was proposed, to be called the King's Council for Marine Causes. This was to consist of seven officers, three of whom already existed, that is the Clerk Controller, Clerk of the Ships and Keeper of the Storehouses. The other four were to be the Lieutenant, or Vice-Admiral, the Treasurer, the Surveyor and Rigger and the Master of Naval Ordnance. All these were to be full-time salaried officials. The Vice-Admiral, for example, was to receive a fee of £100 a year, 1s. 8d. a day for two clerks, 10s. a day for travelling expenses and £10 a year for 'botehire'—a total of £275 a year. The others were to be paid less, down to the Clerk of the Ships whose fee was £33. 6s. 8d.[50]

This Council was to assume full responsibility for all dockyards and other shore facilities, and for all ships in harbour. When the ships were at sea, they were to remain under the direct control of the Lord Admiral, to whom the Council was also responsible. Most importantly, all money allocated for naval expenses was to be paid by warrant to the Treasurer, whose books were to be checked by his fellow officers before they were returned into the Exchequer. How quickly this new structure was implemented is not quite clear. John Winter, originally named as Treasurer, died in December 1545, and it is probable that the final form of the Council was not settled until the patents of appointment were issued in 1546. The Admiralty thus became a fully-fledged Department of State, akin to the Chancery or the Court of Augmentations— although smaller. It had its full-time payroll of clerks, master ship-wrights and other local officers, and was responsible for recruiting workmen as and when these were needed for the repair and mainten-ance programme. Ships continued to be built on contract in private yards, but increasingly even this work was being carried out in the royal dockyards, using direct labour. It was the most sophisticated and cen-tralized naval administration in Europe, and gave the King a long start when it came to mobilizing ships for active service.

At the end of his life, Henry's military machinery was in good work-ing order. The Admiralty had been reorganized and experience had shown that a large 'auxiliary navy' of privateers was available to be called upon when necessary. For example, in March 1545 Robert Reneger, a merchant of Southampton, had demonstrated his 'sea dog' potential by taking a Spanish cargo worth over £4,000 off the Azores, an operation that he carried out in revenge for years of harassment by the Inquisition. There were howls of protest from the Imperial ambas-sador, but Anglo-Imperial relations were poor at the time, and Reneger was rewarded with the command of one of the King's ships.[51]

The campaigns of 1544–5 have been described as the 'last hurrah' for the longbow and the noble retinue, but in truth both were obsolete before then. In 1542 a new foundry for the casting of iron guns was established in Kent, and encouraged by the King with an order for 200 cannons. This marked the beginning of a new era in English gun-founding, greatly reducing dependence on continental suppliers.[52]

Henry's image also survived his declining years of corpulence and ill-health. He was, as he had always been, larger than life. No longer the *preux chevalier*, he had become the Great King. A merciless tyrant to those who opposed him, he had at the same time become a national leader of a new kind. When Henry Howard, the Earl of Surrey, tried to claim a role in the royal minority that was clearly impending on the basis of his own royal ancestry, in November 1546 Henry struck him down without mercy. Surrey's lineage pretensions ended on the block on 21 January 1547, and in spite of a lifetime of loyal service his father, the Duke of Norfolk, would have followed him if it had not been for the demise of Henry himself just a week later. The slightest hint of a status based on ancestry alone carried a terrible retribution with it. Obedience and dependence were what was required of a nobleman. Henry had defied the Pope, the Emperor and the King of France. He had become King of Ireland in 1541, and had put down rebellions both there and at home. He had defined his own succession, reorganized his Church and realigned his nobility. There seemed to be nothing that he could not do, and his court had displayed a magnificence the equal of any in Europe. His last military action had been to seize Boulogne from under the nose of the King of France, and he presided, like a ghost in armour, over the years that followed.

In his last will and testament of 30 December 1547, as well as a previous Act of parliament, Henry restored both his daughters Mary and Elizabeth to the succession. Realizing that he was not going to live until Edward reached adulthood, he entrusted the government to a list of executors who were to act as a Privy Council until his son reached 18. A few days after Henry VIII's death on 28 January 1547 this Council chose the new King's uncle, Edward Seymour, to be Lord Protector of England. Seymour was created Duke of Somerset, and it was his policies that were to shape the first years of Edward VI's reign.

CHAPTER FIVE

EDWARD VI

❖

THE CHILD
KING

MINORITIES always presented an image problem, and never more so than in the case of Edward VI. Unless you lived in London, or on one of the court's regular routes through the Home Counties, the chances were that you would never have seen his formidable sire in person, but you would have known what he looked like. Someone you knew would have seen a portrait, and in any case you would have known his reputation—a gigantic, awe-inspiring and terrifying figure. But his son was a child, a boy of nine; robust enough, and looking remarkably like his father, but quite unable to fill such large shoes. Holbein portrayed him as an infant, with a flattering Latin inscription, urging him to grow up like his father, and there are two or three pictures of him as a child, by unknown artists. However the only portraits that make any effort to create an image were painted after his accession by Wilhelm Scrots. These show him as a self-possessed youth, with his left hand on the handle of his dagger, in a conscious imitation of his father's famous pose.[1]

No doubt the courtiers and ambassadors who actually saw these portraits were suitably impressed, but to the great majority of his subjects he would have remained a shadowy figure in the background of public life. His coronation in February 1547 was sufficiently imposing, but the child at the centre of it had no personality of his own—and again the imagery did not reach beyond those who were actually present.[2] However, he was a studious, pious child, who, well before his premature death, was turning into a zealous (if not bigoted) Protestant, and who appointed Knox, Latimer and Hooper to preach to his court. This gave the reformed publicists their cue, and he became the Godly Imp and the New Josias.[3] Whether this image would have made him popular at the time it is hard to say, but it stuck to him in subsequent historiography, and is how he was known to the readers of Camden and Foxe. It was probably the best that could be done to make him distinctive.

None of this had anything to do with martial arts. Like his father he grew up keen on field sports, but Henry seems to have taken no particular pains to train him in aristocratic pastimes such as jousting. Perhaps he was just too young. After his accession, when he started keeping a journal, we know that Edward was keen on jousting's juvenile relation —running at the ring—and on more plebeian pastimes such as running, leaping, and shooting (with both bow and gun).⁴ In spite of his godly reputation, he strikes the observer as being a thoroughly normal boy—insofar as anyone in his position could be normal. As he began to grow up, he showed an absorbed interest in wars and battles. Under September 1547 his journal records

> There was great preparation made to go into Scotland, and the Lord Protector, the Earl of Warwick, the Lord Dacre, the Lord Grey [of Wilton], and Mr. Bryan went with a great number of nobles and gentlemen to Berwick, where the first day after his coming, he mustered all his company, which were to the number of 13,000 footmen and 5000 horsemen. The next day he marched on into Scotland...⁵

There then follows a brief but specific account of the campaign, including the battle of Pinkie, and over the next few years tournaments and other martial feats are described in loving detail. In January 1552, for example, the complete list of Challengers and Defendants at the New Year jousts is recorded, and a detailed description given of a debate *cum* joust between teams representing Youth and Riches.⁶ The journal shows a young man very much in touch with the world about him, and although it was in a sense a school exercise, not at all reluctant to disclose the real nature of his interests and loyalties. It is, however, entirely innocent of military experience. Edward was never taken, either by the Lord Protector or by his subsequent minders, on any kind of campaign or military exercise. The most that he ever did was to inspect the gendarmerie, and the impression given is that if he had lived to be a man his interest in war would have remained academic. In spite of his concern with tactics and the number of casualties, there is no sign of that yearning for the warrior's life that his father had displayed at a very similar age.

Nevertheless, war was never very far away, and in a sense the politics of Henry's last months had made it more likely. The reformers had triumphed, and this guaranteed not merely the continuance of the Royal Supremacy, but a steady movement towards Protestantism now that the old King's restraining hand was removed.[7] Relations with the Emperor, which were difficult in any case, were now set to become more so. Also, two months after Henry's death his old sparring partner Francis I followed him to the grave, and it was well known that the Dauphin (now Henry II) regretted the treaty of Camp, and was anxious to secure the recovery of Boulogne. The summer of 1547 was therefore no time for England to be lowering her guard, and the Lord Protector carried out musters and mobilized his fleet as though he was expecting trouble. However, the trouble that came was almost entirely of his own making. Scotland, as we have seen, was unfinished business, and it was later alleged that Henry on his deathbed had urged the Earl of Hertford to see it completed. On 16 April muster commissions were issued on the wholly spurious grounds that the Scots were preparing for war 'by sea and land'. Weapons were to be checked, and noblemen and gentlemen bound to maintain great horses were to have them at an hour's readiness by 20 May.[8] In the course of July forces were selectively recruited from these musters, again on the pretext that the Scots were already mobilizing, but in reality provoked by the fact that attempts to resurrect the treaty of Greenwich were having no success at all. The Lord Protector, the Duke of Somerset (as the Earl of Hertford had become in February 1547) seems to have decided, as Henry VIII had done in 1542, to settle with the Scots before the French launched their anticipated strike to recover Boulogne. By late August some 18,000 men and 24 fighting ships had been assembled at Berwick, and there, on the afternoon of 27 August he joined them. Meanwhile Lord Wharton was prepared to lead 2,500 men from Carlisle into the western borders as a diversion.[9]

THE BATTLE OF PINKIE CLEUGH, 1547

M Y LORD MARSHALL [*William, Lord Grey*], *notwithstanding whom no danger detracted from doing his enterprise, with the company and order afore appointed, came full in their faces from the hill's side towards them.*

*Herewith waxed it very hot, on both sides, with pitiful cries, horrible roar, and
terrible thundering of guns besides. The day darkened above head with smoke
of shot. The sight and appearance of the enemy, even at hand, before. The danger of death on every side else. The bullets, pellets and arrows flying each where
so thick, and so uncertainly lighting, that nowhere was there any surety of
safety. Every man stricken with a dreadful fear, not so much, perchance, of
death as of hurt: which things, though they were but certain to some, were yet
doubted of all. Assured cruelty at the enemy's hands, without hope of mercy.
Death to fly and danger to fight… But my Lord Marshall and the others, with
present mind and courage, warily and quickly continued their course towards
them: and my Lord's Grace [the Duke of Somerset] was then at his post by the
ordnance aloft… Therewith then turned all the whole rout, cast down their
weapons, ran out of their Wards, off with their jacks, and with all that ever they
might, betook them to the race that their Governor began. Our men had found
them at the first (as what could escape so many thousand eyes?) and sharply
and quickly with an universal outcry 'They fly! They fly!' pursued after in
chase amain…*

[William Patten, *The Expedition into Scotland* (1548).

Pollard, *Tudor Tracts*, pp.123–5.]

The subsequent events were recorded for posterity by one of the
judges of his 'marshalsea court', William Patten (see above), and later
published under the title *The Expedition into Scotland of the most worthily
fortunate Prince Edward, Duke of Somerset, uncle unto our most noble sovereign Lord, the Kings Majesty, Edward VI…*[10] As the title reveals, this was
as much about the glorification of Somerset as it was about the record-
ing of events, but the narrative is none the less of great interest. On 2
September the Earl of Warwick led the vanguard of 4,000 men across
the Tweed. Behind him Somerset commanded the main army and
Lord Dacre the rearguard. On 7 September there was a skirmish as the
army crossed the North Tyne, in the course of which (according to
Patten) the Earl greatly distinguished himself.[11] Having had plenty of
warning of Somerset's intentions, the Scots had mobilized a suitable
response, and by 9 September the two armies were encamped within a
couple of miles of each other on Falside Brae, near Musselborough. A
cavalry skirmish ensued in the course of which (again according to
Patten) 1,300 of the Scots were killed, and a number taken prisoner.

The battle of Pinkie Cleugh that ensued on the following day is described in great detail. The Scots abandoned their strong position on the Brae, with the intention of taking the English camp by surprise, but the latter had been 'stirring the timelier', and they were frustrated.[12] The English then managed to get several of their cannon into position on the Brae, which wrought havoc amongst the Scottish cavalry. 'Hackbutters they have few or none', Patten observed, drawing attention to a serious weakness of the Scottish infantry, because the English arquebusiers clearly did great execution. Archers are also mentioned, but this must have been one of the last occasions upon which they were engaged. When it came to the point the battle was decided less by the tactical skill of the commanders than by the fighting quality of the troops, and by the inspirational moves made by individual captains in the thick of the fighting. At length the Scottish infantry broke under the superior firepower of the English, and fled. Once their formation was broken they became easy meat for the English cavalry, and many were cut down before they could escape. The pursuit went on for about five miles, almost to the outskirts of Edinburgh.

> Thus, through the favour of GOD's bounty, by the valiance and policy of my Lord Protector's Grace, by the forward endeavour of all the nobles and council there besides; and by the willing diligence of every captain, officer and true subject else; we most valiantly and honourably won the victory over our enemies.[13]

The casualties were heavy, particularly on the Scottish side, although Patten's estimate of 13,000 dead (including 2,600 lairds and gentlemen) is certainly an exaggeration, as is his account of the quantity of armour and weapons abandoned on the field, 'of jacks especially and swords, above thirty thousand'.[14] It was a decisive victory, and Scotland's field army was destroyed, but that did not mean that the country was subdued, as was soon to be demonstrated. Following the battle, Somerset moved towards Leith and began siege works, but without much conviction, and on 20 September the English army began to withdraw. As they went Scottish heralds visited the camp, offering negotiations. English commissioners were appointed, but 'These Scots ... neither came nor belike meant to come'. The English army recrossed the Tweed on 29 September and the camp was broken up. After waiting for some time, the English commissioners also gave up and went home. Somerset returned to London, covered with the glories of victory, but with very little else achieved. The treaty of Greenwich remained unfulfilled, and unless the Protector could devise a better follow up strategy than his late master, the battle of Pinkie Cleugh would have achieved no more than that of Solway Moss. Realizing that he had failed in his main objective, Somerset decided to take advantage of Scotland's temporary military weakness to plant garrisons across the lowlands to maintain pressure on the Regency government.[15] This had already been started during the Pinkie campaign, when ships commanded by Lord Clinton, the Vice-Admiral, had taken Inchcolm in the Firth of Forth and Broughty Castle near Dundee. There was still an English party among the Scottish nobility, and the divisions of that class were notorious. It was probably for that reason rather than out of any deliberate attempt to deceive that the Scottish commissioners had failed to turn up at Berwick, so there was a reasonable chance that a policy of steady coercion would prove fruitful.

For the next two years the garrisons dominated English policy towards Scotland. Some were successfully established, others failed but few were actively resisted. Nor did the French immediately intervene. Between Leo Strozzi's bombardment of St Andrews Castle in July 1547, which forced the surrender of Cardinal Beaton's assassins, and the arrival of André de Montalembert with 6,000 men at Leith in June 1548, their role remained potential only.[16] In April 1548 there was a plan to inhibit access by the western route by planting a garrison in Kirkudbright, but it was abandoned because of supply difficulties. Other plans also came to nothing. An ambitious project to capture Edinburgh Castle was abandoned in January, and in March the planting of a garrison in Dundee was similarly aborted because of the large number of men that would be needed. An attempt to capture Dunbar Castle failed in May. However, many were established, some on the initiative of English border officials, and some on direct instructions from London. In the former category came the bands of light horse established at Ayton, Lochwood Castle, Jedburgh, Kelso, Cockpool and Dumfries, while Somerset directly ordered the planting of Yester Castle, Lauder and Haddington.[17] In contrast to those established by local initiatives, these latter garrisons consisted partly of English forces drawn from outside the borders, and partly of Italian and Spanish mercenaries. In April 1548 Haddington was selected as the main base for operations in the Lowlands. It was fortified and manned with 2,500 soldiers, who were to be provisioned out of England. A 'burnt zone' was created round about it to discourage siege operations.[18]

The arrival of the French force changed the balance of power, but did not immediately affect English strategy. In August 1548 a naval expedition under Lord Clinton attempted, and failed, to establish further garrisons in Fife. Dundee was briefly reoccupied, but in mid-September a gale scattered Clinton's fleet, and Dundee fell again to the Scots. In November the whole Tay garrison project was abandoned, and the remaining strong points were put onto the defensive for the winter. Nevertheless the initiative was not entirely surrendered; a new garrison was established at Fast Castle in February 1549, and at Inchkieth on the Firth of Forth in July. In July also a force of mercenaries was established at the Hermitage in Liddesdale, a fortress ceded by agreement with the Earl of Bothwell.[19] What had changed was that by late 1548 such garrisons were being actively ejected, as distinct from merely failing to establish themselves. Dumfries, Yester Castle and Cockpool had all fallen to Franco-Scottish assaults by the autumn of 1548, and Jedburgh, Inchkieth and Hume Castle by early 1549.[20] Others were abandoned as being impossible to sustain; Inch Castle in February 1548, and the main base at Haddington in September 1549. A mere handful survived into 1550, when they were eventually surrendered by the terms of the treaty of Boulogne.

This marked the end of any forward English policy in Scotland. The Protector had fallen from power in October 1549, but his Scottish policy had been effectively killed over a year before, which makes his persistence in early 1549 very hard to understand. As soon as he landed, Montalembert had proceeded to the siege of Haddington. That siege had not succeeded, but it provided the location for a Franco-Scottish treaty that redefined the whole political situation. The French commander was empowered to negotiate not merely a guarantee of Scottish integrity, but an alliance that embraced the marriage of the young Queen Mary (then aged six) to the Dauphin Henry and, more important, her immediate transfer to France.[21] This treaty was signed on 10 July 1549, and Mary departed for France by the western route the following month. The treaty of Greenwich was not merely dead, but buried, and it not therefore surprising that, having secured control of the Council in December 1549, the Earl of Warwick should have decided to cut his losses in Scotland.

The final quietus had been given to the Protector's hopes, not by the treaty of Haddington but by the outbreak of civil disturbances in England, which put paid to any hopes of raising a new army in the north, and caused the mercenary bands already active in the borders to be recalled to the south. Apart from the deployment of these foreign troops, the military significance of the campaigns needed to suppress these risings was not great. The main danger was that the levies that had perforce to be used for the most part would desert or defect to the rebels, but that did not happen. It may be that the retinues of councillors and other nobles that were also employed provided sufficient stiffening. Lord John Russell, sent against the rebels in the West Country, was inexperienced and over cautious. It was only after more than a month, and substantial reinforcements led by Lord Grey and Sir William Herbert, that he moved to relieve the siege of Exeter. He finally confronted the main rebel force at Clyst St Mary on 5 August 1549, and after a hard fought engagement in which his artillery played a significant part, routed his numerous but ill-equipped opponents.[22] The rising in Devon and Cornwall had been largely caused by resentment against the Protestant direction of government policy over the previous two years, and was particularly directed against the Prayer Book, which had been officially introduced at Whitsun.

Elsewhere, and particularly in East Anglia, the motivation was 'enclosure', which is a catch-all term for a variety of changes of land use introduced mainly by gentry land holders. In some cases arable land was converted to pasture by evading the customary security that the manorial system was supposed to confer on tenants.[23] This could result in depopulation—families being forced off the land—and although that was comparatively uncommon, it caused great resentment. More often the change involved the engrossing of common land, that is the seizure of more than their fair share by greedy landlords when commons came to be enclosed. These grievances caused a 'camping movement' that spread across Norfolk and Suffolk, resulting in the destruction of hedges and other acts of moderate violence.[24] The focus of this movement was in Norfolk, where the Kett brothers, local landowners, created a great camp on Mousehold Heath outside Norwich, destroyed numerous enclosures and imprisoned some particularly unpopular landlords. The Lord Protector had some sympathy with these protests, and needed to be persuaded that it was unacceptable for men to take the law into their own hands in the way that was happening.[25] The local justices having failed to contain the situation, on 21 July 1549 the Council offered Robert Kett negotiations, but at that point his forces were multiplying rapidly, and he refused. On 30 July, therefore, the Marquis of Northampton was sent against him with several gentlemen and their retinues, and what should have been an adequate force. He occupied the city of Norwich, meeting no resistance, but was then attacked over two days by the rebels using guns that must have been looted from gentlemen's armouries, and driven out with considerable loss of life. Northampton was humiliated and the Council deeply worried by this untoward development, but the only alternative now was to try again, using a more effective agent.[26]

On 15 August the Earl of Warwick, who was probably England's most skilful soldier, was sent against them with 6,000 foot (including 1,400 mercenaries) and 1,500 cavalry. He reached Norwich on the 23rd, and immediately attempted to enter into negotiations. It seems that Kett was willing, but his men were not, and discipline broke down in the rebel camp. Kett was no soldier, and had lost control of his followers, so he may not have been responsible for the fatal decision, taken on 26 August, to break up the fortified camp and move to lower ground.[27] Unprotected by any kind of defensive works, on the following day the rebels were attacked and slaughtered by Warwick's cavalry and his mercenaries. The English levies were left in possession of Norwich, where, over the next few days, a number of rebel fugitives were caught and hanged. Warwick, who was a shrewd man, resisted calls for indiscriminate revenge, and retreated, leaving the mopping up to the local magistrates. He did not, however, disband his troops, and their existence gave him a commanding voice in the politics of the next month, including the military clout to depose the Lord Protector in early October.[28]

The disastrous events of 1549 were viewed with dismay by the King's Council, who laid the blame for them squarely at the Duke of Somerset's door. The Lord Protector was removed from office, and was in effect replaced by John Dudley, the Earl of Warwick, who became Leader of the Council but never took the title 'Protector'. Partly because of the circumstances of his overthrow, the Duke of Somerset quickly developed a legend. He became the 'Good Duke', who had understood the commons grievances, and who had summoned them in vain to protect him against his noble enemies.[29] In fact he was a self-opinionated man, and a very bad manager, who fell because he lacked any judgement in dealing with people. His attitude towards Scotland showed a similar lack of understanding, because he seems to have been quite oblivious to the adverse affects that his coercive tactics were having, and how rapidly his support north of the border was being dissipated. In January 1548, when there was still a lot at stake, he published both in English and in Latin *An Epistle or Exhortation to Unity and Peace*, aimed at convincing Scottish opinion, and probably European opinion in general, of the enormous advantages to be gained from a peaceful union of the crowns.[30] This epistle entitles him to be regarded as something of an idealist—the man who created the idea of Great Britain—or would do if it were not so blatant a piece of political propaganda. It made some impression in Scotland, and converted James Harrison, who then spent his time and energy trying to persuade his fellow countrymen of the virtues of Union, but in the diplomatic battle which was then being waged between the agents of England and France, it could not outweigh the effects of French gold, and Somerset was forced back on the policy of coercion, which made his epistle appear to be just so much hot air. The Protector was trying to overcome Scottish defiance by alternative methods, and they did not work, but he deserves the credit for having tried.

WAR WITH FRANCE, 1549

THE FRENCH KING *perceiving this [risings across the south of England], caused war to be proclaimed and, hearing that our ships lay at Jersey, sent a great number of his galleys and certain ships to surprise our ships; but they, lying at anchor, beat the French [so] that they were fain to retire with a loss of a thousand of their men. At the same time the French king passed by Boulogne to Newhaven with his army and took Blackness by treason and the Almain [German] camp, which done, Newhaven surrendered. There were also in a skirmish between 300 English footmen and 700 French horsemen, six nobles slain. Then the French king came with his army to Boulogne, which, they seeing, rased Bolemberg. But because of the plague he was compelled to retire, and Chatillon [Gaspard de Coligny] was left behind as governor of the army...*

[W.K. Jordan, ed., *The Chronicle and Political Papers of King Edward VI*, 1966, p.13.]

Henry II of France had intervened successfully in Scotland as early as the summer of 1548, but the English command of the seas had deterred him from serious operations against Boulogne. Then, in the late summer of 1549, the general mess that England seemed to be in with civil disorders in several parts of the south, and garrisons being liquidated in Scotland, made the opportunity too good to miss, and he declared war on 8 August. It soon transpired, however, that appearances were deceptive, and that however weak England might appear to be, the surrender of Boulogne was not an option. While Henry gathered his forces at Montrueil for an assault on the town, there was action at sea.[31] The English fleet, under the overall command of Sir Thomas Cotton (there being no Lord Admiral at this point), was divided into three squadrons. The first, under Sir Thomas Wyndham, was operating out of Newcastle, and was largely concerned with maintaining the garrison at Broughty Castle; the second, under Cotton himself, was operating out of Dover 'to guard the Narrow Seas'; and the third, commanded by William Winter, was operating out of Portsmouth. It was this third squadron that encountered Leo Strozzi near the Channel Islands on about 14 August 1549. Strozzi had 12 galleys, several transports and about 2,000 men, his objective being a seaborne assault on Jersey. However, his galleys proved no match for Winter's heavy guns, and he was decisively defeated, several of his ships being sunk and one (the *Black Galley*) captured. Renamed the *Galley Mermaid,* this was recruited to the Royal Navy, and continued to appear in the records down to 1562.[32] Privateers also sprang into action on both sides with the declaration of war, but the effects of their operations are impossible to quantify. Probably the English had the better of these exchanges, being the more experienced, but that cannot be determined.

Meanwhile the French attack on Boulogne was developing promisingly. Several probing attempts had been made on the outworks even before war was declared, and in mid-August the fort of Blackness was betrayed by its German mercenary garrison. On 17 August 1549, after a sharp engagement, the remaining outfort of Bolemberg was also captured.[33] This brought the attackers face to face with the main fortifications, and Henry, having no taste for siege operations, handed over the command of the army to Gaspard de Coligny, Sieur de Chataillon. Chataillon set about bombarding the jetty, to discourage the arrival of seaborne supplies which our men seeing, set upon them by night and slew divers Frenchmen and dismounted many of their pieces. Nevertheless the French came another time and planted their ordnance towards the sand side on the sand hills and beat divers ships of victualers at the entry of the haven; but yet the Englishmen at the King's adventure came into the haven and refreshed divers time the town...[34]

The Emperor, appealed to for assistance, reluctantly agreed to allow the English to recruit 4,000 foot and 2,000 horse within his dominions, provided that they were shipped out directly, and even more reluctantly renewed the treaty of 1543, by which he had guaranteed Calais against French attack. Frustrated in this way of an intended attack on Guisnes, and making no further progress against Boulogne, Henry became bored and inclined to negotiate. Early in November, while he was still pumping reinforcements into the beleaguered town, the Earl of Warwick was coming to the conclusion that Boulogne was not worth the massive expense, which he could so ill afford, and sent one Anthony Guidotti to Paris to sound out the possibilities.[35] Although it might seem that the French held all the cards at this juncture, that was not in fact the case. The English were bullish about their success in supplying the besieged garrison, and about the command of the sea that made this possible, while the French army was suffering from plague and desertion. Guidotti met with a cautious but favourable response, and kept up his shuttle diplomacy for more than two months, until in mid-January formal negotiations could be opened. By that time Warwick (now firmly in control of the Council) was looking a little further ahead. He was well aware that his decision to continue his predecessor's Protestant policies—a decision related to the young King's developing convictions—would cause further offence to the Emperor. Charles's hesitancy in responding to English requests during the previous autumn had given a fair warning of his attitude. The alternative was better relations with France, and if the issue of Boulogne could once be settled, that was a distinct possibility.[36]

The English commissioners were therefore authorized to cede Boulogne, effectively for the best terms they could get, and when negotiations finally got under way on 19 February 1550, there were few sticking points. On 24 March it was agreed that Boulogne would be returned upon the payment of 400,000 crowns in two instalments, but that the English would keep the artillery and other military stores held there. The English garrisons would be withdrawn from Scotland, and Somerset's policy was effectively written off.[37] News of this agreement was received with mixed emotions. At a popular level with 'bonfires and great cheer' because an unpopular war was over, but with shame and hostility among the military aristocracy. Henry VIII's great conquest had been sold like a huckster's pack, and the great dream of union with Scotland was dead and buried. On the other hand there were those who pointed out that the position in Scotland was hopeless anyway, and that Warwick had extracted from Henry II far more than he would willingly have paid. The celebrations attendant upon the ratification of the treaty in May generated more good will than could reasonably have been expected, and the French delegation was entertained with lavish banquets, and 'a pastime of ten against ten at the ring'.[38] At the same time the Scots also ratified, and a rather nervous peace descended upon the realm.

Boulogne had been a heavy financial liability, and it had cost the Council £30,000 in back wages and other debts before the place could be handed over. The relief from that burden was considerable, but in spite of the new-found friendship of France, Warwick still regarded the international situation as fragile. Perhaps he had no great trust in Chataillon's professions of regard, but he thought it necessary to strengthen the defences of Calais, and worked hard through a boundary commission to make sure that no conflict over the extent of the Pale should provide a pretext for disruption.[39] He also maintained the navy on what was virtually a war footing. Only four ships were added to the fleet during the entire reign, and most of the rowbarges were sold, but it is clear from the accounts of Robert Legge — and of Benjamin Gonson who followed him as Treasurer in 1548 — that there was a regular maintenance programme.[40] The rowbarges were replaced with four pinnaces (which don't count as ships), three of which were built and one probably purchased. A survey of the navy carried out on 26 August 1552 shows that only one ship of any size, the 500-ton *Marion* of Danzig, had been disposed of since 1548. Some 24 vessels were listed as being 'in good case to serve', and three others were already dry-docked to await rebuilding. Four were thought 'meet to be sold', six others 'not worth the keeping' and a further four unclassified — a total of 41.[41]

The recommendations for sale or disposal seem not to have been implemented, but most of those listed as being in good case were actively at sea during that period, as the victualling accounts of Edward Baeshe and Richard Wattes, taken in June 1550, and subsequently those of Baeshe alone, demonstrate.[42] The survey went on to point out that every ship should be docked and caulked every year, with more substantial repairs as needed, and drew attention to the special needs of the galleys 'if your Lordships' pleasure be to have them kept', about which there was apparently some doubt.

Warwick had surrendered his office as Lord Admiral on being appointed Lord Great Chamberlain in February 1547, and been replaced by Lord Thomas Seymour. Seymour had proved less than satisfactory, staying at home during the Scottish campaign of September that year. Later he was accused of collaborating with the pirates he was supposed to be suppressing, and in January 1549 he was arrested for high treason. He had, allegedly, been plotting against his brother the Lord Protector, and scheming to marry the Princess Elizabeth, the King's sister.[43] He was executed in March 1549 and the office had then been left vacant until it was resumed by Warwick on 28 October. On 14 May 1550 it was bestowed upon Edward, Lord Clinton.[44]

There were also some changes to the Admiralty. Benjamin Gonson moved from being Surveyor to the Treasurership, and was replaced as Surveyor by William Winter. On 28 June 1550 Edward Baeshe was added to the Council as Surveyor General of the Victuals, and on 16 December 1552 William Woodhouse was appointed Vice-Admiral in succession to Sir Thomas Clere. All these men were experienced sea captains, and Baeshe's appointment filled an obvious gap in the competence of the Council. The provision of victuals was one of the most important (and expensive) functions of the Admiralty, and it is surprising that it took nearly five years to bring it under central control. The vested interests of the purveyors at the respective ports may have been the cause. Gonson presented a single account from 29 September 1548 to 24 October 1551, and that shows him to have dispensed £66,250 in a little over three years, an average of about £22,000 a year. Of that sum £30,000 was spent at Deptford, which was the main dockyard, and only £1,150 at Portsmouth, which was the 'advanced base' used mainly in wartime.[45] Ships at sea were separately accounted, but it seems clear that most of the action during these years was focused on the Thames.

Apart from the defeat of Strozzi in the Channel Islands, the navy did not cover itself with glory during this reign. The *Mary Willoughby* was recaptured during the 1547 campaign, and Thomas Wyndham did a decent job in maintaining the east coast garrisons down to the end of 1549, but the North Sea fleet was nowhere to be seen when Montalembert arrived with his French troops in June 1548, and no attempt was made to intercept the ships bearing the young Queen to France later in the same year. As usual, the navy concentrated its strength in the Narrow Seas, and although this strengthened Warwick's hand when it came to bargaining over Boulogne, it left little trace in the annals of warfare.

On the 23 April 1551 the King of France was elected to the Order of the Garter, and accepted the honour, reciprocating by bestowing the Order of St Michael on Edward, who was absolutely delighted.[46] Henry did not apparently mind that the terms and conditions of the Order had recently been amended on Edward's instructions to exclude the 'remnants of Popery'. A few days later the Marquis of Northampton was appointed to bear the insignia to Paris, where he was lavishly entertained and appropriate courtesies were exchanged. On 11 July the Marechal St André arrived in London to return the compliment, and he turned out to be a courtier of great charm. The King was quite captivated, and left a detailed description of the ceremony, and of the hospitality that he provided:

> The next morning [20 July] he came to see mine arraying and
> saw my bedchamber and went a-hunting with hounds and saw
> me shoot and saw all my guard shoot together. He dined with
> me, heard me play on the lute … came to me in my study,
> supped with me, and so departed to Richmond.[47]

Neither the Marechal nor his entourage had objected to receiving Holy Communion after the order of the Church of England, and he had indeed gone out of his way to be gracious in every respect. This was no doubt partly intended to facilitate the negotiations that were by then in hand for Edward's marriage to Elizabeth — the young daughter of the French King. These had commenced towards the end of June with somewhat ritualistic posturings on the English part about Edward's commitment to the Queen of Scots. The French had brushed these aside, as they were no doubt expected to do, and proposed the alternative of Elizabeth. After a great deal of haggling over the dowry, an agreement was reached and the pair were formally betrothed.[48] However, nothing would happen until the bride reached the age of 12, and by that time the English King would be dead.

Edward clearly enjoyed being the centre of attention. On 4 July 1551 he recorded with satisfaction that he had been to Deptford to see the new *Primrose* (a ship of 300 tons) launched, and had been banqueted by Lord Clinton.[49] It is not clear whether he carried out the launching ceremony himself, but probably not, as he would surely have recorded the fact. In July and August 1552 he went on progress, through Surrey and into Sussex, noting that he was 'marvellously, yea rather excessively' banqueted at Cowdray. At this point his journal is interspersed with comments on the fortification of Berwick, and on a clash between the Flemings and the French near Thérouanne, but he returned to his main theme with notes upon his visit to Portsmouth, where he observed that 'two forts were to be made upon the entry to the haven'.[50] His letters to his friend Barnaby Fitzpatrick are more informative about this progress than the journal itself, which is mostly on the lines of 'Removing to Southampton… Removing to Beaulieu…', and does not suggest any great curiosity about the countryside through which he was passing. On 21 August, the day upon which he visited Woodlands in Dorset, the seat of Sir Edward Willoughby, there is no comment upon his reception there, but rather an extended note upon the peace that had been recently signed between the Emperor and Duke Maurice of Saxony.[51] It seems that by this time the keeping of his journal had become a somewhat onerous political duty, because we know from his letters that he was enjoying himself a good deal.

Edward's journal could do nothing for his image. It was a private document, and although his tutors may have been delighted at his precocious political awareness, this could not translate onto the public stage. As a public figure, the King remained a problem, which was one of the reasons why the Earl of Warwick (who became Duke of Northumberland in October 1551) took such pains to 'bring him on' in the last two years of his life. He was encouraged to write political papers, to discuss issues with his Council, and to be more prominent in diplomatic exchanges. How much difference his interventions made is not clear, but the fact that he was becoming more visible was undoubtedly significant.[52] It was just as this emergence was to be put to the test that he succumbed to his final illness, and left behind him the image, not of a great king in the making, but rather of a pious, sickly youth, dominated by the Duke of Northumberland.

Just as the military adventures of 1547–9 were more about the heroic image of the Duke of Somerset than they were about the King, so the last three years of the reign were overshadowed by the growing 'Black Legend' of John Dudley. In its final form this was determined by the failure of his bid to alter the succession in 1553, and his subsequent renunciation of his Protestant beliefs, but it was already in existence while he was in power. He was alleged to have betrayed Thomas Seymour with false advice, and to have plotted the overthrow of the Duke of Somerset for several years, going back into Henry VIII's reign.[53] No substantive evidence supports either of these accusations, indeed he seems to have been on good terms with the Protector until the outbreak of the East Anglian revolt. Most particularly, he was charged with gratuitous malice in bringing about the execution of the former Protector in January 1552, on charges that he later admitted were fabricated. However, although not guilty as charged, the Duke of Somerset had been intriguing to secure a renewed ascendancy in the Council, and Northumberland had decided that he could not risk a split in the Council during a minority. Having done his best to warn his rival— although unsuccessfully—he felt that he had no option but to strike.[54] These factional quarrels hardly touched the King, except that as a nine-year-old he had been innocently guilty of encouraging Thomas Seymour's bid to marry his stepmother, the recently widowed Queen. But they did a great deal of harm to the image of the realm.

Of course it depended a bit on where you were coming from. If you were a religious reformer, such as Martin Bucer or Peter Martyr Vermigli, driven out of your homeland by persecution, then England was a refuge and a haven of Godliness. If, on the other hand, you were a Roman Catholic, and perhaps also an exile, like Richard Smith or Reginald Pole, then England was in the grip of heretics. Whereas the former praised the 'Godly Imp', the latter blamed his evil councillors, among whom the Duke of Northumberland featured prominently. Even the Princess Mary, constantly at odds with the reforming policies of the Regency governments, tried very hard to maintain that her brother was merely an innocent victim of these evil men. This delusion was particularly hard to maintain when Edward personally rebuked her for her obstinacy, but politically she had nowhere else to go.[55] The regime that held England in the most hatred and contempt was that of the Emperor, Charles V. He had even refrained at first from exchanging greetings with the newly crowned Edward in the hope that Mary (in his eyes Henry's only legitimate child) would put forward her own claim. She had not done so, and being a pragmatist, he had held his nose and done business with the Protectorate. As long as England was at war with France, she was an ally — of a sort — but when peace led to a growing friendship, his hostility intensified. In early July 1550 he had even countenanced a plan to spirit Mary out of England to save her from the pressure to which she was being subjected, but at the last moment the Princess had had second (and wiser) thoughts.[56] By the autumn of 1551 Charles was intermittently incapacitated by gout, and policy was being increasingly directed by his half-sister Mary of Hungary, the Regent of the Netherlands. Mary had her own reasons for disliking the English, and was looking for an additional base for the Flemish fleet. In her enthusiasm, she rather let her contempt run away with her. In September she wrote to Charles's trusted councillor the Bishop of Arras,

> We must therefore have a port in that country [England] at our disposal, either by force or through friendship. Many people are of the opinion that the kingdom of England would not be impossible to conquer, especially now that it is a prey to poverty and discord...[57]

It was just a thought, and nothing came of it, but it was symptomatic of the way in which outsiders regarded England during the minority governments. It was an understandable but false perception. Militarily England was not weak, as the tough defence of Boulogne demonstrates. It was strong in artillery and in cavalry, and its infantry was not lacking in fighting qualities, as had been demonstrated at Pinkie. The English navy controlled the Channel throughout the reign, and intermittently dominated the North Sea. Its naval gunnery was second to none, and its privateers swarmed thickly, whether they were called upon or not. The weakness was political, and came less from internal faction than from the inevitable lack of leadership during a minority. The Duke of Northumberland was as effective a ruler as any was likely to be, and suppressed internal dissent, both popular and aristocratic — but he was not the King.

Because of the dominant position occupied by the Dukes of Somerset and Northumberland, and because of the role of aristocratic retinues in the suppression of the revolts of 1549, it has been suggested that the minority of Edward VI resulted in something of a revival of noble power. A reaction, in fact, against the centralizing policies of Henry VIII. However, neither Somerset nor Northumberland (let alone their fellow peers) were over-mighty subjects in the fifteenth-century sense. Their landed estates were comparatively recently acquired, and Northumberland in particular never put down roots in any single place.[58] They lacked the tenant loyalty and generations-old affinities that had characterized the Neville Earls of Warwick or the Percy Earls of Northumberland. Their soldiers, when they raised them, expected to be paid at the going rate, and showed no particular attachment to their commanders. The private armies that had fought the Wars of the Roses were, and remained, things of the past. When Somerset was assailed by the Council in 1549 those who came to his aid were not his clients and dependants, but disorganized and ill-equipped bands of peasants, who were more of a liability than an asset. Similarly, when Northumberland was faced with the disaffection of the Council as he tried to confront Mary in July 1553, his men deserted without the slightest compunction. There was not even a suspicion of the bastard feudal retinue about his force, and he knew that he could call upon no such resources. There could be no going back on the achievement of the Tudor Kings, and had Edward lived to achieve his majority, there is every sign that he would have been as ruthless and opinionated in this respect as his father. But it was not to be, and he died on 6 July 1553, just over a month short of his 16th birthday, and leaving an uncertain succession.

CHAPTER SIX

MARY I

❖

THE FIRST
RULING
QUEEN

ALTHOUGH she had spent much of her life as the acknowledged heir
to the English throne, first during her parents' marriage and then during her brother's reign, Mary's succession was by no means straightforward. Unwilling for England to be returned to the old religion, Edward
VI chose Lady Jane Grey, the granddaughter of his father's sister Mary,
to succeed him. Jane was the daughter-in-law of Northumberland,
who quickly moved to have her proclaimed Queen on 10 July 1553.

The strong card in Mary's hand, as she faced this challenge, was that
she was the acknowledged heir by Henry VIII's last Succession Act of
1543, an Act that would have had to be repealed if her rival were to have
a legal claim. It was this factor, more than anything else, which furthered Mary's cause. Support for the young claimant quickly collapsed,
and Mary rode triumphantly into London to take the crown. Jane was
imprisoned in the Tower, although her life was spared for the time
being; Northumberland was executed for treason.

Despite this dramatic start, Mary still had a problem with her image:
she was a woman and therefore born to be a consort rather than a ruler.
Although there was no Salic law in England, the issue had not been
tried since the twelfth century, and then the female candidate had been
rejected. Mary was 37, unmarried and of questionable legitimacy when
her brother died.[1] In spite of having submitted to her father in 1536, she
continued to regard herself as his legitimate daughter, and based her
claim on that.[2] She also symbolized the popular concept of 'religion as
King Henry left it', because it had been in defence of that settlement that
she had conducted her high profile campaign of defiance against
Edward's ecclesiastical policy. In short, she represented the 'right and
proper course', and her gender did not immediately matter.

On 1 October 1553 Mary was crowned with traditional splendour, only the usual anointing on the breast being omitted.[3] However, the whole ceremonial had been designed for a man, and sat uneasily upon her. For the first (and last) time during the century, there was no coronation tournament, and the revels were distinctly subdued. This was partly because the court did not know how to respond to a female ruler, partly because its whole composition had changed since the summer, and it was filled with inexperienced courtiers, and partly because Mary had no sexual panache.[4] She could perfectly well have presided at the jousts, as Elizabeth was to do, as the inspirer of great deeds, superior, beautiful and unattainable. But such a thought was not within her reach. The only acceptable face of sexuality was within marriage, and that was a problem that had still to be faced. For the time being she was the lawful Queen (the little matter of her technical illegitimacy having been sorted out by parliament), the sovereign of her hereditary patrimony, and the pious restorer of the godly Mass. She was also a hard-working ruler, whose lack of practical political experience was compensated for by the presence in council of Stephen Gardiner, the Bishop of Winchester, her Lord Chancellor, and William, Lord Paget, who had been her father's secretary.[5]

However, the question of her marriage could not be long delayed. In the normal course of events she should have been married 20 years since, and have been the mother of a growing brood of children, but politics had dictated otherwise. This had probably helped her cause over the succession, because a *femme seul* was well known to the law, and could hold her own patrimony, whereas the *femme couvert* existed only in the person of her husband. Had she been married in July 1553 the presence of her husband would have complicated her position in a way that might well have proved fatal. She made discreet remarks about being wedded to her kingdom, but she was now free to exercise her own choice of man in a more conventional union.

It is hard to know how Mary looked at the personal aspect of marriage. As a spinster of a certain age, she may well have regarded the whole prospect of sexual intercourse with terrified fascination; but she knew her duty, and that was to provide for the succession if it should be possible.[6] It was this aspect that made the situation so urgent. Within a year or two, it would be too late; and although she probably knew little of these matters herself, she had the benefit of the best and most experienced advice. Politically the choice was not enormous, or overwhelmingly attractive. The only domestic candidate with the right credentials was Edward Courtenay, the 26-year-old son of the Marquis of Exeter, who had been executed in 1538. Courtenay had been imprisoned with his father, and had grown to manhood in the Tower of London. He had managed, somehow, to remain a Catholic, and had been carefully educated, but was totally inexperienced in the ways of the world. Mary had released him and restored him to the Earldom of Devon on 3 September 1553, but never showed the slightest interest in marrying him. He had a little Plantagenet royal blood, and was warmly backed by a group on the Council led by Stephen Gardiner, but he was a feckless young man and to have married him would have been disparaging, as well as an encouragement to faction.[7]

Then there was Dom Luis, the younger brother of the King of Portugal. Luis had been mentioned before: he was of royal blood, and an impeccable Catholic, and might even have been prepared to come and live in England, but his candidature was blocked by the only man who mattered in these discussions — the Emperor Charles V. The only reason why Charles was important was that Mary sought his advice. Years before, when he had been using diplomatic pressure to protect her from her father, she had sworn never to marry without his consent, and now she remembered her oath.[8] It was a serious mistake, because the Emperor, writing off his own prospects as a widower on the grounds of age (he was 53) and ill-health, put forward the name of his only son, Philip. Philip was 26, but already both a widower and a father. In a sense, Philip was the ideal choice. A zealous Catholic, he was both politically and sexually experienced, and came of the most impeccably royal family in Europe. However, he was his father's immediate heir in respect of Spain and the Indies, and he was a thoroughgoing Spaniard, steeped in the culture and language of that country.[9] Moreover, Charles was not much interested in the well-being of England in proffering his advice. He wanted Philip to become King of England in order to secure his rights in the Low Countries when the time should come for him to take over there. Mary did as she was bidden, and chose Philip, against the wishes of most of her Council, and the majority of her subjects.

Her decision was dutifully accepted by her Council, but there were mutterings in parliament, and full-scale rebellion in Kent, when

Thomas Wyatt, a local gentleman, helped lead a popular uprising with the aim of forcing Mary to change her mind. The revolt, which took place during the early months of 1554, was put down and the leaders were executed, along with the Queen's innocent but dangerous young cousin Jane Grey.[10] It began to be remembered that Mary was half-Spanish by blood, and another, altogether less flattering, image was created. She became 'the Spanish woman' and her dependence on the Imperial Ambassador Simon Renard for advice was viewed with great disfavour.

The Queen's forthcoming marriage created a number of problems early in 1554—some more obvious than others. What effect would her prospective transition from *femme seul* to *femme couvert* have upon her authority as sovereign? A private woman entering into such a contract would automatically surrender her property to her husband, but it was quite unclear whether the realm of England constituted a property in that sense or not. Only parliament could resolve such an issue, which it duly did on 5 May by passing an Act declaring that the Queen's authority in England was the same as that of any of her predecessor 'Kings of this realm'.[11] In other words, her gender became irrelevant as far as her power was concerned—which was fine, except that it left the problem of her image unresolved. Whatever the law might say, she was not a man, and was about to become a wife. By international custom, her husband would become King, so how would their images relate? By the terms of the marriage treaty, confirmed by parliament in the same session, Philip's authority was strictly limited. He could not act executively without her, take her out of the realm, or involve England in his perpetual struggle with France.[12] It was known that he was not happy with this situation, and was determined to escape from the restrictions of the treaty as soon and as far as possible.

Philip could not complain that he was not received with royal honours, and his father made him King of Naples on the eve of his marriage, so that the couple could wed as equals, but the symbolism of the ceremony was heavily stacked against him. Mary took the right-hand side, normally the man's position, and the sword of power was only borne before him after the wedding was complete. The King's servants even complained that he was compelled to eat off silver, while his wife used gold![13] More significantly, he had to get rid of most of his Spanish servants because they were stirring up trouble in the court, and he discovered to his chagrin that he would have to pay all his bills out of his Spanish revenues, because he had been allocated no English patrimony. Nevertheless he went through the motions of being a loving husband to everyone's satisfaction (and his father's surprise), and Mary showed every sign of being completely captivated.[14] Once the marriage was over, the English court and its hangers-on got on with the bad job of having a foreign King as best they could. While the treaty was still under negotiation, a genealogy had been published, showing that Philip was an 'honorary Englishman', being descended in the female line from Edward III, and this was a theme also picked up in the pageantry which greeted his first entry into London.[15] In spite of the problems that it was to create, Mary was seen as having done 'the right thing' by marrying, and the event was celebrated in a number of popular ballads, hailing her as 'the marigold', a flower also, and somewhat incongruously, associated with the Blessed Virgin. When in November she announced that she was pregnant, the joy of her loving subjects was complete. They would soon have the image of a mother to add to that of royal matron.

This expectation partly concealed the fact that her confusion continued. She simply did not know how to blend the roles of English sovereign and Habsburg wife. Philip for the time being did not want to take advantage of that, although he chafed under the dishonourable constraints of his situation. He was given an important job to do, namely negotiating the reconciliation of the English Church with Rome, and that occupied most of the time that he had available for English affairs between September 1554 and January 1555.[16] In that connection he consulted regularly with the Council, but his eye was also very much on contemporary events in Europe, and for that purpose he used his own personal council, in which the Queen's servants played no part. When the reconciliation was complete, he was anxious to join his father in the Low Countries, but the latter dissuaded him on the grounds that it was imperative that he should be on hand when the Queen gave birth.

While Mary's pregnancy moved forward, apparently with no complications, Philip decided to try to create an image for himself. He did not know how to be an English king, but he did know how to be a chivalric and military leader. He recruited English captains for his continental armies, and gave pensions to selected noblemen whom he thought might be useful in that connection. He also took part in tournaments and other martial games. He had been created a Knight of the Garter on his arrival in England, and knew perfectly well that there was a school of thought among the English nobility that looked to him for real manly leadership while the Crown was worn by a woman. On 18 December 1554 he staged 'a great triumph' at the court gate, assisted by 'divers lords both Englishmen and Spaniards', which consisted of running on foot with spears and swords at the tourney '[for] the which the king and his company were in goodly harness'.[17] On 19 March 1555 he tried again. 'In the morning the king's grace ran at the tilt against other Spaniards, and broke four staves [lances] by 8 o'clock'. Philip was not a man of imposing physique, or great skill, and he was better with his sword on foot than he was with a lance on horseback, but he was certainly prepared to try.[18] The spectators were duly impressed, and his image was suitably enhanced. The sporting gentry were even prepared to forgive him for being a Spaniard, but unfortunately his engagement with the country did not extend as far as learning its language. That was one reason why he stayed in the background, even as Mary's condition made her own involvement in politics fitful. While the King nursed his military image, the Council got on with the business of running the country.

Mary, naturally, did not have a military image to foster. When she had challenged the Duke of Northumberland for the succession in July 1553 (see p.118), she had an army, but her own role was that of figurehead, or 'cause'. What seems to have happened is that the gentry of her affinity, which extended all over East Anglia, had been warned of what was likely to happen when Edward VI died, and had mobilized their retinues to respond immediately when summoned.[19] Anxious to gloss over this state of affairs, her 'praise writer' Robert Wingfield, concentrated upon her own role.

> However, this attempt should have been judged and considered one of Herculean rather than womanly daring, since to claim and secure her hereditary right, the princess was being so bold as to tackle a powerful and well prepared enemy, thoroughly provisioned with everything necessary to end or to prolong a war, while she was entirely unprepared for warfare and had insignificant forces...[20]

Such words were misleading to the point of being downright inaccurate. It was reports of her gathering strength, first at Kenninghall and then at Framlingham, which compelled the Duke of Northumberland to march against her. The Duke was a formidable soldier, but it was he rather than she who was unprepared. His troops consisted of about half the royal guard, his own retinue and the followings of some of his fellow councillors. Many of the latter, and most of the levies that he had hastily raised, deserted as he advanced to Cambridge.[21] It was reported that Mary had as many as 30,000 men at Framlingham, and although that is no doubt an exaggeration, she far outnumbered Northumberland's dwindling force, and her army was competently led and well provisioned. On 19 July, undermined by the defection of his colleagues in London, the Duke simply gave up, so no trial of strength resulted, but if it had there could only have been one outcome. Even if his soldiers had remained loyal, he had no more than about 1,500, and his small artillery train was overmatched by the guns from the ships that the Council had sent out, ostensibly to prevent Mary's escape to the Low Countries. These had defected to her cause on about 15 July, and sent both men and weapons to Framlingham.[22] So Mary was not called upon to play the soldier, even when the circumstances seemed to threaten such a role.

When parliament was convened in November 1554, the King and Queen both attended the state opening, and publicly processed to mass on several occasions. On 25 January Philip alone attended a special mass at St Paul's, accompanied by Cardinal Pole, and on the 23 April with the other Lords and Knights of the Garter, went in procession at Hampton Court, while 'the Queen's grace did look out of a casement, that hundreds did see her grace after she had taken her chamber'.[23] Mary had gone into confinement, presumably on medical advice, on the 4th of the month, to await the expected birth. However she waited, and waited, and nothing happened. The rumours began to fly; she was sick, or bewitched, or even dead.[24] Eventually, in July she emerged, shaken and exhausted, but without a child. Her pregnancy had been a phantom, and neither her marriage nor her political prospects were ever the same again.

Philip, disappointed of his dynastic hope, immediately departed for the Continent, and began to reassess his relationship with England, while Mary in due course resumed her royal duties. For months she wrote pleading letters to him to return, and tried to persuade his father to use his influence, but the King made excuses. Finally he offered to return, but only on the condition that she give him a proper coronation. It may be that he was trying to secure the succession in the event of her death, or it may be that he just wanted the symbolism to strengthen his position.[25] Probably it was a question of image rather than substance, and he wanted to reassure the world of Catholic Europe that he really was the King of England. Whatever his thinking, Mary would not comply. She took refuge behind the inevitable opposition of parliament, but the real reason seems to have been her own reluctance. She might still want to be a good wife, but the benefits of that were now more questionable, and since he had chosen to leave her, she now had to place her own duties first. By 1556 Philip was being ruthlessly assailed by hostile propagandists such as John Bradford.[26] While Mary was left to do her best alone, her husband was a-whoring in Brussels, and his image (never good with Englishmen at large) went into terminal decline.

None of this had much to do with the waging of war, and the marriage treaty had carefully protected England from involvement in the ongoing Franco-Habsburg war. Nevertheless relations with France remained tense, and the ambassador in London, Antoine de Noailles, did his best to encourage opposition and dissent, narrowly escaping implication in the Wyatt rebellion of February 1554.[27] Apart from the Queen's own improvised forces, which were quickly disbanded, the only troops in England in August 1553 were the small permanent garrisons in Berwick and Calais, neither of which played any part in the crisis. The navy, however, was always present, and as we have seen, several of its ships, led by the 200-ton *Greyhound*, were directly involved.[28] Which way the Admiralty itself would move at that stage was unclear, and Mary improvised a command structure, using first Sir Richard Cavendish, and then a few days later Sir William Tyrell, both more conspicuous for their loyalty to her than for their naval expertise. However the Lord Admiral, Lord Clinton, obviously succeeded in making his peace with the new regime pretty quickly, because when Tyrell was appointed on 25 July 1553 it was as Vice-Admiral. Tyrell was immediately instructed to take two of the ships then available and proceed to the Narrow Seas to intercept any fugitives from the recently failed coup who might have been thinking of taking refuge in France.[29]

As far as we can tell, the Marine Council simply carried on as though nothing had happened, the Council authorizing warrants to Gonson amounting to £7,000 between July and December 1553.[30] Only the Mastership of the Naval Ordnance was vacant, Sir Thomas Wyndham having died during a trading voyage to the West Coast of Africa during the summer. On 25 August the old *Great Harry*, recently renamed the *Edward*, burned at her moorings at Woolwich, 'through negligence and lack of oversight', but that is the only sign that anything might have been wrong.

Clinton, however, was not secure in the royal favour, and in October Mary decided to replace him with Lord William Howard. She did not apparently, inform the Lord Admiral, who found out by other means and was not pleased. He had no alternative but to obey, and Howard joined the Council as Lord Admiral on 3 January 1554.[31] Not very much is known about the nature of naval operations during the winter of 1553–4. On 11 January four small ships were 'equipped with speed for Spain', presumably in anticipation of Philip's early arrival, but they must have been stood down as his journey was delayed for over six months. Routine patrols obviously continued, as well as the maintenance programme, because we know that Gonson was paid £10,967 between October 1553 and May 1554, as well as a further £15,159 between May and September.[32] During this latter period 29 men-of-war were commissioned to go to Spain as an escort for Philip, and to deter the French from attempting to intercept him—a task in which they were entirely successful. Philip landed at Southampton on 20 July, and none of his escorts saw any action. The only untoward development during this period was the arrest of William Winter, the Surveyor and Rigger, on suspicion of having been involved with Wyatt. He spent eight months in the Tower before being pardoned and resuming his naval duties in November. As Wyndham had still not been replaced, the Marine Council was operating at two-thirds strength though most of 1554.[33] A total of 14 ships were sold during the year, but apart from the nearly-new *Primrose* these were all small and old, fetching altogether a total of £181. Their sale was therefore merely good housekeeping, and not in any sense a running down of the navy.[34]

Philip had a keen interest in the English fleet, because it was the only military asset of value that the country had to offer. He rewarded the naval officers who had escorted him to England, but his departing in

September 1555 seems to have taken the Admiralty by surprise. Perhaps they shared the Queen's illusions about his intentions, but of the 13 ships earmarked to convoy him to the Low Countries, only about half were actually ready by 4 September, and Ruy Gomez (the King's Secretary) felt it necessary to bring over six sail from Flanders to make up the numbers. Philip was not pleased.[35] Later in the month the Select Council wrote to the King reporting that they were withdrawing the ships presently on patrol duties, which had been badly mauled by the weather, and replacing them with others. In reply Philip suggested that these repairs should be carried out at Portsmouth rather than in the Thames, so that the renovated ships could be more readily available, but it seems from the accounts that his advice was ignored.[36] Two new ships were laid down in the autumn of 1555, later named *The Philip and Mary* and the *Mary Rose*, but it is unlikely that the King's initiative was behind this move, or that he contributed towards the cost. In the same letter of 24 September the Council reported that the Queen was determined to have her navy augmented, and (not to be caught napping a second time) to have the existing fleet 'armed and manned against his Majesty's return'. This last was a broad hint that, as we have seen, Philip was in no mood to take.

By the end of 1555 neither the Queen nor her Council were satisfied with the way the Admiralty was being run. The cause of their concern is hard to identify, but seems to have been connected with expense, and the hand of the Lord Treasurer, the Marquis of Winchester, may be detected behind it. On 11 January 1556 a 'secret' survey of the navy was ordered, and monthly musters of the men warned for service. 'Secret' seems in this case to have meant without advance warning, and particular attention was to be paid to victualling, and to the repairs presently under way.[37] Over the next few months the Privy Council showed an unprecedented interest in the working of the Admiralty, even specifying for what purpose particular warrants were granted, instead of leaving this to the discretion of the officers. The only visible short-term consequence of this interest is that the naval debt, which had been running at about £5,000 a year, was by December 1556 reduced to £1,154.[38] Having apparently investigated to their satisfaction, on 8 January 1557 the Privy Council came up with its own solution. Overall responsibility was to be transferred from the Lord Admiral to the Lord Treasurer, and the latter was to receive an Ordinary (or budget) of £14,000 a year, paid to Benjamin Gonson in two equal parts. In return he would ensure that all routine repairs were carried out, and that victuals would be held on standby for 1,000 men for one month, being replaced as necessary. He would also receive warrants for timber from suitably located royal manors to carry out the repairs.[39] However, there is no sign of these reforms being implemented before the outbreak of war in June, and the first block warrant was not paid to Gonson until March 1559, when the war was coming to an end and Elizabeth was on the throne.

REFORM OF THE NAVY, 1557
8 January, Greenwich. Resolution of the Privy Council
for the reform of naval administration

THE QUEEN, *having been often troubled with signing warrants for money for the navy, this day, on consultation with certain of the council, desired the Lord Treasurer, with the advice of the Lord Admiral, to take on this matter, who was content on these conditions.*

£14,000 by year to be advanced half yearly to Benjamin Gonson, treasurer of the admiralty, to be defrayed as prescribed by the treasurer with the advice of the admiral. For which the treasurer took upon him: [1] To cause such of her majesty's ships as may be made serviceable with caulking and new trimming to be repaired. [2] To cause such of her majesty's ships as must be made new with speed; he to have meetest timber of the queen's parks, forests, chases and manors by her warrant. [3] To see all ships sufficiently furnished with sails, anchors, cables, and other tackle and apparel. [4] To cause the wages and victualling of the shipkeepers and workmen in harbour to be paid and discharged. [5] To cause victuals to be always ready for 1,000 men for a month to be set to sea. [6] To cause the ships to be repaired and renewed as occasion requires. [7] When the ships are repaired and the whole navy furnished, to continue this service for £10,000 yearly advanced.

Gonson and Edward Baeshe, surveyor of the victualling, shall make full accounts once a year at least, and as often as thought convenient by the council. If upon their accounts at the end of the year any money, grain or other victuals remain in their hands, the same to remain to the queen's use for the next year or otherwise as it shall please her highness.

[TNA PC 2/7, pp. 565-6. C.S. Knighton,
Calendar of State Papers, Domestic, Mary (1998), no. 536.]

HENRICI · VII

I AN IMAGINATIVE
representation of Henry VII
as a young man, from the
English school, probably late
sixteenth century.

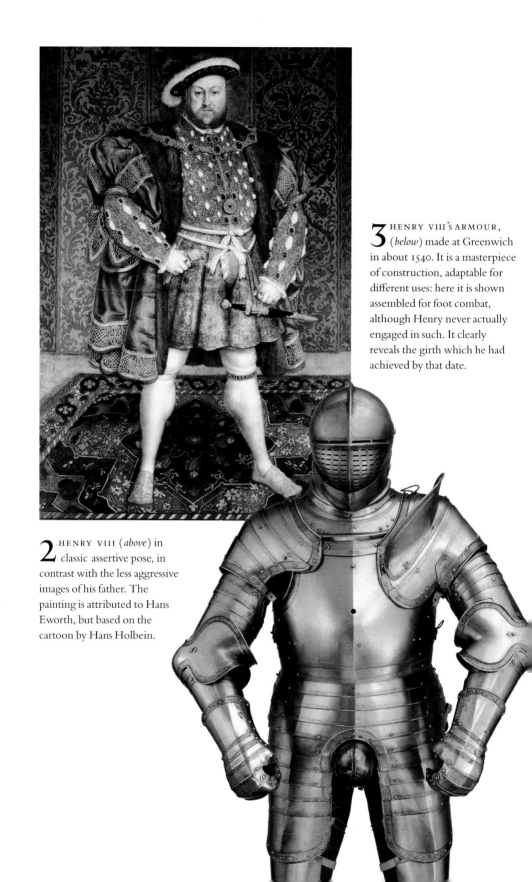

3 HENRY VIII'S ARMOUR, (*below*) made at Greenwich in about 1540. It is a masterpiece of construction, adaptable for different uses: here it is shown assembled for foot combat, although Henry never actually engaged in such. It clearly reveals the girth which he had achieved by that date.

2 HENRY VIII (*above*) in classic assertive pose, in contrast with the less aggressive images of his father. The painting is attributed to Hans Eworth, but based on the cartoon by Hans Holbein.

4 DESIGN for an elaborate royal pavilion in the Tudor colours of green and white. It was intended for the Field of Cloth of Gold in 1520.

5 NAVAL ACCOUNT rendered by John Hopton, Clerk Controller of the navy, showing money expended for furnishing and shipkeeping aboard the Mary Rose around 1512–15.

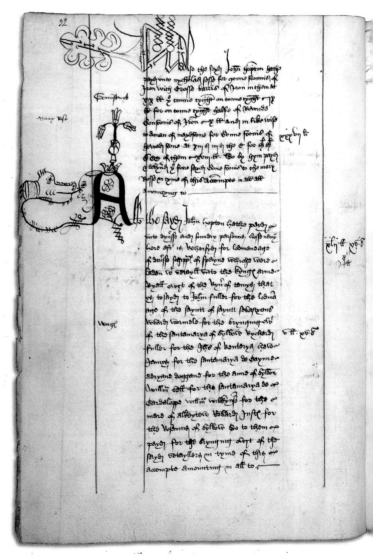

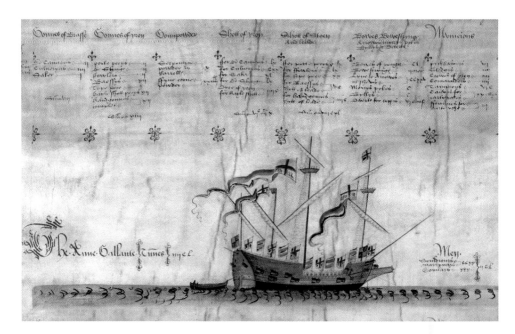

6 THE ANNE GALLANTE, (*top*) a 450-ton sailing warship, with particulars of her armament and manning. Taken from the Anthony Roll, an illustrated inventory of Henry VIII's navy prepared in 1546.

7 ST MAWES CASTLE, (*above*) Cornwall. One of a string of artillery forts that Henry VIII built along the south coast at the time of the invasion scare of 1539. It was based on a French design.

8 EDWARD VI (*right*) imitating his father's pose; a late copy derived from an original by Wilhelm Scrots.

9 MARY I (*below*) looking slightly less grim-faced than in other portraits. From the school of (or possibly by) Antonio Moro, an artist in Habsburg service.

10 A SYMBOLIC representation (*right*) of Philip and Mary, taken from the initial capital of the Placita Coram Rege (King's Bench Plea Roll) for the Hilary Term 1558.

11 ELIZABETH I born aloft by her courtiers (*above*). This group, allegedly by Robert Peake in 1580, includes a number of portraits of men not otherwise known to have been painted.

12 EXTRACT (*below*) from Elizabethan Treasurer Valentine Browne's account, 'The charge of an army sent into Scotland for the aid and assistance of the Scots against the French', 1560. It shows the organizational complexity of the force going to Scotland.

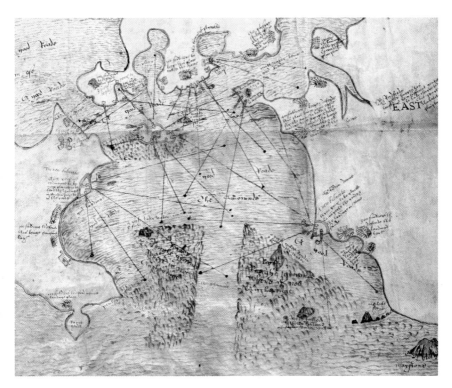

13 THIS ELIZABETHAN defence map (*above*) of Plymouth Sound shows the positioning of cannons and musketeers, and the range of their weapons.

14 AN ENGLISH ARMY in Ireland (*below*) 'in warlike wise', led by Sir Henry Sidney, Lord Deputy from 1565 to 1568. Taken from *The Image of Ireland* by John Derricke, 1581.

15 A DETAIL (*above*) from a contemporary painting and tapestry design of the Spanish Armada.

16 THE ARMADA MEDAL, (*right*) struck in gold to commemorate the defeat of the Spanish Armada in 1588. The inscription on the obverse reads 'Flavit deus et dissipati sunt' (God blew and they were scattered).

There is only fragmentary evidence of how the navy was operating during these days of peace. A rather piecemeal intervention in Ulster took place under the pretext of 'fishing the Ban'. This eventually involved four royal warships in April 1556, in what appears to have been an operation to deter the Scots of the Isles from settling and interfering in Ireland. The coast was to be blockaded and tribal warboats (known as galleys) were to be destroyed. This seems to have originated in a private initiative that won official approval, but how successful it was is not known.[40] However, all the royal warships returned safely.

There were also successful operations against pirates in the Channel. These were both of the ordinary and of the political variety. The latter consisted of fugitives from the Wyatt rebellion, and later the Dudley conspiracy of 1556, who were operating out of French ports, and with French connivance, attacking English and Flemish shipping. They even boasted a ship, the *Sacrette*, which they claimed had been given to them by the French King.[41] These last were a nuisance that bordered on a menace, and in July a squadron of about a dozen royal warships was sent out to deal with them. Eight of the pirate ships were caught off Plymouth later in the month, and after a sharp engagement six were captured. The prisons were filled and interrogations went on for a long time.[42] The dissidents' activities were not ended by this success, but they were very drastically reduced. The *Sacrette* was among the ships captured, and Henry had the nerve to ask for it back!

PIRACY
Deposition of Peter Killigrew, 21st August 1556

H ARRY KILLIGREW *has always been with the vidame [Francois de Vendome]. At his first coming to France we were suitors to the French king to have the Sacrett for two years in recompense of the others we lost. Which suit within seven or eight days we obtained, and had the admiral's letter to Le Havre to trim the ship and put her into our hands. With which letter I came to Le Havre and ordered the trimming, leaving Henry and Thomas at Paris, who remained there till the ship was ready and then came and so we went to sea... At our going to sea he willed us, if we had good fortune, that we might have somewhat to pay our debts at home and get another pardon—which we were never able to get... the lord admiral promised me after Thomas [was] hurt, and upon my going to sea, that after my return we should have the state of their captains, which is 400 francs a year, who willed me in no wise to sue for it, for he willed me always to serve at liberty, and not bound to any of them…*

[TNA SP 11/9, no.25. C.S. Knighton, *Calendar of State Papers, Domestic, Mary* (1998), no. 486.]

Then in March 1557, Philip returned. This had little to do with Mary's needs, physical or otherwise, and everything to do with getting England involved in the renewed war with France, which had broken out again in September 1556, after a truce of eight months. England was one of Philip's dominions, and his honour required that she become engaged. Mary supported her husband, but the Council (or most of it) was vehemently opposed. He had arrived on the 20th of the month, suitably escorted by the ships of the Winter Guard, augmented by others provided from the Cinq Ports. Philip was touchy on this subject after his previous experience, and no effort was spared to get it right.[43] His negotiation, however, got bogged down in arguments about cost, and it was only an apparently fortuitous event that rescued him. On 23 April a band of English adventurers led by Thomas Stafford, an eccentric who believed that he had a claim to the English throne, landed from two French ships at Scarborough on the Yorkshire coast, and captured the castle there. There are a number of odd features about this exploit, but it was taken at the time as a blatant piece of French provocation, and resistance to the war was overcome.[44] The Lord Admiral was put on standby on 22 May, and war was declared on 7 June.

Howard had 20 ships under his command, which were deployed down the coast from Dover to Falmouth, and he was instructed to 'clear the seas' of enemy shipping, concentrating particularly upon the ports of Le Havre and Dieppe, which were notorious for sending out privateers. For about a fortnight he 'chased shadows' because no French warships emerged to challenge him, and on the 22nd complained that his reinforcements from Portsmouth had not arrived, and nor had his Flemish allies.[45] If the French did come in strength, he would not be able to tackle them. He would, however, continue scouting operations until his victuals ran out, which would be about 10 July. Partly for this reason, the departure of the King, with the Earl of Pembroke and his expeditionary force was brought forward to 5 July, and Howard was able to muster sufficient transports from the Cinq Ports and other harbours in the area to get them across to Calais. Having done this, and because there was still no sign of a French naval presence in the Channel, eight of his ships were then diverted to the North Sea, to keep an eye on the Scots and to convoy naval supplies coming from Scandinavia. Additional ships were raised for this purpose from the east coast ports, and Sir John Clere seems to have been commanding about 30 ships on this northern station by the end of July.[46] Then on 12 August, disaster struck. Clere had taken most of his fleet around to the west coast of Scotland to meet the returning Icelandic fishing fleet, and decided, very ill-advisedly, to land on the Orkneys. His boat was caught in fierce cross-currents, and overturned. Clere and three of his captains were drowned. His fleet retreated in some disarray; the auxiliaries were paid off and most of the royal ships returned to the Channel, where the crews were paid off at Portsmouth.[47] Pembroke's army returned in dribs and drabs from Calais during October, and about 10 ships were kept on station to ensure their safe passage. Of the French navy during 1557, there had been no sign.

When Calais fell in January 1558, the navy were not much more than bystanders. An emergency mobilization was ordered on 31 December 1557, but by the time that the Earl of Rutland and his reinforcements had embarked, Ruysbank had already fallen and the harbour was inaccessible. An immediate attempt to redeem the situation was made, and Sir William Woodhouse was ordered to mobilize any ships that he could find. However, his gathering fleet was scattered and badly damaged by a great storm on the night of 9/10 January, and the rescue bid was abandoned.[48]

THE LOSS OF CALAIS

THE DUKE OF GUISE *being general of the French army, proceeded in this enterprise with marvellous policy. For approaching the English frontier under colour to victual Boulogne and Ardes, he entered upon the same on a sudden [on 1st January 1558] and took a little bulwark called Sandgate by assault. He then divided his army into two parts, sending one part with certain great pieces of artillery along the downs by the seaside towards Risbank; and the other part, furnished also with battery pieces, marched straight forth to Newnham Bridge; meaning to batter the two forts both at one time. Which thing he did with such celerity, that coming thither very late in the evening, he was master of both by the next morning... The next day the Frenchmen, with five double cannons and three culverins began a battery from the sandhills next*

Risbank against the town of Calais, and continued the same the space of two or
three days, until they made a little breach in the wall… So that while our peo-
ple travailed fondly to defend that counterfeit breech of the town wall, the Duke
had in the mean season planted fifteen double cannons against the castle.
Which castle being considered by the rulers of the town to be of no such force as
might resist the battery of the cannon, by reason that it was old, and without
any rampires; it was devised to make a train with certain barrels of gunpowder
to this purpose, that when the Frenchmen should enter, as they knew well that
they would, to have fired the said train and blown up the keep; and for that
purpose left never a man within to defend it. But the Frenchmen, at their entry,
espied the train, and so avoided the same. So that device came to no purpose;
and without any resistance they entered the castle, and thought to have entered
the town by that way…

['The winning of Calais by the French, January 1558 A.D.
by George Ferrers the poet', Pollard, *Tudor Tracts*, p. 291.]

By this time Howard had ceased to function as Lord Admiral, and on
10 February he was replaced by the return of Lord Clinton, clearly on
the King's initiative. A routine mobilization was ordered, and on 15
March he was issued with instructions that concentrated on the taking
of prizes.[49] The main object of the summer campaign of 1558 was
intended to be an Anglo-Flemish attack on Brittany, and Clinton was
summoned to Brussels for consultations. On 22 May a deployment was
drawn up which shows 13 royal ships allocated to the Lord Admiral at
Portsmouth, 13 others to the Channel Guard and one to escort duties,
in each case to be supported by armed merchantmen.[50] By the end of
June about 140 ships had been assembled for the main campaign, and
these were joined by 30 from Flanders.

The outcome was a sad disappointment, because although there was
again no sign of the French navy, all that was accomplished was a landing near Brest at the end of July, which was fiercely resisted. A combination of bad weather and disease then forced the abandonment of the
rest of the venture, and by 24 August Clinton was back at Portsmouth.
Only the action of a captain called John Malen redeemed an otherwise
gloomy season. Malen had been detached with a squadron of 10 ships
to assist the Imperial defenders of Dunkirk against a French attack.
Before he could get there, the siege had been lifted by the Count of
Egmont, and a battle had developed on the shore near Gravelines. In an

inspired moment of improvization, Malen brought his ships close into shore, and bombarded the French positions.[51] Taken by surprise and badly mauled by the big guns, the French broke and Egmont was totally victorious. It was, however, a small return for a lot of effort and expense, and the Imperialists' poor opinion of English military efforts was not much diminished.

On land, it seemed at first as though better fortune might be found. The parliament that lasted from 20 January to 7 March 1558 passed two Acts designed to clarify and partly to reorganize the mustering of the militia. The first 'An Act for the taking of Musters' was to give statutory authority to the traditional commissions, and to prevent the large number of absentees who had evaded the summons in the previous year. The second, 'An Act for the having of Horse armour and weapons' divided the whole community into 10 income groups, with those worth less than £10 a year at one end and those worth over £1,000 at the other.[52] The former were expected to provide a bill, a helmet, a longbow and a sheaf of arrows, while the latter were to equip 16 horsemen and 60 footmen. If a man's wife wore a silk petticoat, he was automatically assessed at £70 a year—a liability that ceased on divorce!

Musters were taken at three times during the war, in May and June 1557, January and February 1558 and May and June 1558. On the basis of the first, Pembroke's expeditionary force was selectively recruited. The second, designed to summon 27,000 men for the relief of Calais, was aborted when the navy was dissipated by storm, and influenza reduced the available men to less than 3,000; and the third, probably intended to support the Brittany expedition, was never taken up. Nevertheless the small army that set off in July 1557 was well equipped and relatively enthusiastic—or at least its leaders were. Philip had already rehabilitated many gentlemen who had been in prison or in disgrace for plotting against the Crown, with precisely this eventuality in mind, and now, like the surviving Dudley brothers, they entered his service as captains. The Venetian Surian sardonically observed that the King's army was full of troublemakers, recruited specifically to get them out of England in case they should cause problems at home.[53] As soon as he landed, Philip made haste to join his main army at the siege of St Quentin, but Pembroke lingered in Calais, which was included within his commission. He spent some time reorganizing the defences there, and it was 30 July before he set off to join the King, in spite of numerous exhortations to make haste. The French were advancing to the relief of the town, and Philip was very anxious to be at full strength to meet them.

In the event, both the King and the English missed the crucial battle: the latter because they had got no further than Cambrai by 10 August, and the former because he held back to wait for them. On that same day the relieving army, advancing without proper scouts, were taken in an ambush by the besiegers and utterly routed.[54] Casualties were heavy, and the Imperialists took over 5,000 prisoners, including many nobles. The town continued to hold out until the 27th, when it was taken by storm. The English, who had by then arrived, 'fought very choicely' according to one Spanish observer.[55] Although placated by this success, Philip continued to complain about Pembroke's dilatory and negligent advance, and did not give him anything else to do. He took the neighbouring fortresses of Han and Catalet, and by the beginning of October began to settle in to winter quarters. The English were mustered on 15 September, at which point they numbered about 6,000, and after that they began to go home, company by company. By 10 October only 500 were left.

When William Wightman, the treasurer of the war, accounted in November, he had spent £48,000, all of which was paid by Philip in one way or another.[56] Only the reinforcements for the garrison of Calais were paid out of the English Exchequer, to the tune of about £5,600. Henry II had been humiliated by the reversal at St Quentin, and decided to take advantage of the winter somnolence of his opponents to secure his revenge. The Duke of Guise had been similarly worsted by Alba in Italy, and returned to the north with the same objective in mind. Discreet soundings having been taken, it was determined that Calais (in theory impregnable) was in fact a soft target. The garrison had been run down to save money, and although reinforced in July, was still at a low ebb; nor had the formidable fortifications been kept in repair. The castle was particularly weak. By 11 December Pietro Strozzi, one of Guise's Italian officers had reconnoitred and declared the task to be possible.[57]

Over the next few weeks, and moving in small numbers to avoid attracting attention, about 20,000 men were assembled on the edge of the Pale. Between 17 and 27 December various warnings were uttered, but the Council in London paid no attention until the 29th, when it decided to send the Earl of Rutland with reinforcements. By the time Rutland reached Dover on 3 January, it was already too late. Guise had moved the day before, crossing the otherwise difficult marshes on the ice, and had taken the harbour fort of Ruysbank by surprise.[58] Cut off by this move, and well aware of the weakness of his defences, Lord Wentworth, the Governor, surrendered after a bombardment on 7 January. Guînes held out until 21 January, when, completely isolated and without hope of relief, Lord Grey also surrendered. Over 200 years of English rule had come to an end, and a perpetual bone of contention between the kingdoms had been removed. A few years later, it was appreciated that this loss was a blessing in disguise. Not only did it save a lot of money, it also directed English thoughts outwards to the Atlantic and a future role in international trade. But it did not seem that way at the time. The humiliation was bitter and the recriminations protracted. Philip found himself, to his rage and bafflement, being blamed for no better reason than that he was a foreign King, and when Mary lay dying a few months later, she declared that Calais would be found written on her heart.

Apart from limited naval operations, after the loss of Calais, the English virtually opted out of the war. The Council pointed out that to field an army of 20,000 men, in addition to maintaining the defences against Scotland and the fleet on a war footing, would cost in excess of £520,000 a year, which was far beyond their resources, even with the taxation recently voted by parliament.[59] Philip metaphorically shrugged his shoulders. He was in acute financial difficulties himself. So, however, was Henry, and when this became apparent towards the end of the summer, feelers began to be put out for peace negotiations. These had actually commenced when news of Mary's last illness and death caused them to be suspended. Philip received the news stoically. It was not unexpected and in many ways was a relief; 'I felt a reasonable regret' as he confided to his sister. At the age of 31 he was now free to get on with the rest of his life—and that did not include being King of England. After the Calais debacle, Philip had just about given up on England. Apart from Clinton, none of the English aristocracy retained his confidence, and he made no serious attempt to come to Mary, even when he knew that she was terminally ill.[60] His hopes were focused on Elizabeth, for whom he had acquired a considerable respect, and he made no attempt to stand in the way of her succession.

In the last few months of her life, Mary was a sad figure. Although she would not admit it until within a month of her death, there was no hope of her having a child, and her achievement, particularly in respect of the church, hung on the thread of her own life. Her popularity, so high at the time of her accession, had withered under the impact of her Spanish marriage, and then the evidence of her childlessness. Before she died her image, which had seemed so triumphant early in 1555, had declined to that of a pious, middle-aged woman, lavishly dressed, but plain and utterly lacking in *maiestas*.[61] She had done her best to restore the faith, and had actually achieved a fair measure of success, but it had been at a cost. Normally a gentle soul, she had steeled herself to deal with the harsh masculine world of high politics, and to persecute heretics. On account of her own chequered past, she had developed a phobia about heresy, which was to her the poison of the soul, and she sent nearly 300 of her subjects to their death on that account. The raw material of Mary's 'Black Legend' was already prepared in her own lifetime. She could not be a warrior, and simply lacked the imagination to create a female image of power, which was why she was left stranded between the figure of a dutiful spouse, to which she aspired, and that of a sovereign lady, into which she was thrust by circumstances.

Philip's main weakness was that he lacked flexibility. He was a Spaniard, and must be accepted on his own terms. He could be, and was up to a point, a soldier, but he only showed a brief willingness to exploit that image in order to build up a following in his island kingdom. For about 12 months he was prepared to give England priority in his affairs, but found that he was given little thanks for his effort, and after the failure of Mary's pregnancy he turned with relief to affairs that he understood. Attempts were made to give him an English identity, but he was never willing to embrace them, or even to appear to do so. On the whole, England's military profile was damaged by the reign, as it had been by that of Edward VI, and again not really fairly. The navy had done reasonably well in both reigns, and Mary's reorganization gave the Admiralty the edge over every other European country, building successfully on her father's efforts. Unfortunately the Queen never showed any public interest in her fleet, and probably damaged its efficiency by getting rid of Lord Clinton. Militarily, most of the reign was passed in peace, and when Mary came to reorganize the defences of the north, she chose to do so by the retrograde step of restoring the

Earldom of Northumberland.[62] Fortunately the new/old system was never put to the test.

In a sense Mary was the exception to the Tudor rule of ignoring lineage in her peerage creations. In addition to restoring Thomas Percy to his uncle's Earldom in the north, she annulled the attainder of the aged Thomas Howard, which enabled him to die as Duke of Norfolk in 1554, and created Edward Courtenay Earl of Devon in September 1553, although she did not restore his father's senior title as Marquis of Exeter. In Ireland Gerald Fitzgerald received in 1554 the Earldom of Kildare, which his half-brother Thomas had forfeited in 1536, and as a consequence of his grandfather's reinstatement, the younger Thomas Howard became Earl of Surrey. However in her brief reign she created no other senior peers, and the small number of barons whom she promoted conformed to the normal pattern that had applied since 1520. Little can be deduced from this about her attitude to claims of noble ancestry, because all these restorations can also be seen as a conscientious righting of what she saw as wrongs inflicted by her father, and none of them, apart from Northumberland, had any military significance. It may have been because he was a Duke that the Council gave the task of leading the royal force sent against Wyatt to Thomas Howard in January 1554, but he was virtually senile by then and the gesture was a serious mistake.

Mary temporarily extinguished by attainder the noble families of Dudley, Seymour and Parr, but that does not appear to have been out of any aversion to parvenu nobles as such. It was rather the result of the regime change that had taken place on her accession. She continued the practice of appointing noblemen as Lords Lieutenant, but that had been initiated by her father and extended by her brother's regents. These were military positions, but they were largely symbolic and none of them saw any action. Mary continued what was by then the usual practice of relying heavily upon the gentry and the Commissions of the Peace for routine government, and when she chose a nobleman to lead the expeditionary force sent to aid Philip in 1557, she chose William Herbert, Earl of Pembroke, who was a first-generation peer.

The modest success of this force at St Quentin was heavily overshadowed by the loss of Calais, the defence of which had been singularly unheroic. By the end of Mary's reign the myth prevailed, both at home and abroad, that England was desperately weak. In fact this was

not the case, but a combination of an unpopular war and a high mortal-
ity rate from influenza gave the impression that England could scarcely
stir in her own defence, let alone undertake aggressive campaigns
abroad. Of course it suited the Queen's enemies, both religious and
political, to foster this image of weakness. And it suited Elizabeth to
perpetuate it, in order to maximize her credit for leading the Great
Recovery—which was equally mythological.

CHAPTER SEVEN

ELIZABETH I

❖

THE 'FEMME
FATALE'

ELIZABETH resembled both her parents. She had her father's red hair, imperious nature and unpredictable temper, but her mother's feistiness and sexuality. Her intellect she derived from both sides, but her willingness to adopt unconventional ideas on gender roles came exclusively from Anne Boleyn. She was 17 years younger than Mary, and belonged, in effect, to a different generation. Whereas Mary had been brought up by her mother, and taught by tutors of a humanist but orthodox persuasion, Elizabeth had been instructed by men such as Richard Cox and Roger Ascham, who were shortly to emerge as Protestants.[1]

Her mother had been executed before she was old enough to know her, but Anne's fate had helped to give her daughter an instinctive wariness in dealing with powerful men. She had been 13 when her father died and, unlike her sister, had never been troubled in conscience by Henry's dealings with the Church. Equally illegitimate by English law, she had likewise been included in the Succession Act of 1543, and had therefore benefited from Mary's success in July 1553. In her own eyes, and in those of the vast majority of English people, she was thereafter the only possible heir to the throne.[2] She differed from her sister, however, in ways that education could not reach. She was, and knew she was, attractive to men. Poor Mary had been the subject of many matrimonial negotiations, many of them before she was old enough to be told about them, but had met only one of her suitors, and then in carefully chaperoned circumstances.[3] No man had ever had the temerity to 'make a pass' at her, and as she faced her marriage early in 1554, sex was a dark mystery to her. By contrast, Elizabeth had had an 'affair' with her married guardian, Thomas Seymour, when she was about 14. Whether this ever went beyond horseplay, we do not know, but it taught Elizabeth a lot about sex and its perils. It also taught her that her attractiveness could be used as a weapon, and this was a lesson of enormous value when she came to the throne.[4]

Mary had eventually, and very reluctantly, recognized her sister's right to succeed about a week before her death. There was no alternative if civil war was to be avoided, because Philip had already made it clear that he was not prepared to mount a challenge, and for several weeks all eyes, including those of Philip's personal envoy the Count of Feria, had been turned to Hatfield. 'These Councillors', Feria wrote on 14 November, referring to Mary's Privy Council, 'are extremely frightened of what Madam Elizabeth will do with them. They have received me well, but somewhat as they would a man who came with bulls from a dead Pope'.[5] Feria had been to Hatfield, and his speculations about the Queen-in-waiting were well informed. 'She is a very vain and clever woman', he wrote, '[who] must have been thoroughly schooled in the manner in which her father conducted his affairs, and I am very much afraid that she will not be well disposed in matters of religion… She is', he continued, 'infinitely more feared than her sister, and has her way absolutely, as her father did.' These opinions would no doubt have been music to Elizabeth's ears, had she known about them, because the one thing upon which she was determined as soon as her accession had been confirmed, was that she was going to have councillors, not minders. 'She is determined', as Feria noted, 'to be governed by no one'. She had every intention of being 'difficult', because that was the way in which a woman could maintain control. Had she listened to the best informed advice, she would at once have entered into negotiations for marriage, and would have confined her religious settlement to the restoration of the Royal Supremacy.[6] Instead of which she opted for a fully Protestant settlement, and when parliament petitioned her to marry, in its very first session, she replied

> To conclude, I am already bound unto a husband, which is the kingdom of England, and that may suffice you. And this, quoth she, makes me wonder that you forget yourselves, the pledge of this alliance which I have made with my kingdom. And therewithal, stretching out her hand, she showed them the ring with which she was given in marriage and inaugurated to her kingdom…[7]

She should not, she went on, be reproached that she had no children, because all Englishmen were her children. Mary had used similar, although less forceful words, but time had shown that she did not mean them. What Elizabeth meant was anyone's guess.

The new Queen was a consummate actress, who relished the applause of the multitude like a genuine thespian. 'She puts great store by the people', wrote Feria, 'and claims that they are her mainstay, rather than the nobility'. Her coronation entry into London became a piece of interactive theatre, as she responded with enthusiasm to the various pageants presented to edify her, particularly the offer of the English Bible, and Deborah taking council for the people of the Lord.[8] It was a masterly public relations exercise, which was immediately published in the words of Richard Mulcaster, and rounded off with her presiding like the Fairy Queen, over the jousts at which her knights unashamedly did battle for the favour of their lady's smile.

ELIZABETH IS RECEIVED INTO LONDON

AND ENTERING THE CITY [*she*] *was of the people received marvellous entirely, as it appeared by the assembly's prayers, wishes, welcomings, cries, tender words, and all other signs: which argue a wonderful earnest love of most obedient subjects towards their Sovereign. And, on the other side, Her Grace by holding up her hands, and merry countenance to such as stood afar off, and most tender and gentle language to those that stood nigh to Her Grace, did declare herself no less thankfully to receive her people's good will, than they lovingly offered it unto her. To all that 'wished her Grace well!' she gave 'Hearty thanks!' and to such as bade 'God save Her Grace!' she said again 'God save them all!' and thanked with all her heart. So that, on either side, there was nothing but gladness! Nothing but prayer! Nothing but comfort!... Near unto Fanchurch, was erected a scaffold richly furnished; whereon stood a noise of instruments; and a child in costly apparel, which was appointed to welcome the Queen's Majesty in the whole City's behalf...*

> '*O Peerless Sovereign Queen! Behold what this thy town*
> *Hath thee presented with, at thy first entrance here!*
> *Behold with how rich hope, she leadeth thee to thy Crown!*
> *Behold with what two gifts she comforteth thy cheer!*'

[Richard Mulcaster, *The Passage of our Most dread Sovereign Lady, Queen Elizabeth... the day before her Coronation*, 1558/9. Pollard, *Tudor Tracts*, p.367.]

Elizabeth, debarred by custom and circumstance from the image of the warrior, had to find (and knew that she had to find) some female equivalent of her father's bravura. So she chose to be a beautiful, elusive dominatrix, at once baffling, frustrating and gracious. She was not yet the Virgin Queen, because for nearly 20 years the demands of foreign policy meant that she had to keep up a series of matrimonial negotiations, with ostensible seriousness, and no one knew what her real intentions (or opinions) were. Nowadays the best scholarly view is that she never decided in principle not to marry, but that the price to be paid in terms of control was always too high when it came to the point.[9] When the political pressure became remorseless, she was constrained to remind her councillors that her natural body was her own to dispose of as she thought fit.

Just as Mary's affinity had mobilized to support her through the crisis that followed her brother's death, so Elizabeth's friends had prepared to back her against the eventuality that her sister would not relent in her hostility. It did not come to that, and on 17 November 1558 the new Queen was accompanied to London merely by cheering crowds. The Queen was dead, long live the Queen! Many must have been wondering in their hearts whether the kingdom could survive another woman on the throne, but no such disloyal thoughts were allowed to appear. The soldiers who had mustered were quietly dispersed on the orders of the Council, and no military display accompanied the first few months of the reign.

England was still technically at war, but there were no hostilities, and after a discreet interval peace talks were resumed with commissioners from the new Queen.[10] Characteristically, Elizabeth made bellicose noises about never surrendering Calais, but when it came to the point, and Spain would not back her, she climbed down. Garrisons had to be maintained, and in December officers on the Scottish Borders had to be reminded that their place of duty was the marches, and not London,[11] but the most interesting military activity of these early months was a stocktaking of the navy, which was carried out in February and March 1559, when it was clear that the war was over in all but name. This came about largely because William Cecil, the new Queen's Secretary and man of affairs, was collecting information about the various functions that he would have to discharge, and realized that he knew next to nothing about the Admiralty. On 12 December he received a memor-

andum telling him that at the moment of Mary's death six royal ships
and seven auxiliaries had been on patrol in the Narrow Seas, and on 20
February 1559 someone, who was probably the Clerk of the Ships,
drew up a check list for his benefit.[12] Three Great Ships were laid up at
Gillingham, nine in the Thames, probably at Deptford, and a further
eight at Portsmouth. Four were docked for repairs and a further six at
sea, two in the north and four in the Channel. In other words, it was
business as usual, but the writer also went on to ask what had happened
to the £14,000 Ordinary that had been approved two years earlier.
Cecil was clearly not in a position to answer that question, but he realized that some forward planning was called for, and the following
month a policy statement was drawn up under the general title of 'A
book of sea causes', in which Sir William Woodhouse and his colleagues laid out their views of where the navy had got to, and where it
should be heading.[13]

NAVAL POLICY
A book for sea causes made by the officers of
the Queen's Majesty's navy, 24 March 1558/9

*… The ships and barks underwritten are thought to be a sufficient number for
her Majesty to have of her own, which may be made and brought to their per-
fection within five years next following; so her majesty's pleasure be to continue
the ordinary. Viz:*

SHIPS OF		
	800 tons	1
	700 tons	1
	600 tons apiece	2
	500 tons	4
	400 tons apiece	4
	300 tons apiece	6
	200 tons apiece	6
		24
BARKS OF		
	80 tons	2
	60 tons	2
		4
PINNACES	*40 tons*	2
		30

[TNA SP 12/3, ff. 131–4. *British Naval Documents, 1204–1960*,
ed. J.B. Hattendorf et al., NRS, 1993, pp.69–70.]

It started with a list of 21 ships 'thought meet to be kept and preserved', and a further 10 'thought meet to be continued' at least until peace was concluded. There were 45 merchant ships available for war service, and if the fleet were to be fully mobilized 20 victuallers would also be needed. In that event, the cost would be £11,363 a month, with a further £4,000 needed for demobilization. There was, of course, no question of such an effort being required in the current political circumstances, but the estimate helps to explain how Gonson had managed to dispense £157,638 between 30 December 1556 and 30 December 1558, most of which period was spent at war.[14] The second element of the 'boke' was an updating of the December report, now showing seven royal ships and eight auxiliaries at sea, an arrangement that would continue until the end of March, after which the Queen's pleasure was requested. The third element tells us that the Ordinary had by then (24 March) been fixed at £12,000, a sum that the authors obviously considered to be inadequate, and gives a list of work in progress 'within the ordinary'. Five ships were being worked on at Deptford, eight at Woolwich and nine at Portsmouth, a total of 22, or two thirds of the fleet. The rest were at sea or 'aflote', either at Portsmouth or in the Thames. We also learn that a new Great Ship (later called the *Elizabeth Jonas*) was also nearing completion—although not within the Ordinary.[15]

The three parts of the book were then followed by two short policy papers, the first relating to the navy in peacetime, and the second to the establishment. In the opinion of the officers, Gillingham was the best 'laying up' place for ships out of commission, and the ships currently at Portsmouth should be brought round to the Medway. This, they reckoned, would save £1,700 a year. They also suggested that the old blockhouse at Sheerness should be rebuilt and kept with six gunners to protect the anchorage. The Summer Guard should continue in operation, although the number of ships required would depend on the circumstances.[16] Finally, they recommended a naval establishment of 30 ships—24 of them of 200 tons and upwards. Cecil obviously listened to the advice he was given. Gillingham did indeed become the principal anchorage (as it had been before Philip's intervention), and a new blockhouse was built, not at Sheerness but at Upnor, and was manned as suggested. The blueprint for the size of the navy was altogether too tidy, and was never strictly adhered to, but it guided Admiralty thinking down to the outbreak of the war with Spain, when there was a major expansion. If the Lord Treasurer did continue in overall charge, as had been laid down in 1557, then he left remarkably few fingerprints after 1558. All the indications suggest that the minister responsible for naval affairs (as for most other things) in 1559 was William Cecil.

Cecil's only military experience had been as a non-combatant. Along with William Patten, he had been a judge of the Marshalsea during the Scottish campaign of 1547, but he had shown a journalist's eye for what was going on around him, and had taken assiduous notes both of the action and of the country.[17] The knowledge that he had thus acquired came in very useful now, in 1559, when the situation in the north again called for military intervention. Although Scotland had been included in the treaty of Cateau-Cambrésis, which had ended the Anglo-French-Spanish war in April 1559, French influence had continued thanks to the Regency of the Queen Mother, Mary of Guise. This was resented by many Scottish nobles, and particularly by those of a Protestant persuasion. Thanks partly to the lack of English interference since 1550, and partly to the Calvinist leadership of John Knox, the Protestants were beginning to pose as the patriotic party in Scotland, and in the summer of 1559 the 'Lords of the Congregation' rose in rebellion.[18] At first it seemed that they might succeed without assistance, but by the autumn it had been demonstrated that their raw levies were no match for the French professionals, who, although few, were well-equipped and well-disciplined. Aware of Elizabeth's Protestant declaration earlier in the year, the Lords appealed for her assistance as a Sister in Christ. The Queen was reluctant. Even more than Cecil, she was absolutely inexperienced in military matters, and was warned by one of her courtiers that

> The Duke of Norfolk's grandfather was sent by the king your father to invade Scotland, well accompanied ... an army also by sea went into the Firth [of Forth] well furnished with victuals to relieve the army by land at their coming to Edinburgh, which the army by land was not able to do... In the Duke of Somerset's time the victory was not followed in Scotland ... [s]o consider what an enemy besides the French men, yea and peradventure the Scots ... the weather will be to your people and to their horses...[19]

However, Henry II of France had died in July 1559, following a jousting accident, and this had brought Francis II to the throne. Francis was married to Mary of Scotland, and the pair began to display the arms of England on their achievement. The threat to Elizabeth was obvious, and the need to get the French out of Scotland therefore the greater. Eventually, the rumour that Francis was sending reinforcements to his mother-in-law forced the Queen's hand, and on 16 December she ordered William Winter to sea with 34 ships and instructions to intercept any traffic coming from France.[20] Cecil was now clearly forcing the pace, and on 24 December the Council ordered the Duke of Norfolk to cross the border with 4,000 men. By 22 January 1560 Winter was deployed in the Firth of Forth, and the French reinforcements, reported to number 10,000 men, had been turned back by storms. The French force already deployed in Fife retreated to Leith in the face of Winter's fleet, and two French galleys, left exposed in the Firth, were captured.[21]

Shortly after, the Duke of Norfolk was permitted to conclude a formal alliance with the Lords of the Congregation, and Elizabeth became Protector of the Liberties of Scotland. The title was a masterpiece of diplomacy, which bears all the marks of Cecil's style. Instead of the image of a feudal overlord, which Henry VIII had displayed, or the midwife of political union, which Somerset had aspired to be, the Queen of England was now guaranteeing those very freedoms that her predecessors had sought to abrogate. By advertising the fact that she had no ambitions north of the border, she transformed Anglo-Scottish relations.

Having succeeded so far, Cecil now took the bull by the horns, and on 28 March authorized (without the Queen's explicit permission) the advance of a second army from Berwick under Lord Grey.[22] Grey and Norfolk then proceeded to the siege of Leith, and were in place by 5 April. The siege was a failure, and encouraged by this success Mary of Guise refused to negotiate, but she died on 11 June 1560, and the whole French position in Scotland crumbled away. Without any further effort, or any notable military success, the English were able to negotiate the treaty of Edinburgh on 6 July, which provided for the mutual withdrawal of all foreign troops, and recognized the government of the Scottish Lords.[23] In order to ensure compliance, Winter then evacuated the whole French force himself in an operation of remarkable efficiency. By the time that he was withdrawn in September, the Admiral had been on station for nine months — an unheralded but remarkable achievement — and had cost his government a little over £11,000.[24]

Elizabeth, however, could only be pressed so far. She had sanctioned

Cecil's initiatives in Scotland, and been well rewarded, but was not prepared to follow up her success by establishing closer relations with the
rulers there, or by scoring further points off the Guises in France. Consequently Cecil missed an opportunity to collaborate with the Earl of
Argyll in Ulster, and was forced to ignore the fact that Francis and
Mary refused to ratify the treaty of Edinburgh.[25] The latter did not
matter greatly, because the French presence in the north had been
eliminated, and France itself was sinking rapidly into that civil turmoil
known as the wars of religion. The Duke of Guise might entertain
ambitions in Scotland, but that was as far as he was likely to go. In
December 1560 Francis II died, and his young successor, Charles IX,
required a Regent. The appointment of the Queen Mother, Catherine
de Medici to that position effectively shut out the influence of the
Guises, and ensured that for the foreseeable future there would be no
further adventures in the north.

Meanwhile, Elizabeth was demonstrating her womanhood in an
unprecedented fashion. Her marriage had been under discussion from
the beginning, and a negotiation was actually underway for a match with
the Archduke Charles, the younger son of the Emperor Ferdinand, but
in the spring of 1560 she fell in love.[26] The object of her affection was
Lord Robert Dudley, a younger son of the late Duke of Northumberland. She had known Dudley since they were both children, and had
made him Master of the Horse before her coronation, but it was only
in 1560 that their relationship began to cause comment. So uncon-
trolled did the Queen's behaviour become that she was in danger of
adding the goddess/whore Aphrodite to her assortment of classical
images. Cecil was appalled, and spoke openly of resigning his office.
The only redeeming feature of the situation was that Dudley was
already married, his wife being kept discreetly out of court while these
antics were going on. Then in September 1560 Lady Dudley died in
suspicious circumstances, and everyone held their breath.[27] 'The
Queen of England', Catherine de Medici is alleged to have scoffed, 'is
to marry her horsemaster'. It did not come to that. Dudley was cleared
of any complicity in his wife's death (by a rigged inquiry it was alleged),
but by a supreme effort of will power, which cost her dear, Elizabeth
the Queen backed off.

Their special relationship continued, and Dudley himself went on
hoping for several years, but it was clear by the end of 1560 that she

would not marry him, and Cecil breathed a huge sigh of relief. It would
be business as usual as far as the Council was concerned, but Elizabeth
had learned in the most painful possible way what a conflict existed
between her duty as a ruler and her instincts as a woman.[28] A King similarly placed would have taken the woman as his mistress, and recognized any bastard that might result. His image would, if anything, have
been enhanced by the experience. But it was impossible for a Queen to
follow a similar course. When she believed that she was dying from
smallpox in 1563, Elizabeth swore that she had never had intercourse
with Dudley, and in the circumstances that disavowal must stand. For a
woman of her sharp sexuality, the frustration must have been immense.

Meanwhile her role as the 'Protector of the Liberties of Scotland'
had come to an end with Francis's death, and the return of Mary to
Scotland in August 1561 promised normality of a kind in that kingdom. At first as Queen, Mary behaved with great discretion and good
sense, and Elizabeth saw no function for herself in the north.[29] This was
just as well, because the situation in France was deteriorating alarm-
ingly. The Duke of Guise had no intention of accepting his exclusion
from power, and constituted himself as the leader of the ultra-Catholic
party, dedicated to the extermination of heresy. As the princely house
of Bourbon was Protestant, and had a large aristocratic affinity, civil
war was inevitable, and by March 1562 the Prince of Condé was in
arms, and had seized the strategic city of Orléans.

Elizabeth's ambassador in Paris, Nicholas Throgmorton, urged her
to become involved, but she was hesitant and her Council was divided.
Both Cecil and the Lord Treasurer, the Marquis of Winchester, were
opposed to intervention, but the Queen demonstrated her independence by ignoring their advice. In this matter the prevailing voice was
that of Lord Robert who, although not yet a member of the Council,
retained great influence.[30] On 20 September 1562 she signed the secret
treaty of Richmond with the Prince of Condé, undertaking to provide
him with 6,000 men and a loan of 140,000 crowns (£45,000). In return
she was to recover Calais, and this was the whole purpose of the operation from Elizabeth's point of view.[31] She was well aware how England's
prestige had suffered as a result of its loss; what a coup it would be if, by
a well-timed military intervention, she could recover so important a
symbol of the country's ancient greatness! Unfortunately, Calais was
not under Huguenot control, so for the time being she would have to

accept Le Havre (Newhaven) as a pledge. Musters had already been held, and the first contingent of troops, commanded by Sir Adrian Poynings, set off for France within a matter of days. The navy was already at sea, although at first it was mainly occupied in ferrying supplies to Berwick and chasing pirates off the coast of Ireland. However, on 6 August Sir William Woodhouse went out with five other ships into the Channel, and this was a portent of what was to come.[32] Between then and early October he was joined by five more, including the *Triumph* and the *Victory* (both new and large warships), and this formidable fleet 'wafted' the Earl of Warwick and the rest of the army over to Le Havre in the course of October. The Channel Guard was changed on 1 December and the Great Ships were withdrawn, but with the onset of winter the English were firmly ensconced in Le Havre.

Unfortunately the Huguenot campaign that this was designed to support was a disaster. On 26 October the Catholic forces took Rouen, and this cut Le Havre off from the main Huguenot army, and then in December Condé was defeated and taken prisoner at Dreux. Imprisonment made him amenable to pressure, and when the Duke of Guise was assassinated in February 1563, the makings of a settlement began to emerge.[33] In March Condé came to terms, gaining very little beyond his liberty, and abandoned his ally. Warwick had played no part at all in these events, but he had not been altogether idle. As soon as the English had taken over Le Havre the French government had declared that all merchantmen from that country were legitimate prizes, which put Elizabeth on the spot because she was trying to maintain the position that she had no quarrel with the French Crown.[34] Remedial action was taken by Warwick and by the Huguenot governor, who issued letters of marque on their own authority, which unleashed a flood of English pirates, posing as privateers. Warwick was certainly not entitled to issue such letters, and the activities of his 'privateers', which were directed at least as much against the Flemings and the Spaniards as against the Catholic French, were a source of major embarrassment to Elizabeth.

On 8 February 1563 she dissociated herself from their activities, but by then the damage had been done.[35] When Condé settled with the government, moreover, Warwick's political position became untenable, and by the beginning of June he found himself besieged by a joint Protestant and Catholic army operating in the name of Charles IX. This would have been sustainable as long as the sea lanes remained open, but early in July plague struck the garrison, and by mid-July Warwick had only 1,200 fit men. Some 20 royal ships were scrambled to go to his relief, but they were held up by contrary winds, and by the time they reached Le Havre on 24 July, he had lost control of the harbour.[36] Reduced to the last extremity, the Earl surrendered on 26 July, and was allowed to leave with full military honours, and such of his men as were still standing. The fleet was demobilized, and all that Elizabeth had gained by holding Le Havre for 10 months was 15 ships that had been taken as prizes and sent over some months before.[37] Any chance of recovering Calais had now gone for good, and the treaty of Troyes, which she was constrained to sign in 1564, was as big a humiliation in its way as the original loss of the Pale. Elizabeth had burned her fingers badly, and would not be tempted to play with the fire of military adventures for another 20 years. Until, in fact, circumstances gave her no alternative.

For many years it had been the custom of the King's Council to rent out his ships for mercantile purposes when they were not required for Crown service. They had originally been useful cargo carriers, and it was better that they should be used, rather than deteriorate at anchor. Every ship so used was leased at a specified rent, and covered by a bond of indemnity in the event of loss or damage. This custom had been continued by Henry VIII, Edward VI and Mary. The specialized nature of sixteenth-century warships made them less useful for cargo, but because of the growing activities of the Barbary corsairs in the Mediterranean, and the dangerous nature of longer distance trade, they were equally in demand as escorts. For the latter purpose they came with a full complement of guns, which were included in the rental.

The use of such ships did not imply any particular royal interest in the venture concerned, and indeed Henry VIII had resisted all pleas to interest himself in voyages to Brazil or West Africa.[38] The Guineas voyage on which Sir Thomas Wyndham had died in the summer of 1553 was not in any sense a royal venture, in spite of his involvement. What had happened under Edward VI was that the Duke of Northumberland, who had good contacts in the City, encouraged his fellow councillors and courtiers to invest in London voyages; and that was how the Willoughby/Chancellor exploration of 1553, which resulted in the foundation of the Muscovy Company, had been funded.[39] Mary had been much concerned to avoid offending Philip, and had discouraged

trading voyages into areas of Spanish or Portuguese influence, which
had seriously damaged her relations with London, whose merchants
complained bitterly that the King constantly favoured their Flemish
and Spanish rivals.[40] Elizabeth reverted to her brother's policies in this
respect (as in others), and friendly relations between the City and the
court were resumed.

In 1561, the Queen went a stage further when she loaned four ships
to Sir William Chester for a voyage to West Africa. Chester paid no
rental because the ships, and £300 worth of provisions, constituted
Elizabeth's investment in the voyage. She would be repaid with an
agreed share of the profits.[41] This was an altogether new departure, and
signified a radical shift in the Crown's involvement—and in its relations
with the maritime community. In 1562 Lord Robert Dudley was permitted to borrow the *Jesus of Lubeck* for a rental of only £250 a year,
which also looks like a concealed investment, although the purpose of
the voyage is not known.

Then in 1564 the Queen shared the venture in John Hawkins' second slaving voyage. Hawkins was already established in this line of
business, having undertaken a successful first voyage in 1562, with both
City and Admiralty support. Lord Clinton, Benjamin Gonson (soon to
be his father-in-law) and William Winter were among his backers.[42] It
was no doubt the profits of this voyage that tempted Elizabeth. West
Africa, where the slaves were secured, was a Portuguese sphere of
influence, although poorly policed. Hawkins had no difficulty in shipping his cargo, but when he tried to sell it in the West Indies he found
the colonists too aware of their King's indignation to trade. It required
the firepower of his warships to change their minds, and Philip's
ambassador in London, Guzman da Silva, made furious protests.[43] He
was turned away with a soft answer, but Elizabeth was sufficiently worried to forbid Hawkins' next planned voyage in 1566. However, politics then supervened, because Margaret of Parma blamed the English
for the unrest in the Netherlands, and imposed an embargo on English
trade. This, it quickly transpired, was more damaging to Antwerp than
it was to London, because it stimulated the Merchant Adventurers to
diversify their trade, and the embargo was soon lifted.[44] This in turn
persuaded the Queen that she had little to fear from Flanders. Also, the
French fleet—so formidable 20 years earlier—had entirely disappeared
under the impact of the civil wars, leaving Philip as the only potential

enemy that she had to be wary of. But the King of Spain had the Low Countries to worry about, as well as defending his Mediterranean coast against the Barbary corsairs and fending off the Ottomans in the Levant. Elizabeth decided that a further calculated act of provocation would be in order.

Hawkins' next venture was therefore quickly turned from being an entirely private enterprise into a quasi-public one. This time its piratical nature could not be disguised, but the Queen nevertheless provided him with two ships, fully armed and equipped, and gave him a royal commission. His status therefore became completely ambiguous, and it seems that the men who sailed with him, and even the officers, did not know whether they were in the royal service or not.[45] He hoisted the royal banner when it suited him, although it seems that he was not entitled to do so. In spite of his commission, the expedition was a private one in which the Queen happened to be a partner, not a naval one, although the colonial authorities in the New World cannot be expected to have told the difference.

He set off at the beginning of October 1567, took several prizes of doubtful legitimacy and secured his payload of slaves in the usual manner from the coastal traders.[46] Then at the end of February 1568 he quitted the African coast and spent two months battling with Atlantic storms on his way to what is now Venezuela. He had at this point, according to his own account, 10 ships and some fairly unreliable prize crews. At Margarita he traded peacefully, not only in slaves but also in the English cloth that he had brought along to give a legitimate gloss to his activities. He then proceeded along the coast to Rio de la Hacha, Santa Maria and eventually to Cartagena. Although he was not welcomed at the last place, he had by then shifted nearly all his trade goods, and was minded to head for home.[47] However, in the straits of Florida he was caught by a severe storm, and was constrained to go to San Juan d'Ulloa, the port town of Vera Cruz, to effect the necessary repairs.

On 16 September he entered the port, and was at first well received; no doubt the surprise of his appearance and the power of his ships made a suitable impression. However the very next day a powerful Spanish fleet turned up, bearing no less a dignitary than the new Viceroy of the Indies, Don Martin Enriquez. Don Martin regarded the English presence as an outrage, and after several days of prevarication and feigned friendship, on 23 September attacked the intruders.[48]

Unprepared and outgunned, Hawkins and Francis Drake (who was his second in command), managed to extract the *Minion* and the *Judith*, with a fair amount of bullion on board, but were forced to abandon the *Jesus of Lubeck*. The two ships lost contact, and the *Judith* sailed straight home, while Hawkins, under-provisioned and overmanned, was forced to land some of his men on the coast of Florida. Having replenished his supplies at Vigo—of all places—he reached home on 20 January 1569, seething with rage against Spanish treachery, and also against Drake for having 'deserted' him.[49] Spanish protests were inevitable, and Elizabeth had burned her fingers again, but Hawkins responded by launching a massive claim for £30,000 in compensation through the Admiralty Court. In the political circumstances, this was sheer wishful thinking, and he must have known that, but it was a gesture to cover the fact that the voyage had not made as much profit as might have been expected— and the Queen had lost the old *Jesus*.

San Juan d'Ulloa marked the end of the road as far as the participation of naval ships in private expeditions was concerned, although not the end of royal interest and investment. The diplomatic backlash meant that Elizabeth was more careful in future to conceal the nature of her participation in piratical activities. She found herself uncomfortably facing both ways on the matter of piracy, because the ordinary domestic variety was clearly unacceptable. On 24 December 1564 the Council issued letters of instruction to all Vice-Admirals of the coasts, and to the authorities in port towns, ordering the arrest of certain named individuals, and minuted in a chagrined tone

> sundry and divers piracies and spoils have been committed upon the seas by the Queen's majesty's subjects of the west parts since the conclusion of the last peace with France, and divers of them apprehended, and not one executed or punished according to their deserts...[50]

The problem was one of collusion. Local gentry, even Justices of the Peace, were turning a blind eye, and even acting as fences for the stolen goods. Special commissions were appointed in 1565 to survey various parts of the coast with a view to preventing these abuses in future, but it is not clear that very much was achieved. In 1564 English pirates were alleged to have relieved Scottish merchants of goods to the value of

£20,717, and 10 years later notorious offenders were being arrested, and even tried, and then released on bonds because they were needed in the Royal Navy.[51] It is not surprising that England's neighbours did not take the Queen's virtuous professions seriously, or that ordinary merchants joined in the racket, becoming part-time pirates when a suitable victim (preferably foreign) hove in view. Elizabeth's ambiguity was shared by the whole maritime community, which is one of the reasons why her relations with that community tended to be good. Going buccaneering against the King of Spain was a favourite occupation long before there was any war to justify such tactics, and adventurers like Hawkins did not have much difficulty in recruiting crews.

England was not officially at war at any time between April 1559 and the summer of 1585, so there were no such things as privateers. However, the seas were dangerous places, and just as some merchant companies persuaded the Queen to provide warships to protect them, so others took steps to protect themselves. Hardly any voyages to the Levant, or north or west Africa, let alone the East Indies or the New World, could afford to go unarmed. Consequently the private warship returned after an interval of more than half a century. Just as Henry VIII had been concerned to control private retinues, and to convert his nobility from a lineage-based group to one that took its identity from service to the Crown, so he had been concerned to impose a monopoly of force at sea.[52] Merchants had been less adventurous in his time, and the navy had provided 'wafters' for the Antwerp cloth fleet and for the Icelandic fishermen. Now English merchants were much more likely to venture into hostile waters in search of a 'vent' for their cloth, and needed protection beyond the navy's resources. Every large merchantman carried guns, which were increasingly available from the flourishing foundries of the Weald, and even quite small ones were coming to be similarly equipped, which made the shift from victim of piracy to aggressor all the easier and more tempting. When war eventually returned, ships such as the *Ark Raleigh* and the *Scourge of Malice* were in the front line, owned by courtiers of impeccable loyalty, but not in any sense controlled by the Admiralty.

By 1570, therefore, England had the reputation of being a loose cannon—a maverick sea power whose pirates were feared even more than its navy. It was upon these privately owned warships that the captains, seamen and gunners who were to serve in the navy during the Spanish war learned their craft.[53] Meanwhile the image of the English soldier marked time. Neither the siege of nor the debacle of Le Havre had done anything for his reputation, and apart from a few captains voluntary service overseas was still in the future. In fact, thanks to the Marian statutes, the 'top end' of the musters was reasonably well equipped, and the archer had been relegated to the lowest levels of availability — or to the Scottish marches. Even there the old game of border raiding was in full decline, thanks to the fact that the authorities in London and Edinburgh were now collaborating instead of being at each other's throats.

Meanwhile, the Queen's image was becoming more clearly defined. In the eyes of the papacy and of Catholic Europe she was a heresiarch, the leader of Christendom's most powerful Protestant state, a perception that was shared by her fellow believers and that generated political pressures of its own. She was also hard to woo, and the image of her being aloof and unattainable was gaining ground. Her servants found her exasperating, subtle and highly intelligent. She would not be taken for granted, and all important decisions had to wait upon her good pleasure. She flirted with her courtiers, and even with her councillors in a way that visiting ambassadors found bewildering or disgusting according to their temperament. Above all, she was in control, and obviously relished the fact — an attitude that those who pinned their hopes on her marriage found increasingly disturbing. Mary Queen of Scots' representative in England, Maitland of Lethington, told Elizabeth, 'Ye have an high stomach, madame, and will brook no master'. In view of what happened to his own mistress when she took a 'master' in the shape of Henry Stewart, Lord Darnley, it would appear that Elizabeth chose the wiser course, but it was to leave her without an heir of her body, and that her most dedicated advisers were finding hard to stomach.[54]

In spite of a well-deserved reputation for caution and indecisiveness, Elizabeth had a gambling streak in her personality. She had shown this in her very different relationships with Robert Dudley and John Hawkins, and at the end of 1568 she demonstrated it again. Several Genoese galleys, bearing bullion to pay the Duke of Alba's troops in the Low Countries, took refuge in Southampton from a mixture of winter gales and French pirates. For the last 18 months Alba had been engaged in squeezing the life out of all political and religious dissent in the Netherlands, and Elizabeth viewed his activities with growing hostility and alarm. The opportunity to embarrass him by purely negative action was therefore too good to resist. By depriving him of his pay, he would at least be temporarily paralysed, and his army might even be induced to mutiny. William Cecil came up with a plan, which Elizabeth approved, and having carefully ascertained that the money remained the property of the bankers until it was delivered, announced that she would borrow it herself.[55] The bankers had (and in the circumstances could have) no objection to such a transaction; all they were concerned with was their rate of interest, and that was guaranteed. Consequently at the end of December the money was unshipped and transferred to the Tower of London. The Spanish agents who had been travelling with the cargo were furious but powerless. Alba got wind of what was intended before it actually happened, and promptly seized all the English shipping within his power. In doing so, he put himself in the wrong, because the Queen was able to assert in her most disarming manner that of course she had had no such intention, until driven to it by the Duke's action.

The result was not mutiny, but rather a serious breakdown in Anglo-Netherlandish relations, and a renewal of the trade embargo of 1566. Again the English merchants were inconvenienced by this, but its worst effects were felt in Antwerp, which was rapidly losing its status as Europe's premier mart. Unravelling these knots took several years. The most notable effect in England was that Cecil's enemies at court began trying to persuade the Queen that her trusted Secretary was a disastrous liability who was driving the country straight into war with Spain. Spain's increasingly numerous enemies, in France, Italy and the Low Countries, were heartened by this evidence of the Queen's courage, even if it was shown in a rather indirect way.

CHAPTER EIGHT

ELIZABETH I

❖

THE VIRGIN
QUEEN

AFTER 1568 Elizabeth became increasingly embattled. In Scotland, Queen Mary had been deposed in the summer of that year in favour of her infant son, James. This followed the murder of Mary's husband in January 1567, and her subsequent marriage to the prime suspect. Escaping from confinement, she had attempted to repudiate her abdication, but was defeated again and fled to England in May 1568. Her quest was for help to recover her throne, but although Elizabeth was sympathetic, she had no desire to disrupt her amicable relationship with the current Scottish government, and the Queen of Scots soon found herself in courteous but strict confinement.[1] The English government did not know what to do with Mary, and took the line of least resistance. In the absence of any heir of the Queen's body, Mary was next in line to the English throne, and Elizabeth never explicitly repudiated that. Mary also had a following in England, especially among the conservative aristocracy, and a plot was hatched to marry her to the Duke of Norfolk.

The Queen of Scots was 26 and a widow (her marriage to Bothwell not being recognized) and the Duke 30 and unmarried, so the scheme had a certain superficial plausibility. Unfortunately, when Elizabeth found out about it, she absolutely forbade any such move, seeing it both as a direct threat to herself and an indirect way of bringing pressure upon her to settle on a husband.[2] Supporters of the match, however, chose to see in the Queen's hostility the influence of William Cecil, the man who was also held responsible for having so upset the Duke of Alba in January 1569. A group of courtiers, which included Robert Dudley, now a councillor and (since September 1564) Earl of Leicester, set out to discredit Cecil and remove him from office on the grounds that he was a danger to the realm. Elizabeth, however, did not prove at all suggestible in that respect, and realizing her intransigence, Leicester made a clean breast of the whole plot. He was forgiven and Cecil was vindicated.[3] The others, including the Duke of Norfolk, ran for cover.

Two of them were not quick enough. The Earls of Northumberland and Westmorland, estranged from the court by the withdrawal of royal favour, had been parties both to the anti-Cecil plot and to the Norfolk marriage scheme. They failed to take advantage of an opportunity for submission, communicated by the Earl of Shrewsbury, and in October 1569 were summoned to court to explain themselves. Fearing the consequences and trusting (misguidedly) to their status as northern magnates, they raised the standard of revolt.[4] Their objective seems to have been the removal of Cecil and a partial retreat from the 1559 religious settlement, but their leadership was weak and the rebellion was hijacked by a more radical group that aimed to replace Elizabeth with Mary immediately, and was prepared to appeal to the Pope and the Duke of Alba for assistance.[5] In the event, the rising merely proved that northern affinities were not the power they had once been, and it was suppressed without undue difficulty and without serious fighting. The Earls took refuge in flight, and their estates were carved up. The Crown kept the majority of the Border properties, and the rest was distributed among the loyal gentry. The Marches would never be the same again. However the most significant outcome of the rebellion was the belated papal response. Against the advice of the King of Spain, Pius V took the opportunity to issue the bull *Regnans in Excelsis*, declaring Elizabeth a heretic, and deposing her. Her subjects were absolved of their allegiance, and this declaration put an end to the 'phoney war' of Catholic against Protestant in England. Anyone henceforth who accepted the Pope's authority was a potential traitor, and that formed the basis of the penal laws against recusants that were to follow.[6]

One indirect result of the papal bull was the Ridolfi plot of 1571, which was a rather confused bid to assassinate Elizabeth, in which the Spaniards, the Guises and the Duke of Norfolk were all involved. Norfolk was executed in consequence, but the main effect was to strengthen the government's hand in its dealing with the English Catholics. It became High Treason to call the Queen a heretic, or to

bring papal bulls into England.[7] Another consequence was the treaty of
Blois with France in 1572, which provided for mutual defence against
the growing menace of Spain. Elizabeth's courtship of the Duke of
Anjou having run into the sand on religious grounds, Catherine de
Medici suggested her youngest son, the 18-year-old Duke of Alençon,
as a replacement, in spite of the fact that the Queen was now 39. This
negotiation was to run, on and off for nearly nine years.[8] Meanwhile,
the Queen's image was undergoing a significant change. While continuing to be baffling and unpredictable, Elizabeth was no longer
either young or beautiful. Her looks had been ravaged by the smallpox
that had almost taken her life in 1563, and had cost most of her hair,
forcing a resort to wigs. She was not disposed to give up on feminine
mystique, however, which was such an essential part of her political
armoury. In the early 1570s someone (and it may not have been her)
decided that she should become the Virgin Queen, and her inviolate
body the symbol for the integrity of her kingdom.

Jousting had been a feature of the life of the court since 1559, and
had originally been organized by her Master of the Horse, Robert
Dudley. Such events had marked the coronation, on 16 and 17 January
1559, and again in July, when the Gentlemen Pensioners had displayed
their prowess. Dudley himself had first participated in November of
that year, and in 1562 the fourteenth-century rules were revised and re-
promulgated.[9] By 1570 tilting was a regular feature of court festivities,
but it had lost any semblance of military significance, mainly providing
occasions for chivalric displays of a theatrical nature, designed to
emphasize the mystery of the Fairy Queen who presided. At about the
same time, and possibly in response to the papal bull, the Queen's
accession day (17 November) also became a focus for celebrations,
both at court and in the country at large. Bells were rung and bonfires
lit in gratitude for the escape from Spanish and papal tyranny. It seems
likely that the connection between these two things was first made in
1572 by Sir Henry Lee, the Queen's Champion, who in that year
devised the Accession Day tilts.[10] These remained relatively low-key
events until 1581, when the Queen finally gave up the pretence that she
would one day marry, and the celebration of her Virginity became
unconfined. Edmund Spenser's *Faerie Queene*, although written later,
articulated the ideal relationship that was supposed to exist between
Elizabeth and her knights, through the mouth of Sir Guyon:

> She is the mighty Queen of Faerie,
> Whose fair retrait I on my shield do beare,
> She is the flowre of grace and chastity,
> Throughout the world renowned far and neare,
> My life, my liege, my Souvereign, my deare…[11]

She was at once the sovereign mistress of all hearts, and the unattainable lady of the courtly love tradition. The fact that she was by this time an aging and irritable spinster only added to the piquancy of the celebrations.

This image-building should probably be construed as ritualized defiance, and certainly played a part in the growing self-identification of England as a unique and Protestant place. However, more tangible provisions for defence were not neglected. The fortifications of Berwick had been redesigned and work commenced during the French war of Mary's reign. Between 1558 and 1570 £130,000 had been spent on completing these bastions, and they remain today as the most complete set of renaissance fortifications in Britain.[12] By 1598 Lord Willoughby de Eresby, then the Governor, had no opinion of their effectiveness, but they were actively maintained throughout the 1570s and 1580s. From the beginning of the reign the Council had also tried to make sure that as many as possible of the potential levies were equipped with arquebuses, which had inevitable consequences for mustering and training. Although the law continued to demand archery practice, by 1560 the day of the longbow was over for practical military purposes.[13]

The musters had been reorganized by Mary's statutes, and Royal Lieutenants had been appointed on an occasional basis since the reign of Henry VIII—although when the Duke of Norfolk had occupied that position in the north of England in 1536 it had been regarded as an emergency provision. The Duke of Northumberland, towards the end of Edward VI's reign, had introduced the office on a regular basis as part of his general scheme of national defence, usually grouping several counties under a single Lieutenant. Such Lieutenants were invariably noblemen who had some established connection with the area, and usually some military experience.[14] Mary had continued this practice, and Elizabeth extended it, so that it by the 1570s it had become normal for each county to have its own Lord Lieutenant, who was responsible for all the military aspects of county government. This meant the con-

duct of musters, the maintenance of muster rolls, the appointment of
Muster Masters, and the provision of regular training. Their powers
were in theory extensive, particularly in times of war or rebellion,
including the administration of martial law, and there is some evidence
that the Queen was uneasy about conferring so much authority upon
noblemen who might have their own priorities.[15] Because the Lieutenants were grandees, inevitably much of the actual work was done by
deputies, but when these were first appointed is uncertain. There are
references to officials who may have been Deputy Lieutenants as early
as 1553, but it seems more likely that regular appointments were first
made in the 1560s. The first complete list dates from 1569, by which
time the practice was clearly well-established.[16] The Deputies—about
half a dozen to each shire—were Justices of the Peace wearing other
hats. Some may have had military experience, but by the 1570s that was
becoming increasingly rare. Usually they were appointed for their general competence, or because of a particular relationship with the Lord
Lieutenant.

The professional soldiers were the Muster Masters, and it was they
who conducted the actual training, at the expense of the counties who
employed them directly. After 1570, the emphasis was very much on
the defence of the realm, rather than making troops available for foreign wars, and this led to a further reorganization of the militia. In 1573
the Council decreed that the available men should be divided into two
sorts—the trained bands and the rest. The former were the elite, more
substantial in terms of wealth, or more reliable from a social or religious
point of view. They were selected by the Muster Masters, and were
required to undergo regular training for up to two weeks every year. In
return they were exempt from service overseas, although they could
volunteer for such service, if they were tempted.[17] In order to ensure
that such bands were properly equipped, those shires that had greater
resources or took their duties more seriously established county
armouries. These were places, sometimes within a Guildhall or parish
church, where weapons that had been purchased by the Deputy Lieutenants on behalf of the county were stored and maintained. The
advantage of the county armoury was that it enabled 'fit men' who
might not have the resources to provide their own arquebuses, to be
equipped, and diminished dependence upon gentlemen's or noblemen's retinues, which were separately mustered and equipped at the

expense of their masters.[18] In spite of the appointment of Lords Lieutenant, Elizabeth had an instinctive mistrust of aristocrats with military
pretensions, even when these were theoretically deployed in her service. The collective entity of the shire provided an additional safeguard,
but the responsibility was strenuously resisted in some quarters, not
because of any disloyalty but simply on the grounds of expense, at a
time when the collection of poor relief and other local taxes was growing. No service outwith the realm was required until 1585, but from
about 1572 onwards volunteers were going in increasing numbers to
serve in the armies of the Dutch rebels. Many of these were motivated
by nothing more noble that the search for adventure or plunder, but
some saw the Dutch as beleaguered fellow Protestants whom they
were anxious to help. Young gentlemen were particularly drawn to this
service, and it was from among men with such relevant experience that
the Muster Masters tended to be recruited. The rank and file soldiers
often turned into hardened long-term mercenaries, and found a warm
welcome in English service when it came to turning the raw recruits
enlisted for the war with Spain into acceptable soldiers.

NAVAL RECRUITMENT, 1568
Instructions by James Humphrey, Clerk of the Ships, to parish constables or
other officials despatching a group of 'prested' men, 12 March 1568

THESE SHALL BE *to charge, as also in the Queen's Majesty's name to
command you upon sight hereof to charge and set forth the eight men here
under written, as you tender the advancement and furtherance of her Highness's
service presently to be done. And that you do command them to be at Chatham
in Kent on Saturday next [20th March], and there to present themselves
before the officers of her Highness's ships, who will place them as it shall seem
good to the same officers. As according to a bill of their names and charge which
you shall receive by this bearer. As also four shillings for every one of them, prest
and conduct money of the said eight mariners whose names be here underwritten. And fail you not this to do, as you and every one of them will avoid her
Grace's displeasure at your extreme perils...*

[Bodleian Library MS Rawlinson 846, f.114. *British Naval Documents*, pp.101–2.]

The navy continued along the lines laid down in 1559. Elizabeth did
not like the Ordinary, and reduced it first to £10,000 a year and then to

£6,000. This was not the result of any exceptional meanness, but rather because she preferred to find the necessary money from whichever pocket happened to be most open.[19] The Ordinary was always drawn on the Exchequer, and that might, or might not, be the most convenient source of supply. As we have already seen, the offices of Surveyor and Rigger and Master of the Naval Ordnance had been merged in 1557, then in 1565 the Lieutenancy had been discontinued on the death of Sir William Woodhouse, reducing the Admiralty from seven officers to six. At that level it remained, although there were changes of personnel. Richard Howlett, the Clerk of the Ships, was succeeded in 1560 by George Winter, William's brother, and William Brooke, the original Controller, died in 1561, to be replaced by William Holstock.[20]

New ships continued to be built and rebuilt; the *Victory*, the *Triumph* and the *Aid* in 1562 and the *Great Bark* as the *White Bear* in 1564. After 1570 the programme accelerated, no fewer than 14 ships being added to the fleet between then and 1584, of which six were rebuilds. Most of these later additions were galleons, a 'race built' design attributed to John Hawkins, but in fact in use well before he took over as Treasurer. It was based upon the early sixteenth-century galleasse, a ship that could be propelled either by oars or sail, and was built with a flat deck, like a galley. By the end of Henry VIII's reign the galleasse was out of favour, and when the *Great Galley* (built 1515 to Henry's own design) was rebuilt in 1538, it was as a sailing ship. It was, however, rebuilt without the towering castles typical of a carrack, such as the *Mary Rose*, and a number of other smaller ships were built with flat decks, as is clear from the Anthony Roll of 1545.[21] Early Elizabethan vessels, such as the *Elizabeth Jonas* or the *Victory*, tended to favour the carrack shape, but by 1570 the galleon had clearly established itself. This change of design was tactically significant, because it indicates a shift from a 'grapple and board' method of fighting (where the high castles were valuable) to a 'stand off and shoot' method (where castles were irrelevant). Once a fighting ship was seen primarily as a gun platform, speed and manoeuvrability became the essential requirements, and the galleon came into its own. It was also probably during the 1570s that private warships were pioneering the synchronized broadside that was typical of English naval tactics by the time of the Armada.[22] Privateers (or more accurately, pirates) were using matching sets of iron guns to maximize the effect of these broadsides, long before similar methods were used by the navy.[23] They tended to be relatively small vessels, which depended on speed and firepower to repel or evade the attentions of hostile warships, and that necessity was the mother of many inventions.

As we have seen, after 1568 Elizabeth backed off from further investment in long-distance piracy, but that of course did not prevent it. Altogether there were 13 such private voyages between 1570 and 1577, none of them made any pretence of carrying on legitimate trade. They were not, for the most part, very successful, although they returned a sufficient profit to encourage their investors to try again, and Elizabeth made not the slightest attempt to stop them. Francis Drake was out three times, in 1570, 1571 and 1572–3, and the third of these voyages was significant although it cost the lives of both his brothers. Operating in loose co-operation with Huguenot pirates from La Rochelle, and with a group of *cimarrones*, or escaped slaves, he ambushed a mule train near Nombre de Dios and relieved it of a small fortune in silver bullion —so much, in fact, that neither he nor his allies were able to carry it all away.[24] How much of this found its way to England is not clear, but one estimate is £20,000, which might help to account for the fact that by 1575 Drake was a very rich man. His reputation was also sky high, and *el draque* was a name to be feared in the Caribbean. Drake had friends at court, and the Queen was well enough pleased with his exploits. She was steering a delicate course, because she had brought her dispute with the Netherlands to an end by 1572, and was not anxious to provoke Philip into further hostile acts.[25] On a global scale they both knew that such pinpricks were insignificant, but the King suspected that these raids were concealed probes, intended to establish the feasibility of English colonies on the mainland of the New World, along the lines of the Huguenot colony in Florida that his servants had eliminated in 1562. Richard Grenville had indeed proposed such a scheme in 1574, which Philip knew about, but the Queen had refused to licence it. Without royal support a colony, as distinct from a raid, would be an impossibility.[26] So Elizabeth blew cold, and the King contained his mounting irritation.

Grenville was in a sense unlucky because he caught the Queen in a cautious mood, and such moods were transient. In 1577 she responded much more positively to another bunch of speculators, although in this case the proposal was not for a colony but for a voyage of exploration.

The idea was to sail through the strait of Magellan and explore the western coast of South America. This was disingenuous because she knew perfectly well that the Spaniards were already settled on the west coast, although in much smaller numbers than on the east coast. Further conflict was inevitable, and it was probably for that reason that she insisted on remaining as a private shareholder, and declined to contribute a royal ship.[27] Drake was given the command, and the only visible sign of Elizabeth's involvement was that she insisted on him naming his new flagship (which he owned), the *Pelican*, that being one of her favourite emblems.

After a false start, this epic and extremely well-recorded voyage finally got under way from Plymouth on 13 December 1577. No instructions were issued, but everyone involved knew that the main objective was piracy, and that cause was very much furthered when Drake took the Portuguese ship the *Santa Maria* off the Cape Verde islands, and recruited its experienced and skilful pilot, Nuno da Silva.[28] Unfortunately, as they progressed south and west, Drake's relations with his second in command, Thomas Doughty, steadily deteriorated. The quarrel is an obscure one, but it became extremely bitter, and when they got to Port San Julian, where Drake was to winter before tackling the strait, he decided to settle with Thomas Doughty. Assuming an authority that his commission did not in fact give him, he put his subordinate on trial, conducting the proceedings in due form. The evidence was inconclusive to everyone except Drake, but he was a charismatic leader and loyalty to him prevailed. Doughty was condemned for mutiny and necromancy, and executed.[29] The fact seems to have been that Francis had become paranoid about any challenges to his authority, and those Doughty had certainly offered. The only justification for his ruthless action was that it would have been impossible for the expedition to have succeeded with a weak or challenged leadership, and that the company must have realized perfectly well.

DRAKE AND THOMAS DOUGHTY

IN THIS PORT [*St. Julian*] *our Generall began to enquire diligently of the actions of M. Thomas Doughtie, and found them not to be such as he looked for, but tending rather to contention, or mutinie, or some other disorder, whereby (without redresse) the success of the voyage might greatly have been hazarded; whereupon the company was called together and made acquainted*

with the particulars of the cause, which were found partly by master Doughties
own confession and partly by the evidence of the fact to be true; which when our
Generall saw, although his private affection to M. Doughtie (as he then in the
presence of all sacredly protested) was great, yet the care he had of the state of
the voyage, of the expectation of her majestie and of the honour of his country
did more touch him (as indeed it ought) than the private respect of one man,
so that the cause being thoroughly heard, and all things done in good order, as
neere as might be to the course of our lawes in England, it was concluded that
M. Doughtie should receive punishment according to the qualitie of the offense,
and he seeing no remedie but patience for himselfe, desired before his death to
receive the communion which he did at the hands of M. Fletcher our Minister,
and our Generall himselfe accompanied him in that holy action; which being
done and the place of execution made readie; he having embraced our Generall
and taken his leave of all the companye, with prayer for the Queen's Majesty
and our realme, in quiet sort laid his head on the block where he ended his life.
This being done, our General made divers speeches to the whole companye,
perswading us to unitie, obedience, love and regard of our voyage, and for the
better confirmation thereof willed every man the next Sunday following to
prepare himselfe to receive the Communion as Christian brethren and friends
ought to, which was done in very reverent sort, and so with good contentment
every man went about his business.

[Richard Hakluyt, *The Principall Navigations, Voiages and Discoveries of the English*
Nation (1589). Facsimile edition 1965. II, p.643D.]

Quitting Port San Julian on 17 August, Drake's three ships made a swift
and relatively uneventful passage of the strait, only to run into a Pacific
gale on the other side. The *Marigold* was lost, and the *Pelican* and the
Elizabeth became separated. The latter ran back into the strait, waiting
for Drake to reappear, and when he did not do so, returned home.
Meanwhile the Captain, assuming his remaining colleague to have been
lost also, proceeded north. He now had just one ship and about 80
men.[30] However, the west coast settlements were virtually undefended,
and towards the end of November he attacked the small town of
Valparaiso, relieving it of gold to the value of 200,000 pesos (about
£30,000). Proceeding on his way, he sacked several other villages,
adding about 25,000 pesos to his loot, and taking such provisions as he
needed. The early months of 1579 were passed in this leisurely progress,
until in August he reached what is now Lower California, then

uninhabited, where he landed. He is alleged to have taken possession of this land in the name of his Queen, but the evidence is more than a little suspect.[31]

He then struck out across the Pacific, reaching the Moluccas in late November, where he was able to careen and resupply his ship—now renamed the *Golden Hind*. He also had a near fatal encounter with a reef in January 1580, which forced him to jettison some of his cargo— but not the gold—and after a further stop for supplies, set out across the Indian Ocean for the Cape of Good Hope, another voyage of two and a half months. He does not appear to have stopped again until reaching Sierra Leone on 22 July, an extraordinary feat of seamanship and endurance. He reached Plymouth at the end of September after an epic voyage of nearly three years, bringing home one ship and a fraction of the men he had started off with.[32] The value of his cargo was officially £307,000, but in fact nearer £600,000, which gave his ordinary investors a 4,700 per cent return on their investment, and the Queen about £300,000—the equivalent of a year's ordinary revenue. It is not surprising that she was delighted to see him, and knighted him on the deck of his ship.[33] His own share of the loot seems to have amounted to some £40,000, and the Spanish ambassador's agitated attempts to invoke the agreement for mutual restitution (which had been signed during Drake's absence in 1579) fell on deaf ears.[34]

Drake had plundered with impunity, but he had found no new lands, nor opened up any new trade routes. What he had accomplished was something equally remarkable, although less tangible to assess. He had demonstrated that the English seaman now had a global reach. Where Drake had gone, others would follow, both their ships and their navigational skills now being equal to the challenge. The treaty of Tordesillas, which had divided the world into Spanish and Portuguese spheres of influence, was a dead letter.[35] By 1580 it was clear to Philip that the English were in a position to challenge his worldwide suprem-acy, from Vera Cruz to the Philippines and West Africa, and he did not like what he saw. Apart from Drake, there had been a lull in piracy. Only 10 Spanish ships had been taken between 1578 and 1581, and the losses had been negligible. Edward Fenton's voyage of 1582, aimed at the East Indies, had disintegrated through poor leadership, but Drake posed a threat that could not be ignored.[36]

By 1583 the King's mind was moving definitively towards war with

England, and he was encouraged in this long-deferred decision by the fact that other political events were moving in his favour. Most notably, in 1580 King Sebastian of Portugal had died, leaving no direct heir. Philip, as his nephew, was the next in line, and by moving swiftly was able to take over the whole country without resistance.[37] Although past its peak, the Portuguese empire, particularly in the Far East, was still extensive and wealthy, and by assuming the Crown of Portugal, the King became the master of a global dominion without any rival. Already very wealthy, Philip became richer still. Between 1571 and 1580 he received 12 million ducats (£3,300,000) in silver from the Americas. From 1581 to 1590 that sum increased to 18.7 million (£4,800,000), and that was not even the greatest part of his income, which came principally from the taxation of Castile. In 1577 alone his total income was 8.7 million ducats (£2,000,000).[38] By contrast, in the early 1580s Elizabeth's ordinary revenue stood at £300,000. A parliamentary subsidy was worth about £150,000, but that might be spread over several years. Philip understood this discrepancy, and it encouraged his thinking. He had enormous commitments, but it would not be difficult to outspend the Queen.

In 1583 the Duke of Parma captured the ports of Nieupoort and Dunkirk, which enabled Philip to re-establish the North Sea squadron, and re-open sea communications with the Low Countries. In 1584 the maverick Duke of Anjou died. Anjou had been interfering in the Netherlands, ostensibly on the side of the rebels, and although this had not done much to assist William of Orange (known as William the Silent), it had confused Parma and distracted his attention.[39] Then in July 1584 William was assassinated, and although there is no reason to suppose that Philip was a party to the plot, it served his purposes very well. The French civil wars had been reignited by the fact that the Protestant King of Navarre was now the next heir to the throne, and the Dutch rebels were temporarily leaderless. Philip signed the treaty of Joinville with the Duke of Guise, effectively paying him to prevent Henry of Navarre from becoming King of France, and turned his main attentions back to the Netherlands.[40]

Meanwhile diplomatic relations between England and Spain had broken down. Mendoza had kept up a barrage of protests against Drake's expedition — demanding exemplary punishment, which Elizabeth had no intention of inflicting. She had retaliated by demanding an explanation of Philip's interference with the perpetually rebellious Irish, and when that was not forthcoming had refused him audience.[41] Partly in revenge for this insult, and partly pursuing his master's interests, the ambassador had then become involved in the Throgmorton plot, which was yet another Guisard conspiracy to free Mary, Queen of Scots and murder Elizabeth. The Queen's spymaster, Sir Francis Walsingham, was well abreast of Francis Throgmorton, and knew all about what was intended. The Catholic zealot was arrested, tried and executed, and Mendoza, compromised to the hilt, was finally expelled in January 1584. There was, consequently, no Spanish diplomatic representative in England when the crisis caused by William the Silent's assassination arose in August of that year.[42] Mary would continue to be a liability until her implication in the Babington plot to assassinate Elizabeth led to her trial and execution on 8 February 1587.

The English feared, with every justification, that if Philip succeeded in suppressing the Dutch, he would next turn his fire on them, irrespective of any further action that the Queen might take. It was this consideration that prompted the cautious Burghley to argue in favour of intervention, writing

> Although her Majesty should thereby enter into a war presently, yet were she better able to do it now, while she may make the same out of her realm, having the help of the people of Holland, and before the King of Spain should have consummated his conquests in those countries … and shall be so strong by sea … as that her Majesty shall in no wise be able … neither by sea nor land to withstand his attempts….[43]

Elizabeth wriggled, trying to initiate direct negotiations with Parma, but the logic of Burgley's argument was irrefutable. If Parma's veterans once landed in England, the levies, well though they might fight, would be no match for them. After some unnecessarily difficult and protracted negotiations, the Queen signed the treaty of Nonsuch with the Estates General in August 1585, agreeing to provide 4,000 foot and 400 horse, plus £100,000 a year, the latter to be repaid once the war was over.[44] She also agreed to send a naval squadron to the West Indies. There was no mention of Spain, but both sides treated it as declaration of war. In fact hostilities had had a rolling start, because as early as the 23 December 1584 the Admiralty had been ordered to mobilize a fleet of 35 ships, far more than would have been needed for a normal Winter

Guard, and a circle of investors similar to that which had supported the circumnavigation had put together a plan for another expedition by Drake in the summer of 1585, this time explicitly aimed against the West Indies.[45] The Queen's promised squadron was already in being before she sent it. The soldiers had been mustered before the treaty was signed, and were despatched within a matter of days. Philip had also made a pre-emptive strike. On 26 May he ordered all English, French and Dutch shipping in Spanish harbours to be seized. The pretext given was that these ships were needed for some undisclosed service, but the real motivation seems to have been to obtain the grain that a number of them were carrying. Again there was no mention of war but, on 1 July, Drake was issued with orders for a rather different kind of voyage than that which had been originally envisaged.

This time he was issued with an official commission, making his voyage a fully sanctioned naval expedition, and he was to proceed to Vigo to negotiate the release of the ships that had been seized.[46] What should happen thereafter was much discussed, and resulted in a delay of some two and half months before Drake could actually sail. If his mission was successful, should he come straight home? Or should he take advantage of the fact that a *de facto* state of war existed to go in search of the *flota* (the Spanish treasure fleet), or renew his raids on the Caribbean colonies? It is possible that the Queen deliberately prevaricated in the hope that Drake would lose patience and simply set off without waiting for instructions, because that is apparently what happened on 14 September, and she made not the slightest attempt to stop him.[47]

It was a major expedition. He had altogether 29 ships and some 4,000 men, the Royal Navy being represented by the *Elizabeth Bonaventure* and the *Aid*. On 27 September he reached Vigo and (perhaps to his surprise) successfully negotiated the release of the ships held there. It was probably then that he decided to proceed to America, because the provisions that he had on board were only sufficient to get him home, and he restocked at the Spanish port, finding the Governor surprisingly complaisant—or perhaps intimidated.[48] While Drake was anchored in Vigo, the *flota* arrived safely at Seville, having fought off another English squadron near the Azores, and that may also have been in the Governor's mind as he kept his formidable guest dangling for his stores. Once Drake had restocked to his satisfaction, about 6 or 8 October, he sailed to the Canaries. Having been met with a cannonade at the entrance to

Palma harbour, however, he did not attempt to land, but sailed on to San Tiago in the Cape Verde Islands. This was a small and relatively defenceless community, which they plundered and set ablaze.[49] As was usual on such voyages, there were quarrels among the English captains and indiscipline among the men, but there was no Thomas Doughty this time, and the Admiral's formidable reputation prevented things from getting out of hand. In the Cape Verde Islands two English seamen were hanged for unspecified, but presumably criminal, offences. On 18 December the fleet made landfall in the West Indies.

By this time a sickness — possibly dysentery — had broken out among the men, which Drake isolated by the drastic expedient of setting the sick men ashore. Heartless though this may have been, it protected the rest of the fleet from infection. Santo Domingo was taken in a night attack on 31 December, and Drake did his best to extract a million ducats in ransom from the settlers.[50] There was no great battle, and no resolute defence, but there was no million ducats either, and the Admiral had to settle eventually for 25,000, plus whatever loot he could carry away. He also helped himself to two replacement ships, some of his original fleet having become leaky and unseaworthy. After leaving Santo Domingo, Drake headed for the mainland at Cartagena, arriving in the harbour on 9 February 1586, and landing his men under cover of darkness about four miles from the town. The defenders here numbered about 600, but they made poor use of their strategic position, and were driven out of the town after some heavy street fighting. The gunners on the battery were far too slow in reloading, and were swiftly overrun.[51] The fort of Boqueron, just along the coast, proved a tougher proposition, requiring three assaults before its defences were overcome. Both sides tried to minimize their casualties and it would appear that, in spite of the reports of fierce fighting, no more than about 30 died on each part. Far more Englishmen died from disease, and eventually about 200 bodies were left behind in Cartagena.

The fighting was over by 10 February, and (as at Santo Domingo) Drake then settled down to try and extract a million ducats in ransom.[52] In spite of staying until 14 April, and trying every coercive tactic known to him, he had to settle eventually for 107,000 ducats, plus some separate ransoms for individual houses that were not actually within the town. At least, that was what was declared. There is a strong suspicion that the ransom actually paid at Cartagena was much higher, but

Drake was too good a pirate to be famous for accurate bookkeeping, and whatever surplus there may have been went into his own pocket and those of his men, without any questions being asked. However, the cities of the Indies were not what they were cracked up to be in terms of wealth. It was partly for that reason that discipline declined during the long stay in Cartagena, and several delinquents were hanged. By the time that they left, morale was not good, and although Drake wanted to go on and attack Nombre de Dios, his captains dissuaded him. So, having stowed most of his guns, he set off for home, pausing at Cabo San Antonio on the extreme tip of Cuba to take on fresh water. Apparently a Spanish fleet was expected at Havana, and there was some debate about whether to lie in wait for it, but the negative voice prevailed and Drake continued to Florida, where he reached the small settlement of San Augustin on 27 May.[53]

In the face of so formidable a fleet, the settlers simply fled, and Drake's men stripped the entire place, including 6,000 ducats of the King's money. After this modest success, Drake, for what reason is not known, decided to pay a call on the newly established English settlement at Roanoake in what was later to be called Virginia. It was as well that he did so. The Governor, Ralph Lane, admitted that they were in a bad way, and asked for his help. It was not, apparently, the threat from Spain that was the problem, so much as the local inhabitants and their own inexperience. Drake offered them supplies, and one of his smaller ships. Lane's colleagues, however, had had enough, and when a storm blew up during his stay, they asked instead for a passage home. The embryonic colony was abandoned, and Drake sailed straight for England, reaching Plymouth on the 28 July 1586.[54]

His voyage had not been in theory an act of war, and its plunder was not even sufficient for the investors to see their money back, but in another sense it had been an enormous success. The capture of Santo Domingo and Cartagena had not been great military exploits, but they had been significant humiliations for Spain, and the pen of Walter Bigges was soon to turn this into a propaganda triumph. *The Summarie and True Discourse of Sir Francis Drakes West Indian Voyage,* published first in 1589 (after the Armada), mendaciously presented him as a Protestant hero of gigantic dimensions, fighting against the tyranny and bigotry of Catholic Spain.[55] Drake was undoubtedly a Protestant. He was a friend of John Foxe, the martyrologist, and forced his unfortunate prisoners to listen to long extracts from the *Acts and Monuments*, but apart from blowing up the cathedral at Santo Domingo—accidentally, he claimed—there was little sign of reforming zeal during the voyage itself. What he had done was to convince Philip that *el draque* had elevated himself from the status of nuisance to that of a substantial threat, and that motivated the King to convert the vague schemes he had formulated for the invasion of England into a concrete plan.

As long before as the end of 1583 the Marquis of Santa Cruz, fresh from his victory over Dom Antonio's miscellaneous fleet at Terciera, had urged on Philip the feasibility of a seaborne assault on England.[56] The plan had been shelved at that time because priority was given to the Netherlands, but now things had changed, and news of Drake's depredations played a part in altering the King's mind. In October 1585 Philip accepted a proposal that the Pope had been advocating for several years, and asked for his financial support. By the end of the year both Santa Cruz and Parma had been requested to submit their ideas, and the former had resurrected his plan of two years earlier. At the end of April 1586 the King had both plans in his hands. The former proposed to ship 55,000 men, complete with guns, horses and other equipment, direct from Spain in a fleet of 150 ships; the latter, much more modestly, suggested bringing some 30,000 troops from the Low Countries to Kent on a fleet of sea-going barges—an exploit that the Duke reckoned would take 10–12 hours and would require the Spanish navy to prevent the English fleet from interfering.[57] Philip turned both these plans over to Juan de Zuniga, his senior adviser, and Zuniga reported in July. He urged that the 'Enterprise of England' should be launched in August or September 1587, and suggested a compromise plan that the King largely adopted. The main force should be sent from Spain, but instead of making a direct landfall, it should rendezvous with the Duke of Parma, whose veterans would also form a part of the invasion force. The whole operation would be protected by the Spanish fleet, which would also escort the troop carriers from Spain. This plan was then communicated to Santa Cruz, Parma and Zuniga as the King's decision, and the former was placed in charge of the preparations.[58] It was supposed to be a secret, but it was poorly guarded and by the autumn of 1586 the English Council knew perfectly well what was intended.

English forces had been deployed in the Low Countries since the

mid-1570s, although as volunteers rather than officially. They numbered several thousand, and were officered by English commanders,
such as Sir John Norris, but they were paid by the Estates General. By
1578 their reputation as good fighting men was well established, and
between 1579 and 1585 they had proved mobile and reliable.[59] In 1582
some of them had gravitated into the service of the Duke of Anjou, but
by and large they stayed together in their companies, locally based as
they had been recruited. The cause was popular in England, and there
is no sign that Elizabeth had any difficulty recruiting the troops to which
she was committed by the treaty of Nonsuch. Within days of that treaty
being signed, Sir John Norris was put in command of 5,000 foot and
1,000 horse, and given custody of the cautionary towns of Brill and
Flushing. The Queen had already exceeded her treaty commitment,
and was pumping money into the army at the rate of £12,500 a month.[60]
When the Earl of Leicester took over the command at the end of 1585,
the English army in the Low Countries was a well-established presence.
Leicester turned out to be a bad choice as commander, largely because
of his total lack of relevant experience. He was inveigled into accepting
the Governor Generalship, which involved Elizabeth further than she
wanted to go, got bogged down in the internal disputes of Dutch politics, and quarrelled violently with John Norris, who had all the experience that he lacked.[61] The English soldiers continued to perform well,
notably at the storming of Axel in May 1586, but Leicester, having
aroused Elizabeth's ire on more than one occasion, was withdrawn in
something close to disgrace in November.

Meanwhile the navy was being placed on a war footing. While
Drake was still at sea in the summer of 1586, Henry Palmer was sailing
as Admiral of the Narrow Seas, and on 6 August John Hawkins went
out with an Atlantic patrol consisting of 18 or 20 ships, four of which
were royal warships of over 500 tons. His firepower would have been
considerable, but his tactics were purely defensive. He was not chasing
pirates or taking prizes.[62] Gonson spent only about £30,000 during
1586, which was not a wartime level, but this can be accounted for in
different ways. In the first place the £20,000 or so that Elizabeth invested
in Drake's voyage did not pass through the naval accounts, and in the
second place both the nobility and the maritime community rallied
behind the Queen and contributed their resources. In general, the military effectiveness of the country had to depend upon the willingness of

parliament to vote subsidies, because there was no way in which the Queen's ordinary revenues could have sustained either an army or an operational navy. But it also depended upon the willingness of men to serve, either in person or by contributing ships and money. Not only had the London merchants invested heavily in Drake's enterprises, but they also contributed armed vessels to both Palmer's and Hawkins' squadrons. Walter Raleigh and the Earl of Leicester both sold their private warships to the Crown at notional prices, and the Earl of Cumberland mobilized a whole fleet of privateers.[63] Other courtiers curried favour by fitting out ships and handing them over for royal service.

This was a struggle like no other. Previous wars had been fought for conquest, or for dynastic ambition, or for limited strategic gains, but this was a war for survival, both political and religious. Elizabeth may not have been a soldier, but in 1585 she was an embattled virgin and a symbol of her peoples' freedom. By not marrying she had escaped the ambiguous imagery that had so bedevilled her sister, and instead had nailed her female colours to the mast. As she sailed into the unknown waters of war with Spain there was a genuine originality about both her politics and her imagery, and even Lord Burghley, who had known her for nearly 40 years, did not know quite what to make of her.

CHAPTER NINE

GLORIANA

❖

THE QUEEN
AT WAR

A FULL-SCALE WAR, such as that which commenced against Spain in 1585, presented the Queen with problems that the more limited confrontations of 1560 and 1563 had not created. In the first place, there was the question of paying for it. The fall of Antwerp, coming within days of the signature of the treaty of Nonsuch, had immediately caused her to increase her commitment to 5,000 foot and 1,000 horse. Quite apart from the loan to which she was also committed, these forces in the Netherlands cost £101,000 in 1586, £175,000 in 1587, and £103,000 in 1588; nor did these sums diminish much in subsequent years.[1] The navy cost £44,000 in 1587, and nearly £100,000 in the following year. Eleven new ships were added to the fleet in 1586, and two more in 1587, quite apart from the enormous cost of the auxiliaries, which was not borne by the Crown. Many of these must have been built specifically with the war in mind, because in 1582 when the merchant marine had been surveyed, only 20 ships of more than 200 tons had been returned, of which a bare half dozen had displaced more than 240 tons, whereas against the Armada several private warships of up to 500 tons were in service.[2] The carefully accumulated 'war chest' of some £300,000 was completely spent by the end of 1590, and Lord Burghley was constantly preoccupied with the raising of money. Between 1585 and 1603, £1,560,000 was realized in the form of lay subsidies, as well as a further £227,000 from the clergy.[3] The Queen's habitual reluctance to spend money became paranoid as the war progressed, and her regular servants, never generously rewarded, found the well of royal munificence almost completely dry.

There was also the question of imagery. As we have seen, Elizabeth had from the start made use of 'military-related' images by presiding at tournaments. She had also used the Garter ceremonial, revised by Edward VI, to present herself as a leader of men, although not in the same sense that her father had done. The virginal imagery had begun to gain ground in the 1570s, and as early as 1576 the well-known 'sieve' portrait represented her as a Roman vestal.[4] Full-scale war, however, offered a different challenge. Precisely because she was not able to lead an army into battle, she was in danger of being upstaged by those who could. An Army Royal could have been a disaster for Elizabeth, because it would have to have been led by a nobleman, who would inevitably have assumed a quasi-royal stature. Professional soldiers were different, because—although they could command small armies and expeditionary forces, in Ireland, for example, or in Brittany—their status was not high enough for them to challenge the royal imagery. This was one of the reasons why the Earl of Leicester in the Low Countries had so annoyed her. By accepting the status of Governor General, he was not only committing her to a position that she did not wish to occupy, but he was also acting as a surrogate king. The Earl of Essex presented a similar problem in Ireland later, particularly because of an over-inflated sense of his own importance. The only time that an Army Royal was assembled, it was on English soil, and Elizabeth squeezed herself into a suit of armour to go and harangue the troops at Tilbury. Her speech on that occasion, if truly reported, was a masterpiece of gender bending. 'I know I have the body but of a weak and feeble woman, but I have the heart and stomach of a king and of a king of England too...'[5] In other words Elizabeth was doing what the statute of 1554 had invited her to do—present herself not as a woman, but as a king who happened to be female. It was not accidental that soldiers of baronial or knightly status commanded all the English armies that fought abroad during this war. Indeed, on the few occasions when noblemen were deployed, they were recalled in disgrace.

ELIZABETH AT TILBURY

M*Y* LOVING PEOPLE, *I have been persuaded by some that are careful of my safety to take heed how I committed myself to armed multitudes for fear of treachery. But I tell you that I would not desire to live to distrust my faithful and loving people. Let tyrants fear: I have so behaved myself that under God I have placed my chiefest strength and safeguard in the loyal hearts and goodwill of my subjects. Wherefore I am come among you at this time but for*

*my recreation and pleasure, being resolved in the midst and heat of the battle to
live and die amongst you all, to lay down for my God and for my kingdom and
for my people mine honour and my blood even in the dust. I know I have the
body but of a weak and feeble woman, but I have the heart and stomach of
a king and of a king of England too—and take foul scorn that Parma or any
prince of Europe should dare to invade the borders of my realm. To the which
rather than any dishonour shall grow by me, I myself will venture my royal
blood; I myself will be your general, judge and rewarder of your virtue in the
field…*

[*Elizabeth I, Collected Works*, ed. Marcus, Mueller and Rose, 2000, pp.325-6.]

This was also an additional argument for fighting as far as possible at
sea. Given the relative resources of the two kingdoms, it made strategic
sense to fight the Spaniards in that way, but there was also the consideration that sea captains had neither the standing nor the resources to
present any threat to the sovereign. Even the Lord Admiral was a mere
baron. John Hawkins, Martin Frobisher, Richard Grenville and Walter
Raleigh were all gentlemen from recognized families. Francis Drake was
not even that, but rather a self-made man and a pirate with no respect-
able credentials.[6] Her favour made him a knight, and a very rich man,
but she could drop him without hesitation when he ignored her instructions in 1589. It was during this last part of the reign that the royal imagery turned most unashamedly to courtly flattery. These were the years
of the Armada portrait, and the Rainbow portrait, of Astrea, Belphoebe,
and above all Gloriana. As the Queen's earlier good looks faded away,
and cosmetics and stiff brocades took over, the serpent of wisdom ruled
the passions of the heart.[7] The courtly poet and royal servant Sir John
Davies likened the whole conduct of public affairs to a stately measure.

> Since when all ceremonious mysteries,
> All sacred orgies and religious rites,
> All pomps, and triumphs and solemnities,
> All funerals, nuptials and like public sights,
> All parliaments of peace and warlike fights,
> All learned arts and every great affair,
> A lively shape of dancing seems to bear.[8]

Since the very early days of the reign, the realm of England had played
lover to its royal mistress, and the fact that she was by this time a very

difficult old lady, made no difference. In this last decade or so, Elizabeth became a virtual goddess, at whose feet her captains laid the symbols of their victories. In a sense she became a very sad figure, as she herself recognized,

> Thus spake fair Venus' son, that proud victorious boy
> And said, 'Fine dame, since that you be so coy,
> I will so pluck your plumes that you shall say no more
> "Go, go, go, seek some otherwhere,
> Importune me no more…"'

> …then lo, I did repent that I had said before,
> 'Go, go, go, seek some otherwhere,
> Importune me no more.'[9]

She also became increasingly isolated as the lovers, servants and friends of her youth died. Leicester departed in 1588, and Burghley 10 years later. Her relationships with the younger generation were different. But she acted out her part with indomitable courage, remaining impenetrable and unpredictable to the end.

Fortunately there were some real successes to give substance to this play-acting. It would have been impossible to have sustained the image of Gloriana in the face of persistent defeat and humiliation, even if the Queen's government had managed to survive such reversals. There were setbacks. The attack on Lisbon in 1589 was an expensive fiasco, the betrayal of Deventer and the defeat at Yellow Ford in Ireland in 1598 were humiliations, but the prevailing atmosphere was one of success. Drake's raid on Cadiz in 1587, the capture of Crozon in Brittany in 1594, the taking of Cadiz in 1596, and above all the defeat of the Armada in 1588, all added lustre to Elizabeth's crown, while the capture of the *Madre de Dios* in 1592 contributed significantly to her treasury. Remarkably, after 18 years of war, when Elizabeth died in 1603 she left £60,000 in the exchequer and assets in the form of uncollected taxes of over £350,000. Against that must be set debts of some £420,000, but that had left a net deficit of no more than £10,000—a quite remarkable achievement that owed a lot to her capacity for making smiles and gracious words do the work of more tangible rewards.[10] Her parliament was not entirely persuaded by the 'golden speech' of 1601, but it was sufficient to induce them to delay their main attack until she had bowed off the stage.

When Drake returned from the West Indies in July 1586, he was unable to declare a dividend. When the accounts were finally made up, he paid his investors only 15s. in the £1 — a net loss of 25 per cent, and even then some of his creditors remained unpaid.[11] However, this was not the whole story. There were strategic reasons for wishing to minimize the scale of Spanish losses, although this was an act of war. The unofficial ransoms collected in Santo Domingo and Cartagena were not declared, and probably amounted to some £12,000, most of which may well have ended up in Drake's own hands. The Spaniards seem to have been better informed about these unofficial accounts than was the English Council, although that may be an optical illusion.

Aware of the preparations being made in Spain, but unsure of their target, Elizabeth could not afford to lower her guard. Within a few days of Drake's return, Hawkins was at sea in the Western approaches, looking out for hostile moves, and possibly the treasure fleet, but finding neither. Sir Francis was apparently a firm believer in the tactical value of Dom Antonio, the Portuguese pretender. In November he went to the Low Countries, trying (unsuccessfully) to solicit Dutch aid for an attempt against Portugal, and in December began to prepare for a new voyage, it was rumoured with the same aim in mind.[12] However, as reports from Spain became more ominous, his destination was changed, and he was given until 20 March 1587 to complete his preparations. As before, most of his ships were provided by the City of London, and most of his money came from the same source. However, this was war and the Queen contributed her authority and four warships. Several others came from private individuals, such as Hawkins and William Winter. Half of any plunder was to go to the investors, and half to the Crown.[13] The Queen seems to have been in two minds about the whole enterprise, and even after Drake had left on 2 April made an unsuccessful attempt to recall him.

It appears that the original intention was to attack Lisbon, but news received at sea caused the operation to be diverted to Cadiz, where the supplies for the intended Armada were being assembled. Spanish intelligence, so good in many respects, was completely wrong-footed by this tactical switch, and when Drake's ships arrived on 19 April his identity was at first mistaken. Once disabused, resistance was offered by one large galleon and by a number of royal galleys, but it was swiftly overcome and the galleon was captured and burned. Most of the merchant

ships in the outer harbour were unmanned and unrigged, although
loaded, and were quickly set ablaze. Such as were mobile then crowded
in to the inner harbour to be under the protection of the guns of Puerto
Real, the main fortress. These guns fired on the intruders, inflicting
some damage, but were unable to save the merchantmen, which were
systematically captured, plundered and burnt. At least two dozen vessels suffered in this way.[14] Drake was not tempted to land, or to attack
the town, which had been reinforced at very short notice by the arrival
of the Duke of Medina Sidonia, and by noon of the following day was
ready to leave. As he did so, the wind failed and he was becalmed in the
entrance to the harbour. This was the signal for a renewed attack by the
Spanish galleys, but again they proved no match for the English warships,
and, the wind getting up, the latter were soon out of reach. Drake had
filled his own ships with looted provisions, and brought away four of
the captured vessels. The rest, ships and supplies, he destroyed.

The Spaniards estimated the damage at 172,000 ducats (nearly
£60,000), but that was only the beginning. Sailing west from Cadiz,
on 4 May Drake landed and captured the castle of Sagres after a spirited
resistance, and seems to have intended using it as a base from which to
prey on incoming shipping. However disease broke out, and the *Golden
Lion* deserted and went home, so Drake sailed instead for the Azores.[15]
There he encountered and captured a great carrack called the *San
Felipe*, loaded with a cargo conservatively valued at 300,000 ducats, and
probably worth a great deal more. With many sick men on board, and
satisfied that he could now pay his investors, Drake duly brought his
prize back to Plymouth. From there he set off for London, armed with
a discreet array of jewellery as presents for his royal mistress, in whose
eyes, at this juncture, he could do no wrong.[16]

Drake had made sure that no Armada would sail in 1587, but he had
not touched the main fleet, which was assembling at Lisbon in the
heavily defended estuary of the Tagus. Philip gritted his teeth and set
out to replace the lost provisions. However, time was not on his side
and the soldiers already assembled at Lisbon were deserting, and con-
suming victuals as fast (or faster) than they could be supplied. There
were also difficulties that owed little or nothing to English attacks. Suitable guns were in short supply, and so various in size that the ammunition often did not fit. Ships levied on the Biscay ports were slow to
arrive, and inadequately prepared. The costs mounted inexorably and

began to tax even Philip's enormous resources.[17] Then, in February 1588, the Marquis of Santa Cruz died. This, as it turned out, was the salvation of the whole enterprise, because the King made his only inspired move in appointing the Duke of Medina Sidonia to replace him. Don Alonso Perez de Guzman was a man of indefatigable energy, and an organizer of genius. Within weeks he had turned around a failing enterprise, found fresh sources of supply, and restored the flagging morale of the captains and men.[18] Although time was to demonstrate that he was a timid and unimaginative commander at sea, on land he was an inspiration.

THE ARMADA FIGHT
Philip's instructions to the Duke of Medina Sidonia, April 1588

I F YOU DO NOT *encounter the enemy until you reach Margate, you should there find the Admiral of England with his fleet alone—or if he should have united with Drake's fleet, yours will still be superior both in quality and also in the cause which you are defending, which is God's—you may give battle, trying to gain the wind and all possible advantages from the enemy; and trusting to the Lord to give you victory. As far as the battle formation and tactics to be adopted in the fight are concerned, I can give you little advice, since those questions must be decided at the time of action by circumstances. I nevertheless urge you to lose no opportunity to improve your position and gain all possible advantages, and to have the armada so drawn up that every unit takes part in the fight and is ready to give its support to the others, without any confusion nor disorder. You should take special note, however, that the enemy's aim will be to fight from a distance, since he has the advantage of superior artillery, and of the large number of fireworks with which he will come provided; while ours must be to attack, and come to grips with the enemy at close quarters; and to succeed in doing this you will need to exert every effort. That you might be forewarned, you will receive a detailed report of the way in which the enemy arranges his artillery so as to be able to aim his broadsides low in the hull and so sink his opponent's ships. The precautions you feel to be necessary you must take against such action.*

[C.C. Lloyd, ed., 'Spanish documents relating to the Armada',
Naval Miscellany, IV, 1952, p.16]

On 30 May, and against all the apparent odds, Medina Sidonia led his fleet of 130 ships down the Tagus and out to sea. As they made their

way north towards Coruna, however, storms struck and the Armada
was scattered. Medina Sidonia took this as a warning that their enterprise was not pleasing to God, and advised its abandonment. The King,
however, remained determined, and the Duke had to assemble his fleet
in Coruna as best he could, repair the damage to his ships, and replen-
ish his supplies—again. The success of this operation restored his confidence, particularly when he discovered that Drake and Lord Howard
had come out against him with 60 ships, and had been turned back by
those same winds that had delayed his own advance. Perhaps God was
on his side after all.[19] On 21 July he led his great fleet out to sea once
more, and moved north on those very same winds that were keeping
Drake and Howard imprisoned in harbour.

However, despite this evidence of Divine approval, all was not well
with the Armada. Too many of the officers were gentlemen with no
seafaring experience, and too many of the troops were raw recruits,
untrained for any kind of warfare. The problem of fitting ammunition
to guns had not been solved, and too much of the artillery was unsuit-
able for use at sea.[20] The handful of galleys that had set off from the
Tagus had had to be abandoned in the storms of the Bay of Biscay, and
no more than 30 of the ships were proper men-of-war; the rest were
urcas, or hulks, used to transport the soldiers, and their slow speed im-
peded progress. Worst of all, the King's confidence in Divine support
had prevented him from facing up to the fact that Parma did not control a deep water port large enough to hold Medina Sidonia's fleet, and
arrangements for their rendezvous were hazy to the point of being
non-existent. Experienced commanders such as Juan Martinez de
Recalde were shaking their heads sadly.[21] They knew the fire power
and manoeuvrability of the English ships, and the skill of their captains,
and feared the worst.

Nevertheless, at first the Armada did remarkably well. Entering the
western approaches to the Channel on 30 July [by the Gregorian calendar, which the Spaniards were using; English (Julian) datings are 10
days earlier] it kept its tight formation, and fought off repeated on-
slaughts by the English galleons. A few ships dropped out and were
captured, and a few others ran for the cover of the French coast, but the
great majority held their positions defiantly. Howard and Drake
engaged off Plymouth on 31 July, off Portland Bill on 2 August, and off
the Isle of Wight on 3 and 4 August.[22] Although the English probably

had the better of the actual fighting, they ran out of shot at an alarming rate, and apart from cutting out one or two stragglers, did remarkably little damage.

However, fortunes were about to change, and his lack of strategic preparation was about to catch up with the Duke. When he reached Calais on 6 August, he found Parma unready to receive him. It would take, the latter declared, another week before he could be ready to embark, and Medina Sidonia had nowhere to go.[23] He could only anchor in the open roadstead at Calais, and hope for the best. Howard did not waste his opportunity. That same night he sent in the fireships, and in spite of the Duke's best endeavours, most of the Armada was scattered; only a handful of ships under the Admiral's direct control managed to hold their positions.[24] With its formation broken, and desperately trying to keep off a lee shore, the following day the Spanish fleet took a tremendous hammering. Only a few ships were actually sunk, but many were rendered unseaworthy and the casualties were appalling as the superior English gunnery at last began to make itself felt. The wind then veered round to the south and the battered remains of the Grand Armada were able to escape into the North Sea.[25]

It had been a decisive victory, and all England celebrated. Musters had been held and two field armies assembled, one at Southampton and the other at Tilbury. Elizabeth had been inspired to make her great oration, probably knowing as she did so that the most pressing danger was past. Had Parma's veterans landed, it is unlikely that the English would have had much to celebrate, but not only was his embarkation frustrated by the scattering of his escorts, it is highly unlikely that he would have been able to defeat or evade the shallow draft Dutch warships that lay in wait for his barges among the Flanders Banks.[26] Objectively, the danger had been severe, but not as severe as it appeared. Only if Medina Sidonia had ignored his instructions and landed on the Isle of Wight would a land battle have ensued, and his troops were not of the same quality as Parma's. From an English point of view the aftermath was worse than the fighting. As the court rejoiced and London breathed a sigh of relief, plague broke out among the English ships, and the hasty demobilization that resulted was a shambles. Men were thrown ashore without money or proper medical care, and as many as half the 16,000 men who had fought and survived the Armada perished in this way.[27] Nevertheless, patriotic fervour reached a crescendo.

O noble England,
fall down upon thy knee,
And praise thy GOD with faithful heart,
Which still maintaineth Thee...[28]

So wrote Thomas Deloney in a ballad registered almost before the
Spanish sails had vanished over the horizon. 'Flavit Deus et dissipati
sunt', proclaimed the commemorative medal. God was undoubtedly
English, and favoured the embattled maiden who so strenuously upheld
His cause. Whatever reservations we may have about the military facts of
the campaign, the defeat of the Armada was a defining point in English
national history, and it cost Philip many hours of anguished prayer
before he convinced himself that the Lord loves whom he chastens.

However, it was not the end of the war. More Armadas would
undoubtedly come unless the King's capacity to wage war at sea could
be crippled for the foreseeable future. Elizabeth did not know that his
Great Enterprise had cost the King of Spain the equivalent of £2½
million, and had well-nigh bankrupted him.[29] She only knew that his
resources were infinitely greater than hers, and that he would be
enraged by his failure. Before the end of September 1588 plans for a
counter stroke were being discussed. Only a few of the Queen's ships
could be ready at short notice, but fortunately, in the euphoria of the
moment there was no shortage of subscribers to a new 'joint stock'
venture against Spain, on the same lines as Drake's successful raid of
1587. By the end of December it had been agreed that the Queen
would authorize such an expedition, providing six ships and £20,000,
while a further £40,000 would be put up by a private consortium.
Lisbon was identified as the target, and musters were held.[30] Contributions of both men and money were solicited from the Queen's Dutch
allies, without success, and as the preparations went ahead, the estimates of cost began to rise above £60,000. The Queen raised her stake
considerably, and on 23 February 1589 issued instructions making it
clear that she saw this primarily as a military operation, to which the
securing of plunder, or the assisting of Dom Antonio, would be
entirely secondary.

Before you attempt anything either in Portugal or in the said
islands [Azores] our express pleasure and commandment is that
you first distress the ships of war in Guipuzcoa, Biscay, Galicia,

and any other places that appertain either to the King of Spain,
or his subjects, to the end that they may not impeach you...[31]

In other words the priority was to destroy the battered remains of the
Armada, before they could be repaired and put to sea again. Sir Francis
Drake and Sir John Norris, the joint commanders of the enterprise,
were summoned before the Council and bound in solemn oaths to
obey these orders. The Queen knew perfectly well that in altering the
priorities of the expedition, she had made it less attractive, both to the
other investors and also to the captains, but as the mobilization neared
completion and the cost rose again, she bailed out the undertakers again,
and thus confirmed (in her own mind) her right to issue whatever
orders she chose. By the end of March 1589 some 97 ships and 17,000
men had been assembled, and having been delayed by contrary winds,
this counter armada was led out to sea on 18 April.[32]

It soon became apparent that the Queen's suspicions were justified.
Making not the slightest attempt to attack the Biscay ports, Drake
sailed straight for La Coruña, ostensibly because a rich merchant fleet
was reported to be there. There was no merchant fleet, and the town,
although taken with ease, yielded very little in the way of plunder. It
was, however, on the direct route to Lisbon, and on 16 May Norris
landed his troops about two days march from that town, the idea being
to rally Dom Antonio's alleged army of supporters, take Lisbon and
rendezvous with Drake who would sail up the Tagus in support.[33] However, there were no supporters, and Lisbon was held in strength. By 26
May Norris had decided to cut his losses, and retreated to Cascais at the
mouth of the Tagus, where he managed to rejoin the fleet. The climate
and unaccustomed diet had wrought havoc with the army, and by 3
June Norris had only 4,000 fit men.[34] It was clear that Dom Antonio
was a dead duck, and that the prospects in Portugal were hopeless, in
spite of the fact that they had encountered only sporadic resistance.
Norris re-embarked and the fleet sailed off to the Azores in the hope of
repairing its fortunes. Even that did not happen. Scattered by southerly
gales, by 19 June many of the ships had lost contact with their commanders, and had turned for home. Drake did succeed in taking Vigo,
but it was an empty gesture as there was nothing there worth the taking; on 3 July he was back in Plymouth. When a count could be taken,
only two small vessels had actually been lost, but casualties from disease

had been heavy, and all the commanders had to show for their efforts was another demonstration of the vulnerability of the Spanish coast. Neither Coruña nor Vigo had been properly defended.[35]

At first the Queen was indulgent. It had been worth something to explode the myth of Dom Antonio. However the men had not been properly paid, and made their grievances known in no uncertain fashion. Patriotism was at a low ebb, and it would never be so easy again to recruit men for such a venture. Moreover, as the accounts for the expedition began to be examined, the extent to which Drake and Norris had ignored their orders became apparent. In October the Council summoned them to answer charges of dereliction of duty.[36] In the event nothing very much happened, but Drake had forfeited the golden opinion of his sovereign, and was not permitted to undertake another voyage until 1595, when he and Hawkins (an ill-assorted pair) went to the Spanish Main, an expedition that failed to deliver and cost both their lives.[37] It would be tempting to declare that the Lisbon fiasco was the sea dogs' last hurrah. In 1591 Lord Thomas Howard achieved nothing but the pointless sacrifice of Sir Richard Grenville and the *Revenge*. Drake and Hawkins both died in the West Indies in 1595, and the Earl of Essex's Islands Voyage of 1597 was another dismal failure.[38] In fact, however, fortunes were more equally balanced. New Spanish Armadas were launched in 1594 and 1596, and both were destroyed by storms at sea without ever reaching their destinations. In 1592 the English brought off the greatest privateering scoop of the century when they captured the *Madre de Dios*, and in 1596 a second attack on Cadiz brought one of the greatest military triumphs of the war.

THE TAKING OF THE *MADRE DE DIOS*

The third of august [1592] about four of the clock in the morning, or thereabout, being some fourteen or fifteen leagues west of the Flowers [Flores], the seven sail of ships being spread north and south, a league and a half one from the other, the Dainty of Sir John Hawkins being the windermost, descried a sail and presently set sail and gave chase… About twelve of the clock the Dainty ran up under the carrack's lee, and shot a piece or two, and ran ahead the carrack and cast about again, and fought very well with her. The Green Dragon came up about two of the clock to second her. The Roebuck about four of the clock, and fought very well with great and small shot…I was up with her and hailed Sir John Burgh and asked him what he would do; who

told me that he would lay her aboard, if I would second him; then I said unto
him there was no way but that, or else we should lose her… There we lay till
one of the clock or past in fight, without any aid; at which time, the fury of the
fight well overpassed, my Lord of Cumberland's [ship] came up and laid her
Majesty's ship aboard in the quarter, her quarter then being as far up as the car-
rack's forecastle; then they had room enough to have boarded the carrack… I
think about two of the clock in the morning we were possessed of her, without
any harm in the entering to our knowledge. And hereunto we offer to depose.

['A true report' by Robert Crosse and Johno Merchant. C.L. Kingsford, ed.,
'The taking of the Madre de Dios', *Naval Miscellany*, II, 1912, pp.119–21.]

The *Madre de Dios* was a Portuguese carrack, homeward bound from
the East Indies, which was intercepted off the Azores by a motley fleet
of English privateers, mostly owned by the Earl of Cumberland and Sir
Walter Raleigh. The fleet was actually commanded in the Queen's
name by Sir John Burgh in the *Foresight* and the merchants of London
had put up most of the capital to launch it, so it was fairly typical of the
warlike foraging going on in the Atlantic at that time.[39] Actually two
carracks were targeted, but one escaped by the simple if drastic expedient of running aground on a friendly island. The *Madre de Dios* was
headed off, and tried to shake off her pursuers at sea, but this turned
out to be futile. The ship was only lightly defended, but the English
had great difficulty getting aboard her because of her enormous size.
She displaced about 1,500 tons, whereas the largest of the English ships
was no more than about 300 tons. However, Sir John Hawkins' *Dainty*
got under her prow, inhibiting her way, and eventually the privateers
got aboard. Her cargo turned out to be enormously rich, consisting
not only of gold but also of precious stones, spices and exotic fabrics
from the Far East. Even its declared value was £150,000, and the true
return was probably nearer a quarter of a million.[40] Sir Robert Cecil was
sent down to Plymouth especially to prevent this wealth from 'walking', and after a great effort he managed to secure the bulk of it. This
time there was no Francis Drake to confuse the issue with imaginative
accountancy. Eventually the Earl of Cumberland got £37,000, Raleigh
£24,000, the London merchants £12,000 (for an investment of
£6,000) and the Queen took the rest. Only Raleigh may have been
out of pocket on this distribution; the rest all did very well. Francis
Seall, a gentleman of the Earl of Cumberland, wrote an account of the

whole adventure, but it remained unpublished until 1912.[41]

The *Madre de Dios* was an exceptional prize; the indications are that most big privateers had such heavy overheads that they did not make a profit on their investments. They continued to operate more to demonstrate their loyalty to the Queen than for the money they made out of it. However the small operators, of whom there may have been as many as 200 operating in the western approaches in the later 1590s, do appear to have made a satisfactory profit. They also seem to have strangled Spain's seaborne trade; only the main treasure fleet, which was heavily guarded, continuing to get through in spite of repeated attempts to intercept it.[42] Captures such as the Portuguese carrack were good for the Exchequer, and for relations with London, but they were not very striking in military terms, and by 1596 the war party on the Council, led by the Earl of Essex, were hankering after some spectacular piece of aggression to carry the war to the enemy in unmistakable terms. Early in April the Spaniards had taken Calais, and a striking riposte was called for, so the summer voyage, which would probably have taken place in any case, was reshaped and diverted to this purpose.[43] The instructions for this expedition were a closely guarded secret, but it was clearly to be no ordinary plundering voyage. In the first place the Queen split the costs, not with her subjects, but with her Dutch allies, who contributed 24 ships to the fleet of about 125 that was assembled for the expedition. The soldiers carried numbered about 7,000, of whom 2,000 had been diverted from service in the Low Countries; in other words, they were the nearest thing to veterans that England afforded. On 3 June 1596 this armada sailed out of Plymouth Sound, and once at sea, opened their sealed instructions. Cadiz was to be their target.[44]

The commanders were the Lord Admiral, Lord Howard of Effingham, and the Earl of Essex, and their orders were explicit,

> By burning of [the King's] ships of war in his havens, before they
> should come forth to the seas, and therewithal also destroying his
> magazines of victuals and his munitions for the arming of his
> navy… [so that] the king be [un]able of long time to have any
> great navy in readiness to offend us…[45]

This time there were to be no confused agendas caused by the need to satisfy investors. Elizabeth had learned that lesson from the Lisbon expedition, and this was to be purely an act of war.

The secret had been well kept. When Howard arrived at Cadiz on 20 June, the surprise was complete. Fort San Felipe at the entrance to the harbour opened fire as soon as the intruders had been identified, but did little to impede their progress. Driven further into the narrowing harbour by Howard's advance, the Spanish ships began to tangle with one another. There was a narrow channel of escape south of the Isle of Leon, but as the action developed Sir John Wingfield in the *Vanguard* blocked that way, and by late afternoon on the 21st, the cornered Spanish ships had been almost totally destroyed.[46] The flagship, the *San Felipe*, blew up, two large galleons were captured, and the remainder sunk, burnt or driven ashore. While this highly successful operation was in progress, the Dutch attacked and captured the Isle of Puntal, lying in the harbour, and an English force took and destroyed the bridges leading from the Isle of Cadiz to the mainland.

CADIZ

THE LOS *that we resaved in this sea service was one flybote unfortunately fired by negligence by some of the same shype: and not 30 slayne by the enemy; and of them but one gentyllman, sonne to Customer Smith: besides one other pinnas of Sr. Robert Sothwell, which in laying the great shyppe abord, whylest she was burning was fired by her, the men all saved. There ships weare laden richly and bownd for the Indies, amongst those that came agrownd the St. Phylyppo and the St. Tomaso sett themselves presently on fyer, to our exceding glory and joy thereby assured of the victorye, the St. Mattew and St. Andrew weare left on grownd abandoned by them and taken by us. This Don the Lord Generall Essex dyd instantly shyp into long boates and Pinnaces aboute 3000 of hys land companyes of every regiment a part, accompanied wyth most of the officers and gentylmen that weare for land service.*

['The journal of the Mary Rose'. Lambeth MS 250, f.353. S. and E. Usherwood, *The Counter Armada, 1596*, 1983, p.142.]

The Earl of Essex, with the main English army, then attacked the city itself. In spite of the fact that it was walled, it was poorly defended, and surrendered after a few hours with remarkably little loss of life on either side. A ransom of 520,000 ducats (£180,000) was then negotiated and the civilian population was evacuated.[47] Meanwhile Howard had sent Sir Walter Raleigh with a squadron of warships to destroy the shipping still remaining in the secondary harbour of Puerto Reale. Thinking that they knew their enemy, the officials at Puerto Reale offered him a ransom of 2 million ducats, but Raleigh responded that his orders were to destroy, not to negotiate, and he proceeded to do just that. By the time Howard and Raleigh had done their work, 13 men-of-war, 11 East Indiamen and a large number of miscellaneous merchantmen had been destroyed, several galleys driven ashore, and two great galleons captured. The Spaniards estimated their losses at 20 million ducats.[48] Essex and Duijvenvoorde (the Dutch commander) wanted to retain and garrison the city for the permanent harassment of the Spanish coast, but Howard and the rest of his council deemed that to be unrealistic in view of the countermeasures that Philip was bound to take. Consequently the fortifications were rased, and the expedition returned home with its loot, its fleet intact, and the Earl of Essex in a foul temper at having been overruled.[49]

The consequences of the Earl's ill-humour were to be serious, and eventually fatal to himself. His attempt to emulate the late Sir Francis Drake in the summer of 1597 was a failure, and after the defeat of the English forces in Ireland at Yellow Ford in August 1598, he manoeuvred himself into the position where he could not refuse to take the Lord Lieutenancy himself (March 1599). He then negotiated illicitly with the rebel Earl of Tyrone, abandoned his post without licence, and forfeited the Queen's confidence completely in consequence.[50] Choosing to blame his self-inflicted wounds on the Principal Secretary, Robert Cecil, he attempted to stage a coup against the court in January 1601, and paid for his folly with his head. He had only himself to blame if his great success at Cadiz was undervalued in the subsequent years.[51]

Cadiz had been mainly a naval victory. The soldiers had done well, but had not particularly distinguished themselves, in spite of the Earl of Essex. Normandy and Brittany, however, were soldiers' wars. Both were relatively small-scale campaigns, and were undertaken on behalf of Henry IV of France against his enemies the Catholic League, and the League's backer, Philip of Spain. Henry had previously been the Huguenot leader and King of Navarre, but he had succeeded to the French throne by hereditary right when Henry III was assassinated in 1589. In the circumstances the English were his natural allies, just as the Catholic League looked to the King of Spain.

The death of the Duke of Parma in December 1592 enabled

Elizabeth to switch her main military priority from the Low Countries to France. A small army in Normandy was briefly commanded by the Earl of Essex, but he exceeded his orders and was recalled.[52] With Henry's conversion to Catholicism in 1593, and the threat from the Netherlands significantly reduced, Elizabeth was then able to turn her main attention to Brittany, where the League remained strong, and where a Spanish force was fortifying Crozon, in order to control the harbour of Brest.[53] Sir John Norris had first been sent to take command there in 1591, while the Queen's eyes were still mainly on Normandy, and the capture of Rouen, for which she hankered in vain. The frustrations involved in that campaign had turned her against the whole idea of becoming more deeply involved in France, and at first Norris found himself very largely ignored. He was short of everything —money, reinforcements, arms, even clothing—and in March 1592 returned to England to argue his case before the Queen and Council. His main point was that the campaign in Normandy was going nowhere, while the Spanish presence in Brittany was growing and becoming more menacing. In making this case he was supported by Lord Burghley, and prevailed in the Council with comparative ease.[54] However, more substantial success had to depend on negotiations with Henry IV, and they proved to be both slow and difficult.

It was not until 27 June that an agreement was finally reached, whereby Elizabeth agreed to provide 4,000 troops, which would include the 900 or so already there, and companies to be transferred from Normandy. The French in turn agreed to deploy 4,000 foot and 1,000 horse into Brittany, and to make no peace without consulting the Queen.[55] Reports that a further 2,000 Spaniards had arrived in the province gave substance and urgency to this agreement. In spite of such concrete-sounding plans, however, nothing was quite what it seemed. The companies from Normandy never arrived at all, and Sir John had the greatest difficulty getting his force up to 3,000, in spite of all the assurances that he had received. It was not until the delayed companies from the Low Countries arrived in January 1593 that he even approached that number. On the other hand, the French were now taking Brittany seriously. Henry appointed one of his best generals, the Marshall d'Aumont, to command there, and d'Aumont immediately made Paimpol on the north coast available to his allies as a base. Paimpol was not ideal, and Sir John had to be bullied by the Council before he would agree to go there. So aggrieved was Norris by this order, and so outspoken were his comments, that Elizabeth was determined to withdraw him, and had to be persuaded otherwise by the Council, which was more used to dealing with this temperamental commander.[56]

Early in November 1593 Norris was finally installed at Paimpol, and had about 1,500 men under his command, the remainder having (mostly) deserted. By then the port had been fortified, and formed a reasonably secure haven, but the news of enemy deployment was becoming increasingly alarming. Aguila, the Spanish commander, now had 5,000 men under his command and had a new agreement with the Catholic League for joint operations. Meanwhile plans for a fort to command the harbour at Brest were well advanced. Aguila commenced building operations at Crozon in March 1594. Norris's despatches to London at this time were understandably pessimistic, but the threat to Brest galvanized the Council into action, and 1,000 troops were transferred from the Low Countries, reaching Paimpol on 13 June.[57] Musters were ordered for 3,000 additional soldiers, and the navy was mobilized to support the operation against Crozon which it was now clearly appreciated would be necessary.

On 7 September Martin Frobisher, in command as Vice-Admiral, began to shell the fort from the sea, while 2,000 French footmen and 1,000 cavalry joined Norris's force as it moved to invest it from the landward side. Norris's optimism, and the confidence of the Council in London, had been remarkably restored during the summer. On 12 September the English captured Morlaix, and began to move against Crozon from the northeast. Although the fortifications were incomplete, they were eminently defensible, and the siege went on for over a month. Guns were mounted against the fort, and gave it a formidable pounding, but repeated attempts to take it by assault were expensive failures, one of which cost the life of Sir Anthony Wingfield, Norris's second in command. On 30 October the Spaniards even made a sally that temporarily dislodged some of the French besiegers. Finally, on 7 November, Norris and d'Aumale agreed on a general assault, and after bitter fighting that went on the whole day the defenders' resistance was overcome.[58] Almost the whole garrison of 350 men perished, and the French also counted their casualties in hundreds. Norris admitted to only 60 deaths among the English, but they included Martin Frobisher, who died later of wounds sustained during the battle. Having completed his assignment to everyone's satisfaction, Norris shipped his cannons back to England and led his men into winter quarters at Paimpol. The Spanish threat to Brittany had not been eliminated, but it had been reduced to a level that d'Aumale was perfectly capable of containing. The threat to England had disappeared, and that was what mattered to Elizabeth. Both Norris and his troops were shortly after withdrawn.

It was to Ireland that Norris and his men were sent. Sir John had served in Ireland before, and did not relish the prospect.[59] Since the rebellion of Silken Thomas in 1536, the country had been in a constant state of small-scale, piecemeal insurrection and tribal warfare. Successive English governors had contained this situation from a secure base in the Pale (around Dublin) by the regular deployment of small numbers of troops. By comparison with the 'wild' Irish, the English soldiers were well disciplined and well equipped, but they could not be everywhere, and the political solution of displacing Irish chieftains with English colonists had only exacerbated the situation. Attempts at conciliation in the latter part of Henry VIII's reign having failed, a policy of plantation was initiated under Philip and Mary, and developed under Elizabeth.[60] England's enemies looked continually to Ireland for a point of entry, and a polyglot force under a papal banner had landed at Smerwick in September 1580, hoping to exploit this constant unrest. That enterprise had been brutally snuffed out, but the danger was always there, particularly after 1585.

Sir John spent about two years struggling with this recalcitrant problem, made worse by the slippery politics and eventual rebellion of Hugh O'Neill, Earl of Tyrone, until he died of exhaustion and old wounds in June 1597.[61] By that time Tyrone was in open rebellion, and he inflicted a serious (and unusual) defeat on the English forces at Yellow Ford in Ulster in August 1598. This provoked the brief and disastrous experiment of using the Earl of Essex in Ireland in 1599, and eventually his replacement with the competent professional soldier and politician, Lord Mountjoy in 1600. It was Mountjoy who contained and defeated the belated Spanish attempt to intervene at Kinsale in October 1601, and who forced O'Neill's eventual submission in the last days of Elizabeth's life, in March 1603.[62] Ireland was the graveyard of reputations, but it was also the testing ground where professional English captains learned their trade and proved their skills. The primitive tactics employed by the Irish were not much use as an introduction to sophisticated continental warfare, but courage and tenacity were at a premium.

By the end of Elizabeth's reign, the image of the English soldier had recovered from the low ebb of the 1560s. In the Low Countries and in Brittany, the English had fought well and earned the respect of their adversaries. Their equipment and training were likewise up to speed. But it was at sea that the islanders were really feared. In spite of setbacks, both the Royal Navy and the English privateers enjoyed a formidable and well-deserved reputation, and it was at sea, against a background of expanding commerce, that Elizabeth's canny cultivation of the maritime community paid its most striking dividends. Of the 130-odd ships that had sailed against the Armada, only about 40 had belonged to the Queen, and that told its own story of a nation at war in a new way.

EPILOGUE

❖

A CHANGING
SOCIETY

IN ITS POLITICAL ASPECT, the Tudor period falls neatly into two halves. For nearly 70 years England was ruled by Kings; and then for 50 years by Queens. The royal image consequently underwent a profound transformation. Henry VII was the prudent King; a competent law-giver and a stern taskmaster, pious and tightfisted. Henry VIII was the warrior, both literally and metaphorically, the King who defied the French on the field of battle, and the Emperor and the Pope in the 'cloth wars' of diplomacy.[1] The child Edward was the young Josias, a paragon of virtue and learning. Had he lived, he might well have been as formidable as his father, but as it was his image remained that of the infant prodigy. And then the whole picture changed. Confused by her gender and its implications, Mary could find no satisfactory compromise between sovereignty and marriage, and left an image constructed by her enemies, while Elizabeth took the whole issue of sexual subordination and turned it on its head. She may not have set out to be the Virgin Queen, but she exploited the symbolism of that virginity remorselessly. Barred by both taste and custom from the image of the Amazon, she became the bewitching damsel of the troubadour romances—cunning, manipulative and unattainable. Her marriage to the realm was real as well as symbolic, and the integrity of her body became the image of a realm increasingly self-confident and at home with its God.

Beneath the splendid pageantry of politics and courtly ceremonial, however, a fundamental change was taking place, which progressed steadily throughout the period, irrespective of whether the ruler was male or female, and had a profound affect upon the military face of England. Nobility, Sir William Cecil observed contemptuously, was nothing but ancient riches, but that was the perception of a humanist trained politician of the late sixteenth century. His grandfather would almost certainly have disagreed. To the fifteenth-century mind, nobility consisted in three things; lineage, honour and wealth, of which the last was the least important. A man's ancestry determined his place in society, whether noble, gentle or common. It was, as we might now say, 'in his genes', and there was nothing that he (or anybody else) could do about it.[2] At the same time honour was a military concept. It was upon his own deeds and those of his forebears that a man's reputation depended, whether those deeds had been executed on a stricken field in the service of the King, or in a private feud pursued in defence of his family interests. The higher the status, the more conspicuous the honour was supposed to be. This, like ancestry, led to all manner of creative fictions, and was deeply embedded in the popular consciousness. As late as the reign of Elizabeth, gentry families that had risen from the yeomanry within living memory were creating bogus genealogies for themselves, and even the Cecils claimed descent from the ancient princes of Gwynedd.[3] All manner of men claimed that their ancestors had fought at Crécy or at Agincourt. After all, the sign of gentility was the bearing of coat armour, the original purpose of which had been identification upon the field of battle.

Henry VII, whose own ancestry was a few degrees short of impeccable, was profoundly sceptical about the claims of nobility. He was well aware that Edward IV had established a firm grip over the creation of peers, and that no one could be a Viscount or above without a patent of creation from the Crown. He also knew that without the appropriate writ, no one could claim to be a baron.[4] There was thus a logical inconsistency about a title of honour. In theory it might depend upon noble progenitors, but in practice it was created at the will of the King. Henry did not ignore the claims of ancestry. He restored Edward Stafford to the Dukedom of Buckingham and Thomas Howard to the Earldom of Surrey. He created his uncle Jasper Duke of Bedford, but in his mind such titles were rewards for loyalty and service—they did not arrive with the rations for those with the right family background. Moreover, service did not mean necessarily, or even principally, service in arms. Thomas Grey was restored to the Marquisate of Dorset and Thomas Stanley created Earl of Derby the first for having facilitated his rise to the throne, the latter because he was his stepfather.[5] Henry's wars were few and small, and no major creations resulted from them. Polydore Vergil thought that he was hostile to the nobility, but what he seems to have been trying to do was to separate their social and courtly function from the government of the country. While he surrounded himself with nobles at court, he governed the country through lesser agents, who had fewer pretensions and who would not wish to claim the autonomy that noble status was still seen to convey.[6] This was the critical point. During the previous half-century the nobility of lineage had set itself up as a kind of alternative government, which paid only lip service to the Crown, and ran its various 'countries' to suit itself. Henry VII was determined to re-establish central control, and the nobility were potentially obstacles in the path of such a policy.[7] This was why so many were placed under recognisances for their good behaviour, and could only retain servants under licence. The culture of honour was seen as inimical to good government, and insofar as it had a military basis, we can see why.

At first Henry VIII relaxed this stringent regime. He wanted to wage war, was devoted to the military cult of chivalry, and needed companions in arms. He chose noblemen to command his armies, created military peers—notably the Dukes of Norfolk and Suffolk—and respected the claims of noble ancestry. Henry Courtenay became Marquis of Exeter, and Margaret Pole Countess of Salisbury.[8] There was a certain sense in this because the nobility of lineage was seriously discontented with the way it had been treated under Henry VII, and could have caused trouble for the new and young King if he had not made conciliatory gestures. However, it was not long before he changed his mind. It may have been the influence of Thomas Wolsey, or it may have been the shock caused by the treason of the Duke of Buckingham, but after 1520 lineage ceased to be a prime consideration in new peerage creations. Outside of the royal family, titles became the reward for service, and service became a political and civilian concept. In 1529 Sir Thomas Boleyn became Earl of Wiltshire for essentially domestic reasons; George Hastings became Earl of Huntingdon and Robert Radcliffe Earl of Sussex primarily because they were his political allies. Thomas Cromwell became Earl of Essex and William Paulet was made Lord St John because they were excellent civil servants and councillors. Edward Seymour became Earl of Hertford because he was Queen Jane's brother rather than because he was a soldier, and John

Dudley became Viscount Lisle in the right of his mother.[9] Hertford and Lisle were the main military men of the latter part of the reign, but neither was made a peer for that reason. Henry made it abundantly clear that all his peers depended upon him for their promotion and their wealth, and that their elevation was conditional upon loyalty and good service. Where that was suspect, the family was destroyed. The Marquis of Exeter, the Earl of Surrey and the Countess of Salisbury were beheaded; the Percy Earls of Northumberland were escheated and the Duke of Norfolk sentenced to death.

In the regular processes of government, Henry bypassed the peerage, just as his father had done, relying increasingly upon the commissions of the peace to control the counties, and upon the musters to replace the noble retinue. By 1547 any claim to noble autonomy based upon lineage could have fatal consequences, as the Earl of Surrey learned to his cost.[10] The nobility of England retained its status and its wealth, but the political importance of individual peers had been drastically reduced. Only in the House of Lords could they exercise their collective force, and that was a very restricted forum. A title was a reward for service, and a sign of royal favour. The changes that took place after Henry's death were more apparent than real. The Dukes of Somerset, Suffolk and Northumberland in the reign of Edward VI were not 'overmighty subjects' in the fifteenth-century sense. They were court peers, whose roots in their countries were shallow, and were ruthlessly exposed when each in turn fell from power.[11] Mary resurrected a few 'lineage' families, notably the Courtenays and the Percys, but this hardly amounted to a consistent policy, and Edward Courtenay, Earl of Devon, soon departed into exile. The remorseless tendency of the gentry to rise at the expense of the nobility continued, fuelled partly by the sale and grant of monastic property in the wake of the dissolutions of 1536 and 1540, a process that Mary was significantly unable to reverse, in spite of her expressed intention.[12] Elizabeth carried on where her father had left off. She made very few peers, and one of the most conspicuous, Robert Dudley, Earl of Leicester, was for strictly personal services. Significantly her military peers were promoted for naval commands rather than soldiering. While her most successful armies were commanded by men such as Sir John Norris, her Admirals became the Earls of Lincoln and Nottingham. Elizabeth's court was Protestant, educated and intellectually sophisticated—none of these characteristics being consistent with a lineage priority. Elizabeth did use peers to command armies, notably the Earls of Leicester and Essex, but did not promote any for that reason, and Essex, for all his military pretensions, was a graduate of the university of Cambridge!

The transformation of the nobility from an elite of lineage to an elite of service was virtually complete by the end of the sixteenth century, and that had a profound effect upon aristocratic culture as a whole. Nowhere was this more visible than in the field of education. The *Liber Niger* of Edward IV expressed the traditional view succinctly. A gentleman should be taught to

> show the schools of urbanity and nurture of England, to learn to ride cleanly and surely, to draw them also to jousts, to learn them to wear their harness [armour] to have all courtesy in words, deeds and degrees...[13]

or, as John Skelton put it in the early sixteenth century,

> noble men born,
> to learn they have scorn...[14]

Book learning was for clerks, not for gentlemen—let alone nobles. However, as a result of steady pressure from the courts of Henry VIII and Elizabeth, by 1586 the received wisdom was quite different.

> Alas, you will be ungentle gentlemen if you be no scholars, you will do your prince but simple service, you will stand your country in but slender stead, you will bring yourselves but to slender preferment, if you be no scholars...[15]

And by 'scholars' the author had in mind what we might understand by the term, a man learned in the history and literature of the ancients. A gentleman, in other words, needed book learning in order to be of service to his prince and to govern his country. A military priority had been replaced with a civilian one, and the whole concept of honour had been transformed in consequence. By the end of the sixteenth century, a university graduate was automatically considered to be a gentleman.

This change did not happen swiftly, or uniformly across the country. As Mervyn James put it, violence was 'in the air' in the sixteenth century because of the concept of honour that legitimated it. Honour, as the late fifteenth-century 'Book of the Order of Chivalry' makes clear, was inseparable from lineage, not only for the nobleman but also for the gentleman, because the *nobiles minor*, no less than the peers, were considered to be sons of Japheth, whereas the commoners were the sons of Ham.[16] This mythology validated a concept of virtue that consisted of fortitude, prudence and skill in arms—a virtue to which learning provided no path, but which was quite consistent with the practice of violence. Virtue also embraced loyalty to a lord, but said nothing about obedience to the King, which was one of the main reasons why Henry VII had looked askance at it, and why Henry VIII came to do the same. It was the knight's duty to punish the wicked with the sword, and to execute the judgement of God, but without reference to the King's laws. So the Tudor emphasis upon obedience needed allies outside the honour culture, and these it found in the humanist emphasis upon a nobility of virtue—a virtue conceived, not in military terms but in terms of classical philosophy, and particularly in the thinking of Seneca. Self-discipline, self-control and obedience to law formed the basis of a new type of honour, and one much more conducive to civil government.[17]

It is not surprising that the Tudors encouraged their courtiers to have their sons taught the laws and history of the Roman republic. The Reformation also helped, because although John of Salisbury had seen the Christian warrior as a vehicle of God's judgement, the competitiveness and emulation inherent in the honour culture were not really compatible with Christian values, as the Reformers were quick to point out. In place of the nobility of lineage they strove to implant the idea of a nobility of virtue, and this was a virtue conceived in strictly New Testament terms, of morality, humility and obedience to constituted authority.

The monarchy itself played a critical role in bridging the gulf between these two cultures, and in enabling a younger generation of courtiers and gentlemen to slip from one into the other. In the first place the Honour of the Monarch could be seen as an essential quality in the commanding of obedience. This was why Henry VIII found his martial imagery so important, and why he continued to play chivalric war games. In outfacing the French upon the field of battle he was in a sense justifying the obedience of his nobles—or at least giving them no excuse to be defiant. Lord Darcy (who was an old man) justified his joining the Pilgrimage of Grace in 1536 on the grounds that the King had dishonoured himself by listening to such upstart advisers as Thomas Cromwell, but even at that time he was isolated in acting upon his conviction.[18] In the second place the image of the Godly Prince did yeoman service in 'selling' the merits of obedience. The Godly Prince was God's Viceregent, whom to disobey was a kind of impiety. This was not necessarily a Protestant idea, because it was used by both Henry VIII and Mary, in slightly different ways, but it came into its own under Elizabeth. The idea that God had chosen the Queen to rule both realm and church was one way of demonstrating that the will of God cannot be constrained by human ideas, but it also gave a quasi-divine sanction to all that she demanded of her subjects. It also, of course, distanced her from her peers, who could command no such status, and welded the notions of civic virtue and Christian virtue into a single compelling model. In short, the politics of morality had replaced the politics of honour.

Although such ideas were prevalent at Court by about 1540, it was to be another half-century before they came to control behaviour in the far north of England, or in Wales. The latter was notoriously addicted to lineage, and violence continued—although at a 'sub-political' level —to afflict the administration of justice in the principality until well into the Elizabethan period.[19] At the same time the culture of the Anglo-Scottish borders was based upon cattle raiding and the blood feud, sustained by the perpetually hostile relations between London and Edinburgh. Once the treaty of Edinburgh had brought about a general alignment of interests after 1560, this violence was generally curbed. As late as 1569 the Earls of Northumberland and Westmorland attempted to appeal to the loyalty of honour in raising the standard of revolt, but they were only partially successful, and the redistribution of land that followed the rising effectively destroyed the great northern affinities.[20] By 1600 the borders were well on the way to becoming the 'middle shires', which they were to be after the union of the crowns in 1603.

Gentility, no less than nobility, had been recast in a service mode. Henry VIII had curbed the heralds by resuming into his own hands the grant of coat armour, and although the heralds were reincorporated in 1555, they were made subject to the Earl Marshall. 'Service done to us or to another' was the criterion upon which arms were to be awarded, and that service was not usually military. Lineage continued to fascinate, and bogus genealogies were a feature of the new men of the 1570s and 1580s, who were mostly lawyers, officials and merchants—witness the pretensions of Francis Drake—but lineage was no longer central to the concept of honour. By the latter part of Elizabeth's reign, honour lay in obedience, to the monarch but equally to the law, both human and divine. As a result the military became professionalized. Although the levies remained as a kind of 'home guard' to be called upon in an emergency, for most men fighting was a career choice rather than a routine obligation. This was particularly true of the officers and commanders. Men like Charles, Lord Mountjoy, Sir Roger Williams and Sir John Norris would have thought of themselves primarily as soldiers rather than as gentlemen of honour. Paradoxically it was because of his old-fashioned notions of the links between fighting and honour that the young Earl of Essex became such a nuisance in the late 1590s, and why he eventually staged a very obsolete kind of revolt.[21] The violence of honour had by the 1570s been corralled into the duel, for which men sought training in the Italian fencing schools that sprang up in London. Significantly, even this remained a very restricted choice, and both Elizabeth and James I set their faces firmly against such actions.

The military imagery of the Tudor state thus focused, first and foremost, upon making violence a royal monopoly. From the reign of Henry VII onward, only the King could make war, and the deployment of military resources for private purposes (even self-defence) was absolutely forbidden. Most of the nobility lost their military function and became instead civil servants, administrators and legislators. The trappings of aristocracy remained, but most of its substance had been drawn away. The beneficiaries of this process were the gentry, who became the governing class, and gentility became a question of wealth and function rather than lineage and honour. In place of a plethora of armed retinues, the army became a professional organization, armed and equipped to the latest standard. The navy was rather different, because the Admiralty retained its strong links with the commercial interests of London and the southwest. A gentleman might be a naval officer, but not all naval officers were gentlemen. Henry VIII had set out to make sea-fighting, like land warfare, a royal monopoly, and the private warship disappeared. However, in this respect he failed thanks to the culture of part-time piracy that pervaded the maritime community.

Elizabeth compromised with this constituency, investing in its efforts and recruiting its services, so that by the time of the Armada more than half the fighting ships to sail under Lord Howard of Effingham were privately owned. The navy proper was highly professional, both in its technology and in its administration, but it remained fairly small. The culture of the sea remained violent, but it was the violence of robbery and greed rather than that of honour. As such it served Elizabeth well, but remained as a problem for her successor. This was aggravated by the fact that the integrity of the naval administration fell apart after John Hawkins' death, and by 1608 was riddled with a corruption that the Lord Admiral had neither the knowledge nor the will to deal with. After so many and such notable successes, the navy ended the period on a down beat, which was to be ruthlessly exposed by the Royal Commissions of 1608 and 1618.[22]

By 1603 a King no longer needed to be a warrior, nor a Queen an Amazon. He (or she) was a divinely appointed sovereign, whose function was to govern under the law, and to defend biblically determined standards of integrity. The monarch was responsible for the general oversight of the Kingdom's defence, but was not expected to take the field in person, or to display the personal qualities expected of a soldier. War remained a political option, but one for which the public resources of the state would be mobilized rather than the private resources of the nobility. Only at sea did private warfare remain a reality, and that was unconnected with that culture of honour that the Tudors had done so much to overthrow. The seamen nodded to the Queen's authority by attacking (mainly) Spanish shipping, and thus combined service to the state with their own private interests. But the honour of a man such as Francis Drake lay primarily in the quantity of his plunder. The demilitarization of England was one of the more important, and least noticed, aspects of the Tudor revolution in government.

NOTES ON THE TEXT

Titles in short form can be seen in full in the Further Reading.

INTRODUCTION: THE FACE OF KINGSHIP

1. For a discussion of these, and other relevant issues, see Keegan (1993), pp.1–61.
2. There are numerous discussions of feudalism in its various contexts, but the best is still Marc Bloch, *Feudal Society* (trans. L.A. Manyon, 1961).
3. Frank Barlow, *Edward the Confessor* (2nd edn, 1997), pp.256–86.
4. See particularly W.L. Warren, *Henry II* (1973), pp.518–55.
5. Keen (1984), pp.146–62.
6. Allmand (1992). It was the drying up of ransoms during the unsuccessful years of Henry VI's regime in France that made the nobility reluctant to serve there.
7. See James Gairdner, ed., *Paston Letters* (1910) for numerous expressions of these views.
8. Loades (1986), pp.1–8.
9. Anglo (1969).
10. Young (1987), p.11, citing Roger of Hoveden, *Annals.*

11. These began with Pope Innocent II's ban of 1130, which was repeated by successive popes down to 1316. Sometimes all the participants were excommunicated. Ibid., p.12.
12. Robert Bartlett, *England Under the Norman and Angevin Kings* (2000).
13. Elizabeth Salter, 'Courts and Courtly Love' in D. Daiches and A. Thorlby, eds., *The Medieval World* (1973).
14. Joanna L. Chamberlayne, 'English Queenship, 1445–1503', (York University PhD, 1999).
15. *ODNB*, Catherine de Valois.
16. Charles Ross, *Edward IV* (1974), pp.85–103.
17. C. Rawcliffe, 'The Insanity of Henry VI', *Historian*, 50, 1996. The fullest discussion of the circumstances of Henry's deposition is to be found in R.A. Griffiths, *Henry VI* (1981).
18. W.M. Ormrod, *The Reign of Edward III* (1990), pp.25–6. Keen (1984), pp.228–32.
19. At Crécy the knights were mounted, and had their horses shot from under them. At Poitiers they dismounted, and were thus less vulnerable to the archers, but were cut down by the English cavalry.
20. Strickland and Hardy (2005).

21. J. Barnie, *War in Medieval Society; Social Values and the Hundred Years War, 1337–99* (1974).

22. W.M. Ormrod, *The Reign of Edward III* (1990), p.120.

23. Henry IV was the son of John, Duke of Lancaster, the third son of Edward III. When Richard II was deposed in 1399, it could be argued that Philippa, the daughter of Lionel, Edward's second son, had transmitted a better claim to her grandson Edmund, Earl of March.

24. C. Richmond, 'English Naval Power in the Fifteenth Century', *History*, 52 (1967). D. Loades, 'The King's ships and the Keeping of the Seas, 1413–1480', *Medieval History*, I (1991).

25. Ship service was a feudal condition upon which the towns received their commercial privileges. They were bound to provide so many ships (and their crews) at their own costs for a limited period—usually 40 days. Ships were raised from selected noblemen by commissions of array, rather than by feudal obligation.

26. C.F. Richmond (1971), pp.96–121. S.P. Pistono, 'Henry IV and the English Privateers', *English Historical Review*, 90 (1975), pp.322–30. N.A.M. Rodgers, *The Safeguard of the Sea* (1997) p.115.

27. S.P. Pistono, 'Henry IV and the English Privateers', *English Historical Review*, 90 (1975), pp.322–30. Rodgers comments 'piracy was the mark of a weak government, unable to defend its subjects or restrain their attacks', see N.A.M. Rodgers, *The Safeguard of the Sea* (1997) p.116.

28. M.W. Prynne, 'Henry V's *Grace Dieu*', *Mariner's Mirror*, 54 (1968), pp.115–28.

29. Ian Friel (1995), pp.139–57.

30. R. Knox and S. Leslie, eds, *The Miracles of Henry VI* (1923). Discussed also in Eamon Duffy (1992), pp.180–81.

31. Alan Young (1987), p.22.

32. Croyland Chronicle, 'Historiae Croylandensis Continuatio' in *Rerum Anglicarum Scriptores Veterum*, ed. W. Fulman (1684), pp.449–592.

33. Charles Ross, *Edward IV* (1974), pp.201–2, 334.

34. Keen (1984), pp.143–62.

35. Ibid., pp.145–6.

36. For a discussion of this pressure (from different points of view) see Williams (1979) and Loades (1997).

37. Charles Ross, *Edward IV* (1974), pp.126–61.

38. Thomas Rymer, ed., *Foedera, conventiones etc.* (1704–35), XII, p.23.

39. Ross (1981), pp.xix–liii. There are many discussions of this subject.

40. Notably Thomas, Lord Stanley, but the Earl of Northumberland was almost equally responsible. Ross (1981), pp.210–27.

41. John Foxe, *Acts and Monuments* (ed. 1583), pp.251–3.

Chapter One
HENRY VII:
THE PRUDENT
KING

1. W. Stubbs, *The Constitutional History of England* (1903), III, p.59. The legitimation of the Beauforts was confirmed on the 10th February 1407, when the clause *excepta dignitate regali* was inserted.

2. Chrimes (1972), p.13. Edmund's death seems to have been from natural causes.

3. Polydore Vergil, *Anglica historia*, ed. D. Hay (Camden Society, 3rd series, 74, 1950), p.135. This was the occasion on which Henry VI is alleged to have prophesied that one day the boy would succeed him.

4. The original intention seems to have been to go to France, but a storm forced them to land at Le Conquet in Brittany. On Henry's education during these years, see Chrimes (1972), pp.17–18.

5. C.A.J. Armstrong, *The Usurpation of Richard III by Dominico Mancini* (1969).

6. Ross (1981), p.117.

7. J. Gairdner, ed., *Letters and Papers Illustrative of the Reigns of Richard III and Henry VII* (Rolls Series, 1861–3), I, pp.37–43.

8. Chrimes (1972), p.34 and n.

9. D. Rees, *The Son of Prophecy* (1985).

10. Polydore Vergil, *Anglica historia*, ed. Hay (Camden Society, 3rd series, 74, 1950), pp.209–16. For the questionable attitude of Anne of Beaujeu and her Council, see David Grummitt (2009), pp.6–7.

11. For a discussion of the sources describing Bosworth Field and its circumstances, see Ross (1981), Appendix II. There are also different accounts of the battle in M.J. Bennett, *The Battle of Bosworth* (1985), and Jones (2002).

12. S. Anglo, 'The foundation of the Tudor dynasty', *Guildhall Miscellany*, II (1960), p.3.

13. This enabled him to attaint 'Richard, late Duke of Gloucester' for treason against King Henry VII on 21 August. *Rotuli Parliamentorum*, (1767–1832), VI, pp.275–8.

14. The English succession was governed by custom, not law. The question of a female heir had not been raised since the twelfth century, and no attempt was made, even by Yorkist loyalists, to promote Elizabeth's claim against either Richard or Henry. The best account of Henry's early impact is to be found in Sean Cunningham, *Henry VII* (2007), pp.43–64.

15. Chrimes (1972), p.76.

16. Polydore Vergil, *Anglica historia*, ed. Hay (Camden Society, 3rd series, 74, 1950), pp.12–26.

17. Ibid. For a fuller account of Simnel's rebellion, see Bennett (1987).

18. M. Oppenheim, *Naval Accounts and Inventories of the Reign of Henry VII* (NRS, 1896), p.xvi.

19. Ibid., p.xxi.

20. Ibid., pp.216–17.

21. B. Dietz, 'The Royal Bounty and English shipping in the sixteenth and seventeenth centuries', *Mariner's Mirror*, 77 (1991). Loades (1992), pp.39–40.

22. M. Oppenheim, *Naval Accounts and Inventories of the Reign of Henry VII* (NRS, 1896), p.155.

23. Ibid., pp.xxvii–viii.

24. Loades (1992), p.43.

25. Rymer, *Foedera, conventiones...etc.*
(1704–35), XII, p.497 et seq. *Statutes of
the Realm* (1810–28), II, p.635. Currin
(2005), pp.14-43. See also Currin
(1996), pp.343–58.

26. Arthurson (1994), pp.42–51.

27. The ease with which this rather motley
army was able to approach London
appears to have been due to Henry's
preoccupation with the north.
Chrimes (1972), p.90.

28. M. Oppenheim, *Naval Accounts and
Inventories of the Reign of Henry VII*
(NRS, 1896), pp.xliv–vi.

29. Ibid., pp.82–132.

30. J. Gairdner, ed., *Letters and Papers
Illustrative of the Reigns of Richard III and
Henry VII* (Rolls Series, 1861–3), I,
pp.104–9.

31. S. Anglo, *Spectacle, Pageantry and Early
Tudor Policy* (1969), p.106.

32. Scarisbrick (1968), p.32. Richard,
Edmund's younger brother, was killed
at the battle of Pavia in 1525.

33. G.A. Bergenroth, ed., *Calendar of State
Papers, Spanish,* I, 1485–1509 (1862),
pp.177–8.

34. D. Grummitt, 'The establishment of
the Tudor Dynasty' in Norman Jones
and Robert Tittler, eds, *The Blackwell
Companion to Tudor Britain* (2004),
pp.13–28.

35. Chrimes (1972), p.298, n.3. For the
context and changes in Early Tudor
law and justice, see Gunn (1995),
pp.72–108; also Sean Cunningham,
Henry VII (2007), pp.150–72.

36. Polydore Vergil, *Anglica historia*, ed.
Hay (Camden Society, 3rd series, 74,
1950), pp.145–7.

37. H. Schubert, 'The first cast iron
cannon made in England', *Journal of the
Iron and Steel Institute,* 146 (1942).
Loades (1992), pp.49–50.

38. W.C. Richardson, 'The Surveyors of
the King's Prerogative', *English
Historical Review,* 56 (1941). T.B. Pugh
(1992).

39. For a case study of this practice, see
W.H. Dunham, *Lord Hastings
Indentured Retainers, 1461–1483* (1955).

40. G.R. Elton (1982), pp.34–7 and n.

41. Statute 19 Henry VII, cap.14. *Statutes
of the Realm,* II, pp.658–60.

42. Ibid., paras. vii and viii.

43. Chrimes (1972), p.190 and n.

44. Ibid.

45. Polydore Vergil, *Anglica historia*, ed.
Hay (Camden Society, 3rd series, 74,
1950), pp.145–7. Sean Cunningham,
Henry VII (2007), pp.150–72.

46. These negotiations resulted in a draft
treaty as early as 7 July 1488. *Cal. SP.
Span.,* I, nos 13 and 14. This treaty was
confirmed at Medina del Campo on 28
March 1489. Currin (2005).

47. Chrimes (1972), pp.285–7.

48. John Edwards, *Ferdinand and Isabella:
Profiles in Power* (2005), p.157.

49. G.A. Bergenroth, *The Supplement to
Volumes I and II of ... State Papers
Spanish* (1868), pp.47–430 contains all
the documents relevant to this matter.

50. J. Gairdner, ed., *Memorials of King
Henry VII* (Rolls Series, 1858),
pp.223–39.

51. Chrimes (1972), p.318.

52. T.A. Birrell, *English Monarchs and their
Books: from Henry VII to Charles II*
(1987), pp.6–7.

53. Thompson (1965), pp.237–8. John
Foxe, *Acts and Monuments* (ed.1583),
p.731.

54. Foxe, loc.cit.

55. For example John Morton at
Canterbury, and Richard Foxe at Bath
and Wells, Durham and finally
Winchester.

56. Chrimes (1972), p.241. F.R.H. de
    Boulay, 'The fifteenth century' in C.H.
    Lawrence, ed., *The English Church and
    the Papacy in the Middle Ages* (1965),
    pp.195–242.
57. Carpenter (1966).
58. For a recent argument in favour of this
    thesis, see Grummitt (2009), where the
    point is made that Henry's tightening
    control over the nobility constituted a
    new approach.
59. Statute 4 Henry VII, cap.12. *Statutes of
    the Realm*, II, pp.536–8.

Chapter Two
HENRY VIII:
THE RENAISSANCE
PRINCE

1. Desiderius Erasmus, *Opus Epistolarum*,
   eds P.S. and H.M. Allen (12 vols, 1906–
   58), I, no.1. Skelton later wrote that he
   had 'acquaint[ed] him with the muses
   nine'.
2. J.S. Brewer et al, eds, *Letters and Papers
   … of the Reign of Henry VIII* (21 vols,
   1862–1910), II, p.395. Rawdon Brown
   et al, eds, *Calendar of State Papers
   Venetian,* II, p.1287.
3. Anglo (1969), p.109.
4. Ibid., p.110. Richard Grafton noted,
   'The king at this time being lusty,
   young and courageous, greatly
   delighted in feats of chivalry, insomuch
   that he made a challenge of Jousts
   against all comers to be proclaimed…'
   Chronicle (1809), p.238.
5. Henry II of France was killed in 1559
   when a splinter of his opponent's lance
   entered his eye.
6. TNA E 36/217, ff.41-55. Edward Hall,
   *The union of the Two Noble and Illustre
   Famelies of Lancastre and Yorke* (1809),
   pp.517–19.
7. Ibid.
8. Gunn (1988), pp.6–11.
9. Loades (1992), p.56.
10. Rule (1982), pp.149–83. There is some
    controversy about the number and
    placing of these guns.
11. TNA E 404/87/2, no.121. Loades and
    Knighton (2002), pp.5–7.
12. 'The ballad of Sir Andrew Barton', in
    C.H. Firth, ed., *Naval Songs and Ballads*
    (NRS, 1908). Spont (NRS, 1897),
    pp.xii–xiv.
13. Rodger (1997), p.476.
14. Spont (NRS, 1897), pp.xxv–xxvi.

15. Ibid., quoting Alain Bourchart, a contemporary Breton chronicler.

16. Grafton, *Chronicle*, pp.246–8. Cruickshank (1990) pp.4–5.

17. According to Grafton, 'The King of Aragon was sore discontent[ed] with their departing ... and said openly, that if they had tarried he would have invaded Guyenne'. Henry took this assurance for what it was worth.

18. News of the French court sent by Spinelly to Henry VIII, 25 February 1513. Spont (NRS 1897), pp.75–6.

19. Ibid., pp.87–8.

20. Ibid., p.xxxviii, quoting Holinshed's *Chronicle*. The original letter does not survive.

21. Grafton, *Chronicle*, p.252. Rodger (1997), p.171.

22. Thomas Howard to Wolsey, 5 June 1513. Spont (NRS 1897), p.170.

23. Cruikshank (1990), pp.29–36.

24. Ibid., pp.102–5.

25. Polydore Vergil, *Anglica historia*, ed. D. Hay (Camden Society, 3rd series, 74, 1950), p.221. Scarisbrick (1968), pp.37–8.

26. BL Cotton MS Vespasian F III, f.15.

27. Robert Macquereau, *Chronique de la maison de Bourgoigne* (1838), p.40.

28. Ibid., pp.40–41.

29. TNA 31/8/144, ff.286–7.

30. Cruikshank (1990), p.135.

31. *Cal. Ven.*, II, 445. Scarisbrick (1968), p.53.

32. This story is probably apocryphal, but it suits the known character of the lady. Scarisbrick (1968), pp.57–8.

33. TNA E 36/13, pp.3–16. Loades and Knighton (2000), pp.113–17.

34. Loades (1992), p.68.

35. Ibid., p.70. *Letters and Papers*, III, 1911.

36. *Anthony Roll*, p.119. See also the inventory of the *Christ of Greenwich*, p.152.

37. This discontent soon erupted into the complicated rising known as the revolt of the *comuneros*.

38. Scarisbrick (1968), pp.68–9.

39. *Cal. Ven.*, II, 1052–3. *Letters and Papers*, II, 4333, 4348.

40. T. Rymer, *Foedera, conventiones etc* (1704–35), XIII, pp.624 ff.

41. Ibid. Scarisbrick (1968), p.73.

42. Ibid., p.99.

43. *Letters and Papers*, III, 302. For the effect of the deep pockets of the Fuggers (an Augsburg banking house) see R.H. Ehrenberg, *Capital and Finance in the Age of the Renaissance* (1928).

44. *Letters and Papers*, III, 551, 728. *Cal. Span.*, II, 274.

45. Scarisbrick (1968), p.75.

46. Ibid., pp.92–3. The traditional figure for Henry VII's legacy is that given by Francis Bacon — £1,800,000. This is not accepted by recent research, which suggests a sum equivalent to about two years ordinary revenue — £300,000. F.C. Dietz, *English Government Finance, 1485–1558* (1964), p.87.

47. Hall *The Union of the Two Noble and Illustre Famelies...*, p.519. He died in February.

48. Mattingly (1963), pp.123–5.

49. Murphy (2001), pp.16–20.

50. For a discussion of Henry's possible sexual problems, see Ives (2004), p.191.

51. Mattingly (1963), pp.132–3.

52. Loades (1992), p.49. L.G. Carr-Loughton, 'Early Tudor Ships' Guns', *Mariner's Mirror,* 46 (1960).

53. Cruikshank (1990), pp.64–5.

54. Loades and Knighton (2000), p.41.

55. For all these creations, see E.B. Fryde et al, eds, *The Handbook of British Chronology* (1986).

56. Cruikshank (1990), pp.30–31.

57. E.B. Fryde et al, eds, *The Handbook of British Chronology* (1986), pp.473, 484.

Chapter Three
HENRY VIII:
POVERTY AND
PREOCCUPATION

1. For a full discussion of this event and its context, Russell (1969).
2. *Letters and Papers*, iii, nos. 702, 704, 869, 870. S. Anglo, 'Le Camp du Drap d'Or et les Entreuves d'Henri VIII et de Charles Quint', *Fetes et Ceremonies au Temps de Charles Quint* (1959), pp. 116 et seq.
3. Russell (1969), pp. 41–4.
4. Scarisbrick (1968), p. 77. This shallow valley was apparently known as the Val d'Or, which may have suggested the name for the whole celebration.
5. *Letters and Papers*, iii, no. 558.
6. Russell (1969), pp. 161–4. Richardson (1970).
7. Ives (2004), p. 31. Anne's mother, Elizabeth, and her brother, George, were also present.
8. Russell (1969), pp. 123–4.
9. *Calendar of State Papers, Venetian*, iii, p. 115.
10. *Letters and Papers*, iii, no. 1176. Knecht (1982), pp. 105–6.
11. *Letters and Papers,* iii, nos. 1462, 1493. For the text of the treaty, see *Cal. Span*, ii, p. 355.
12. *Letters and Papers*, iii, no. 2574. Scarisbrick (1968), p. 126.
13. *Letters and Papers*, iii, no. 2296. Orders for the fleet. Loades (1992), p. 105.
14. Ibid., p. 106.
15. *Letters and Papers*, iii, nos. 2333, 2360. Scarisbrick (1968), p. 95.
16. Hoyle (1993), p. xv.
17. Fissel (2001), p. 10.
18. John Pound, ed., *The Military Survey of 1522 for Babergh Hundred* (1986). Fissel (2001), p. 9.

19. Loades and Knighton (2002), p. 82.
20. Ibid.
21. *Letters and Papers*, iii, no. 3123. A. Levey, *Le Connetable de Bourbon, 1490–1527* (1904), livre ii.
22. Gunn (1986), pp. 596–634.
23. Ibid.
24. *Letters and Papers*, iii, 3659; iv, 26, Scarisbrick (1968), p. 130.
25. The English did not stay long enough to capitalize on this situation. Gunn (1986).
26. *State Papers of Henry VIII* (1830–52), vi, 221, 233.
27. F.C. Dietz, *English Government Finance, 1485–1558* (1964), p. 94. Bernard (1986), pp. 53–5.
28. Scarisbrick (1968), pp. 130–31.
29. *Letters and Papers*, iv, no. 384. The King wanted to send money, but Wolsey managed to persuade him that there wasn't any.
30. Knecht (1982), pp. 165–72.
31. Bernard (1986), pp. 110–36.
32. *Cal. Span.*, iii, p. 82. Scarisbrick (1968), p. 136.
33. Bernard (1986), pp. 136–52.
34. Knecht (1982), pp. 183–7.
35. *Cal. Ven.*, iii, 1401. Wolsey's relations with Pope Clement VII became strained in consequence.
36. *Letters and Papers*, iv, nos. 5710, 5744. Scarisbrick (1968), pp. 232–3.
37. Barbara Harris, *Edward Stafford, third Duke of Buckingham, 1478–1521* (1986).
38. Peter Gwyn, *The King's Cardinal* (1990), pp. 159–72.
39. Miller (1986), pp. 254–7.
40. Fissel (2001), pp. 8–13. Miller (1980).
41. Loades (1992), pp. 110–13.
42. TNA E 315 / 317, ff. 41–5.
43. BL Royal MS 14 B xxii D. *Letters and Papers*, iv, 2, 2635.
44. Loades and Knighton (2002), pp. 95–7.
45. *Letters and Papers*, v, no. 321. Loades (1992), p. 115.

46. TNA E 315/317, f.58. The maintenance pattern can be only imperfectly reconstructed from these accounts.

47. The *Mary Willoughby*. Rodger (1997), p.179.

48. Chapuys to the Emperor, 24 November 1533. *Letters and Papers*, vi, no.1460.

49. Hoyle (2001), pp.282–305.

50. Loades and Knighton (2002), pp.96–7. The archaeological evidence shows that the frame of the ship was significantly strengthened at that time, and that additional gunports were added. Rule (1982), pp.103–7.

51. Loades (1992), p.113.

52. Loades (2007), pp.88–111. There is an enormous literature on the subject of Henry's 'divorce'.

53. For a full examination of this event and its repercussions, see Hook (1972).

54. Henry's support derived very largely from recognition that something had to be done to secure the succession, as well as from the fact that Rome was a distant and foreign power.

55. Scarisbrick (1968), pp.365–7.

56. Loades (2007), pp.208–10. G.W. Bernard (2005).

57. Ibid.

Chapter Four
HENRY VIII: YOUTH REVIVED

1. Scarisbrick (1968), pp.355–6.

2. *Letters and Papers*, XIV, ii, 400. Words reported by George Constantine, and not necessarily accurate.

3. For the papal bull see D. Wilkins, *Concilia*, III, 840. The Cleves negotiation is illustrated by Christopher Mont's report of March 1539 (*Letters and Papers*, XIV, i. no 920), and Cromwell's fears of invasion by his memorandum of May. (*Letters and Papers*, XIV, I, 580).

4. Fissel (2001), p.37. Colvin (1982), pp.369–77.

5. Dietz, *English Government Finance 1485–1558* (1964), pp.137–8.

6. Scarisbrick (1968), p.362. Hughes and Larkin, *Tudor Royal Proclamations*, I, no.190. 28 February 1539.

7. Pierce (2003), pp.115–40.

8. Warnicke (2000), pp.63–93.

9. Ibid.

10. Charles Wriothesley, *A Chronicle of England During the Reigns of the Tudors … 1485–1559*, ed. William Hamilton, (Camden Society, 1875), I, p.109.

11. Warnicke (2000), p.255.

12. Elton (1990).

13. D. Loades, *Henry VIII and his Queens* (2000), pp.127–8. Smith (1961), pp.175–81.

14. Scarisbrick (1968), pp.434–6. Loades (2007), pp.76–7.

15. *Letters and Papers*, XIII, ii, nos.1135–6.

16. Fissel (2001), p.26.

17. Loades (2007), p.76.

18. Loades (1996), pp.53–5.

19. *ODNB*—Mary, Queen of Scots.

20. Catherine had been married twice before: to Edward Borough in 1529 and, following Borough's death in 1532, to John Neville, Lord Latimer. Lord Latimer was still alive when Henry first met Catherine in the spring of 1543, when she was about 30. He died at the end of March. Loades, *Henry VIII and his Queens* (2000), pp.135–6. James (1999).

21. Hughes and Larkin, *Tudor Royal Proclamations*, I, no.243.

22. Scarisbrick (1968), 442.

23. *Letters and Papers*, XIX, I, no.86.

24. Loades and Knighton (2008), pp.62–3, 79–82.

25. Ibid., and pp.85–6.

26. BL Add.MS 32654. *The Hamilton Papers*, ed. J. Bain (1890–92), II, pp.361–6.

27. *Letters and Papers*, XIX, I, no.481.

28. BL Add.MS 32654, ff.189–92. *Hamilton Papers*, II, pp.371–5.

29. TNA SP 49/7, no.15. Loades and Knighton (2008), pp.94–5.

30. Loades (1992), p.92.

31. Fissel (2001), p.14.

32. *Letters and Papers*, XIX, I, nos.529–30.

33. Ibid., no.741.

34. Richard Grafton, *Chronicle* (ed.1809), II, p.492. 'The xviii day the kings highnesse having the sword borne naked before him by the Lorde Marques Dorset, like a noble and valyaunt Conquerour rode into Bulleyn, and all the Tompetters standing on the walles of the towne, sounded their Trumpets'.

35. Scarisbrick (1968), p.448.

36. *Letters and Papers*, XIX, ii, no.353.

37. Clowes (1897), I, pp.461–2. Hall (*The Union...*, p.863) says 200 sail and 26 galleys.

38. Loades and Knighton (2002), p.109.

39. Ibid.

40. Rule (1982), pp.103–16. The debate on the reconstruction of the ship continues.

41. Wriothesley's Chronicle says 'all the men that were in her, saving 40, were drowned, which were above 500 persons'. *Chronicle*, I, p.158.

42. Loades (1992), p.134.

43. Loades and Knighton (2002), p.111.

44. Scarisbrick (1968), p.452.

45. *Letters and Papers*, XXI, I, nos.85, 91, 122, 124, 218, 221, 251–2, 272.

46. Ibid., nos.507–8, 527, 577, 586. Loades (1996), p.76.

47. BL Egerton MS 2603, f.31. *Letters and Papers*, XXI, i, 610.

48. Ibid., 1405. The text of the treaty is printed in Rymer, *Foedera etc*, XV, p.98.

49. Rodger (1997), pp.477–8.

50. TNA C 66/788, mm. 27–30. C.S.L. Davies, 'The Administration of the Royal Navy under Henry VIII: the origins of the Navy Board', *English Historical Review*, 80, 1965, pp.268–88.

51. Rodger, *Safeguard*, p.182.

52. H. Schubert, 'The first cast iron cannon made in England', *Journal of the Iron and Steel Institute,* 146 (1942), pp.131–5.

Chapter Five
EDWARD VI:
THE CHILD KING

1. Strong (1969), II, plates 164, 165, 166, 172 and 173. Other portraits of Edward are also illustrated.
2. Grafton, *Chronicle*, p.500. Jordan (1968), pp.65–72.
3. MacCulloch (1999), pp.14, 18. Josias was the young king who had turned Israel from its addiction to idolatry.
4. For example on 1 April 1551, Edward's Journal records 'The first day of the challenge at base, or running, the King won'. W.K. Jordan, *The Chronicle and Political Papers of King Edward VI* (1966), p.57.
5. Ibid., p.7.
6. Ibid., pp.102–5.
7. Bush (1975), pp.100–127. Loach (1999).
8. TNA SP 10/1, no.36.
9. Jordan (1968), pp.250–52.
10. London, 1548. [*RSTC* 19476.5] Reprinted in A.F. Pollard, *Tudor Tracts, 1532–1588* (1903), pp.53–157.
11. Ibid., pp.90–95.
12. Ibid., p.107. '[T]his at first, was so strange in our eyes that we could not devise what to make of their meaning … that they would ever forsake their strength, to meet us in the field.'
13. Ibid., p.133.
14. Ibid.
15. Bush (1975), pp.13–23.
16. In May 1546 a Protestant 'commando group' had broken into St Andrews Castle and murdered Cardinal Beaton. They had defied all attempts to eject them until Strozzi's arrival on 31 July 1547. S. Haynes and W. Murdin, eds, *A Collection of State Papers … left by William Cecil, Lord Burghley* (1740–59), I, pp.43–54.
17. *Calendar of State Papers Relating to Scotland*, ed. J. Bain etc. (1898–1952), I, 129, 143, 146, 155, 156, 161.
18. Ibid., 240, 251, 269.
19. Bush (1975), p.17. BL MS Cotton B.VII. f.385.
20. Ibid., p.18. TNA SP 50/4, no.21.
21. Jordan (1968), p.283.
22. Inner Temple, Petyt MS 538, f.435-6. Jordan (1968), pp.464–5. Loades (1996), p.121.
23. All copy-hold tenants were supposed to be protected by the custom of the manor, which required a decision of the manor court before enclosure could be carried out. However, there were ways around this, such as obtaining unity of possession. These issues are fully discussed by Eric Kerridge, *Agrarian Problems in the Sixteenth Century and After* (1969).
24. D. MacCulloch, 'Kett's rebellion in Context' in P. Slack, ed., *Rebellion, Popular Protest and the Social Order in Early Modern England* (1984), pp.39–76. MacCulloch (1986), p.302. Wood (2007).
25. Jordan (1968), pp.448–50. Hughes and Larkin, *Tudor Royal Proclamations*, I, nos. 333, 334.
26. Raphael Holinshed, *Chronicles*, III, pp.972–4. Jordan (1968), pp.487–90.
27. BL Harley MS 523, no.43. Russell (1859), pp.146–50, 213-5. Loades (1996), p.127.
28. Ibid., pp.129–30.
29. Parry (1989), pp.370–80.
30. *RSTC* 22269.
31. Clowes (1897), I, p.469.
32. Rodger (1997), p.478.
33. Jordan (1968), p.303. Once the Germans had surrendered, the position at Bolemberg became untenable, and the garrison withdrew.
34. Jordan, *Chronicle and Political Papers*, p.16.

35. Guidotti was a Florentine merchant, resident in London. *Cal.Span.*, IX, p.490. Loades (1996), p.153.
36. Ibid., pp.155–7.
37. D.L. Potter, 'Documents Concerning the Negotiation of the Anglo-French Treaty of March 1550', *Camden Miscellany*, 28 (1984), pp.59–180. For the treaty itself see Rymer *Foedera*, XV, pp.212–15.
38. Jordan, *Chronicle and Political Papers*, pp.23–5.
39. *Acts of the Privy Council*, III, p.156. *Calendar of State Papers, Foreign, Edward VI*, ed. W. Turnbull (1861), pp.61–3.
40. TNA E 351/2588.
41. TNA E 351/2194
42. TNA E 351/2353
43. TNA SP 10/6, nos.10–15. Loades (1996), p.115.
44. Jordan, *Chronicle and Political Papers*, p.29. Until its surrender, Lord Clinton had been Captain of Boulogne.
45. TNA E 351/2194.
46. Jordan, *Edward VI: The Threshold of Power* (1970), p.128.
47. Jordan, *Chronicle and Political Papers*, p.73.
48. The English originally demanded 1,400,000 crowns, then 800,000. The French offered 100,000, and then raised to 200,000, which was eventually agreed. Ibid., pp.68–9.
49. Ibid., p.70.
50. Ibid., pp.138–9.
51. This was the peace of Passau, signed on 2 August.
52. Loach (1999), pp.97–102. Loades (1996), pp.200–202.
53. 'Certayne Brief Notes of the Controversy between the Dukes of Somerset ... and Nor[t]humberland', *Religion, Politics and Society in Sixteenth Century England*, ed. Ian Archer et al, (Camden Society, 5th series, vol.22, 2003), pp.35–136.
54. Loades (1996), pp.183–6.
55. Loades (1989), pp.164–5.
56. Ibid., pp.153–7.
57. *Cal.Span.*, X, p.377. Mary of Hungary to the Bishop of Arras, 5 October 1551.
58. Loades (1996), pp.288–99, which tracks the gathering and disposal of his lands.

Chapter Six
MARY I:
THE FIRST
RULING QUEEN

1. Mary's legitimacy was doubtful because she had been bastardized by Henry VIII's first succession act of 1534 (25 Henry VIII, c.22), which had been confirmed by the second act in 1536 (28 Henry VIII, c.7). In 1543 a third succession act had restored her to the order (35 Henry VIII, c.1), but had not legitimated her. On the other hand, by Roman Canon Law, she was his only legitimate child.

2. Mary always regarded herself as legitimate, and seems to have taken the pragmatic view that her brother Edward was legitimate also, because her own mother was dead before he was conceived. This did not, apparently, imply any consistent view of either statute or the Canon Law.

3. J.G. Nichols, ed., *The Chronicle of Queen Jane and of Two Years of Queen Mary* (Camden Society, 48, 1850), pp.27–32. Hoak (2003).

4. Mary's attitude towards her sexuality was extremely reticent. She clearly regarded her gender as a liability, whereas Elizabeth used it as a weapon. Loades (2006), p.12.

5. Loades (1991), pp.404–11. Redworth (1990), pp.289–310. S.R. Gammon, *Statesman and Schemer: William, First Lord Paget* (1973), pp.189–213.

6. Mary declared to Renard that, given a free choice, she would not have married, but in her circumstances that was not possible.

7. Loades (1989), pp.201–2. There is no satisfactory life of Edward Courtenay, but see Anne Overell, 'A Nicodemite

in England and Italy; Edward Courtenay, 1548–1556', in *John Foxe at Home and Abroad*, ed. D. Loades (2004), pp.117–37.

8. Loades (1989), pp.104–5.

9. For (somewhat different) assessments of Philip at this stage of his career, see Kamen (1997), pp.50–79; and M.J. Rodriguez-Salgado, *The Changing Face of Empire* (1988), pp.73–100.

10. Nichols, *The Chronicle of Queen Jane*, pp.35–45. David Loades, *Two Tudor Conspiracies* (1965).

11. 1 Mary, sess.3, c.1. Loach (1986), pp.96–7.

12. 1 Mary, sess. 3, c.2. It was unprecedented to have a royal marriage treaty confirmed in this way, but it was also unprecedented for a ruling Queen to marry.

13. *Cal. Span*, XIII, p.11.

14. Loades (1989), pp.226–7.

15. John Elder, *The copie of a letter sent into Scotlande* (1555), reprinted in Nichols, *Chronicle of Queen Jane*, appendix X. Anglo (1969), pp.327–38.

16. Loades, 'Philip II as King of England', in *Law and Government under the Tudors*, ed. C. Cross, D. Loades and J. Scarisbrick (1988). G. Redworth, '"Matters Impertinent to Women"; Male and female Monarchy under Philip and Mary', *English Historical Review*, 112 (1997), pp.597–613.

17. J.G. Nichols, ed., *The Diary of Henry Machyn* (Camden Society, 1848), p.79.

18. Ibid., p.83.

19. 'The Vita Mariae Angliae Reginae of Robert Wingfield of Brantham', ed. and trans. D. MacCulloch, *Camden Miscellany*, 28 (1984), pp.205/53.

20. Ibid., p.252.

21. Tighe (1987), pp.1–11.

22. Alsop (1992), pp.577–90.

23. Machyn, *Diary*, p.85.

24. John Foxe, *Acts and Monuments* (admittedly a hostile source), devoted a whole section to 'the childbed of Queen Mary as it was rumoured among the people', and printed several of the prayers used for her safe delivery. *Acts and Monuments* (1583), pp.1480–82.

25. Loades (1989), pp.257–9.

26. *The copy of a letter sent by John Bradforthe to the right honourable lordes the Earles of Arundel, Derbie, Shrewsburye and Penbroke* (?London, 1556) is an extreme example.

27. Harbison (1940). David Loades, *Two Tudor Conspiracies* (1965).

28. TNA PC 2/5 (*APC*, IV, p.295). Alsop (1992).

29. TNA PC 2/6, pp.5, 6. (*APC*, IV, pp.416–18).

30. TNA SP 11/1, no.14. *APC*, IV, pp.339-378 (Council warrants).

31. His patent of appointment was not issued until 8 April. *Calendar of the Patent Rolls, 1553–4,* p.262.

32. TNA E 101/63/5, f.11. Sir Edmund Peckham's accounts.

33. William Winter added the Mastership of the Naval Ordnance to his existing office of Surveyor and Rigger in July 1557. Loades (1992), p.169.

34. TNA E 351/2/195.

35. *Calendar of State Papers, Venetian*, VI, I, nos.200, 204.

36. Pepys Library, MS 2876, pp.158–9.

37. *APC*, V, pp.219–20.

38. TNA E 351/2196.

39. *APC*, VI, pp.39–41.

40. Loades (1992), pp.163–4. *APC*, V, pp.183–4.

41. Peter Killigrew's examination. TNA SP 11/9, no.25.

42. David Loades, *Two Tudor Conspiracies* (1965), pp.225–6.

43. Machyn, *Diary*, p.129

44. Stafford was the grandson of the last Duke of Buckingham, and a nephew of Cardinal Reginald Pole. It is quite likely that he was lured into this operation by Jean Ribault (who arranged his transport). Ribault had been closely associated with Lord Paget, who was in favour of the war. Loades (1989), pp.275–7.

45. TNA SP 11/11, no.14.

46. TNA SP 11/11, no.35

47. There is an account of this incident in John Strype, *Ecclesiastical Memorials* (1822), III, ii, pp.86–7. Loades (1992), p.171. Glasgow (1967), pp.321–42.

48. TNA SP 11/12, no.35. Davies (1980), pp.159–85.

49. TNA SP 11/12, no.51. For some reflections on the replacement of Howard by Clinton, see *The letters of William, Lord Paget of Beaudesert, 1547–1563*, ed. B.L. Beer and S.M. Jack (Camden Society, 4th series, 13, 1974), pp.130–31.

50. William Winter to Secretary John Boxall. TNA SP 11/12, nos.11, 11(i).

51. Glasgow (1967), p.336.

52. 4 & 5 Philip and Mary, cs. 2 and 3.

53. *Calendar of State Papers, Venetian*, VI, pp.1085–7.

54. Rodriguez Salgado, *Changing Face of Empire*, pp.176–9.

55. Juan de Pinedo to Francis de Vargas, 12 August 1557. *Cal.Span.*, XIII, p.317.

56. BL Stowe MS 571, f.78.

57. Giovanni Michieli to the Doge and Senate, *Cal Ven.*, VI, nos.1389–90.

58. Potter (1983), pp.481–512.

59. BL Cotton MS Titus B.II, f.59. Loades (1991), pp.320–21.

60. Loades (1989), pp.310–12. Philip's comment was made in a letter of 4 December 1558. *Cal.Span.*, XIII, p.440.

61. Her portraits, both by Antonio Moro and Hans Eworth, are very revealing in this respect.

62. Paul Boscher, 'The Anglo-Scottish Border, 1550–1560' (Durham Univerity Ph.D, 1985).

Chapter Seven
ELIZABETH I: THE 'FEMME FATALE'

1. Mary's tutors, such as Richard Fetherstone, were later in trouble for their opposition to the Royal Supremacy. Richard Cox became the Bishop of Ely in December 1559. Cox and Ascham both tutored Edward as well as Elizabeth. At what point they became Protestants is not clear, but they only admitted it after Henry's death.

2. Margaret Clifford (daughter of Eleanor Brandon) was Mary's choice because of her Catholicism, but the only real alternative to Elizabeth was Mary Stewart, who was unacceptable alike to Philip and to the people of England.

3. This was Duke Philip of Bavaria, the son of the Elector Palatine, who came a-wooing to England in December 1539. He did see Mary, but he was a Lutheran and his suit made no progress. Loades (1989), pp.127–9.

4. Loades (2003), pp.68–9. Bernard (1992), pp.212–40.

5. 'Feria's dispatch of 14th November 1558', ed. and trans. M.J. Rodriguez-Salgado and Simon Adams, *Camden Miscellany*, 28 (1984), p.329.

6. See particularly C.S. Meyer, *Elizabeth I and the Religious Settlement of 1559* (1959), and Jones (1982). The Queen was bombarded with advice (most of it anonymous) on this subject.

7. *Elizabeth I: Collected Works*, ed. L.S. Marcus, J. Mueller, and M.B. Rose (2000), p.59, taken from William Camden's printed Latin translation of 1615.

8. [Richard Mulcaster] *The Passage of our Most Dread Sovereign Lady, Queen Elizabeth, through the City of London to Westminster the Day before her Coronation* (1559), in A.F. Pollard, *Tudor Tracts, 1532–1588* (1903), p.387. Biblical images of female power were few and far between, so Deborah was called upon frequently.

9. Doran (1996), pp.195–210.

10. MacCaffrey (1969), pp.41–2.

11. Hughes and Larkin, *Tudor Royal Proclamations*, II, no.449.

12. BL Add.MS 9294, f.1. Glasgow, 'The Maturing of Naval Administration, 1556–64' (1970), pp.3–26.

13. TNA SP 12/3, no.44, ff. 131-4. J.B. Hattendorf et al., eds, *British Naval Documents, 1204–1960* (1993), pp.62–70.

14. TNA E 101/64/1.

15. Glasgow, 'List of ships in the Royal Navy from 1539 to 1588' (1970), pp.299–307. Work on the *Elizabeth Jonas* (called at that stage *The Peter*) seems to have ongoing in the spring of 1558.

16. Glasgow, 'The Maturing of Naval Administration, 1556–64' (1970), p.18.

17. W. Patten, *The Expedition into Scotland*, in A.F. Pollard, *Tudor Tracts, 1532–1588* (1903), p.155.

18. Gilbert Burnet, *History of the Reformation of the Church of England* (1715), p.285. Marshall (1977), pp.224–6.

19. Fissel (2001), pp.114-5.

20. TNA SP 12/7, ff.169-71. Glasgow (1968), pp.23–37. Winter was at first instructed to act as though on his own initiative (!).

21. Loades (1992), pp.210–11.

22. Read (1955), pp.164–6. The Queen's permission is nowhere recorded, but must have been granted.

23. S. Haynes, *The State Papers of Lord Burghley* (1740), pp.351–2.

24. TNA E 351/2197. Gonson's account from 1 January 1559 to 31 December 1560.

25. Dawson (2002), pp.111–42.

26. Doran (1996), pp.40–45.

27. Ian Aird, 'The Death of Amy Robsart', *English Historical Review*, 71 (1956), pp.69–79.

28. Doran (1996), pp.69–72. Elizabeth's state of mind at this point was reflected in a poem which she wrote many years later:

    'When I was fair and young, favour graced me,
    many was I sought unto, their mistress for to be,
    But I did scorn them all, and said to them therefore,
    "Go, go, go, seek some otherwhere, importune me no more"...'
    Elizabeth I: *Collected Works*, pp.303–4.

29. She confined her diplomatic efforts to attempts to find a 'safe' husband for Mary. Read (1955), pp.301–25.

30. D. Loades, *Life and Career of William Paulet* (2008), p.144.

31. TNA SP 70/42., ff.582–3.

32. TNA E 351/2199. Bod.Lib. MS Rawlinson A.200, f.153.

33. Sutherland (1984), p.38.

34. Loades (1992), p.215.

35. *Tudor Royal Proclamations*, II, no.499.

36. Loades (1992), p.216.

37. TNA E 351/2199, m.9d. Bod.Lib. MS Rawlinson A.200.

38. R.G. Marsden, ed., 'The voyage of the Barbara to Brazil, Anno 1540', *Naval Miscellany*, II, (1912), pp.1–66.

39. Loades (1996), p.246. Sir William Foster, *England's Quest of Eastern Trade* (1933), pp.3–13. The Muscovy Company was founded in 1555.

40. Loades (2000), pp.65–6.

41. TNA SP 12/17, no.43.

42. Kelsey (2003), pp.12–33.

43. Ibid., p.36. Guzman da Silva to the King, 4 February 1566.

44. Herman Van der Wee, *The Growth of the Antwerp Market and the European Economy*, III (1963).

45. Kelsey (2003), pp.56–7.

46. TNA SP 12/49/40.i, f. 85. *A true declaration of the troublesome voyadge of M John Haukins* (London, 1569), f. A ii.[*RSTC* 12961].

47. Kelsey (2003), pp.82–3.

48. Ibid., pp.88–90.

49. *A true declaration*, f.B v.

50. *APC*, VII, pp.180–82.

51. Loades (1992), pp.225–6.

52. Miller (1986). Loades (2007).

53. Andrews (1964), p.3.

54. Read (1955), pp.229–30.

55. Read (1933), pp.443–64. D. Loades, *The Cecils: Privilege and Power behind the Throne* (2007), pp.69–73.

Chapter Eight
ELIZABETH I: THE VIRGIN QUEEN

1. Mary's ambiguous role in her second husband's death was used as an excuse to keep her in prison, but the real reason was that she was extremely dangerous to Elizabeth. She was suspected of involvement in numerous plots against the Queen, and was eventually tried and executed for her part in the Babington conspiracy of 1586. Parliament had been campaigning for her death for many years. Fraser (1969). Wormald (1988).

2. Read (1955), pp.431–54.

3. Adams (2002), pp.32–3.

4. MacCaffrey (1969), pp.221–2. Fissel (2001), pp.123–8.

5. Sir Cuthbert Sharp, *The 1569 Rebellion; the Rising in the North* (1840, reprinted 1975), pp.275–87. The ringleader of this group was Richard Norton, known as 'Old Norton', who was a survivor of the 1536 rebellion.

6. P. McGrath, *Papists and Puritans under Elizabeth I* (1967). Philip Hughes, *The Reformation in England,* III, (1954), pp.337–56.

7. Statutes 13 Elizabeth c.2, 23 Elizabeth, c.1.

8. Doran (1996), pp.130–94.

9. Young (1987), pp.32–7.

10. Strong (1977), pp.130–33.

11. E. Spenser, *Faerie Queene*, Book 2, 2, xlii.

12. H. Colvin, ed., *History of the King's Works*, IV, ii, pp.613–64.

13. Fissel (2001), p.93. Archers continued to be used in Ireland down to the end of the century.

14. Gladys S. Thomson, *Lords Lieutenants in the Sixteenth Century* (1923). Fissel (2001), pp.50–53.

15. Ibid., pp.53–6.

16. Ibid., p.62.

17. Cruickshank (1966), pp.24–5.

18. Ibid., pp.1–5.

19. Loades (1992), pp.183–4.

20. Ibid., p.182. Glasgow (1977), pp.253–63. Ibid., 'The maturing of naval administration' (1970), p.21.

21. For example the *Hart* and the *Antelope*, both of 300 tons. Loades and Knighton (2000), pp.66–7.

22. Martin and Parker (1988), pp.224–5. The use of the synchronized broadside can only be deduced from comments made by Spanish officers at the time. The first set of matching guns to have been recovered and scientifically examined come from the Alderney wreck and date from 1592.

23. The navy maintained a preference for bronze guns into the seventeenth century, possibly because they were less inclined to fracture in use. N.A.M. Rodger, 'The development of broadside gunnery, 1450–1650', *Mariner's Mirror*, 82 (1996), pp.301–24.

24. Kelsey (1998), pp53–6.

25. Loades (1992) p.223.

26. Grenville's petition to the Queen. TNA SP 12/95/63.

27. Valderama to Antonio de Guaras, 20 August 1577. TNA SP 94/8 f.101.

28. Kelsey (1998), pp.83–93.

29. Ibid., pp.95–110. John Cooke, 'Sir Francis Drake, anno domini 1577', BL Harley MS 540, ff.93–102.

30. Kelsey (1998), p.137 and n.1.

31. This issue is examined in great detail by Kelsey (1998), pp.172–190.

32. 'The regester of suche as is dellevered unto Xtopher hanes…', TNA SP 12/144, no.17 f.142. Rodger (1997), pp.244–5.

33. Mendoza's report of 9 January 1581. BL Add.MS 26056, f.138.

34. Mendoza to the King, 23 October 1580. Ibid., f.121.

35. This treaty between Spain and Portugal followed a papal bull dated 25 September 1493, which declared that Spain should not infringe Portugal's right to the West African coast. The parties agreed a boundary between their spheres of influence 370 leagues west of the Cape Verde islands, supposedly the mid point between the Azores and the West Indies.

36. E.G.R Taylor, ed., *The Troublesome Voyage of Captain Edward Fenton, 1582–3*, Hakluyt Society, second series, 113 (1959). Elizabeth Donno, *An Elizabethan in 1582; the Diary of Richard Maddox, Fellow of All Souls,* Hakluyt Society, second series, 146 (1976).

37. Kamen (1997), p.172.

38. Rodger (1997), p.248.

39. Parker (1977), p.207.

40. Ibid., p.226.

41. Loades (2003), pp.219–20.

42. Read (1925), III, pp.82–3.

43. Raphael Holinshed, *Chronicle* (ed.1878), IV, p.536.

44. Parker (1977), p.217.

45. It was only in February 1585 that the objective had been switched from the Moluccas to the West Indies. TNA AO 1/1685/20A. Mendoza, by this time in Paris, was well informed. *Calendar of State Papers, Spanish, Elizabeth,* III, pp.531–2.

46. TNA AO 1/1685/20A.

47. TNA SP 12/183, f.22. Kelsey (1998), pp.242–3.

48. Loades (1992), p.234.

49. Kelsey (1998), pp.253–6.

50. BL Royal MS 7 C, xvi, f.169. 'The discourse and description of the voyage of Sir Francis Drake and Master Frobisher'. M.F. Keeler, *Sir Francis Drake's West Indian Voyage,* Hakluyt Society, second series, 148 (1981), pp.191–3.

51. Walter Bigges, *The Summarie and True Discourse of sir Francis Drakes West Indian Voyage* (1589), pp.16–17.

52. Kelsey (1998), pp.264–5.

53. Deposition by Francisco Hernandez, 30 June 1586. Translated and printed by Irene Wright, *Further English Voyages to Spanish America,* Hakluyt Society, second series, 99 (1951), p.183.

54. Walter Bigges, *The Summarie and True Discourse of sir Francis Drakes West Indian Voyage* (1589), pp.35–6.

55. *RSTC* 3056.

56. Martin and Parker (1988), p.109. 'The captains who accompanied the Marquis of Santa Cruz … said openly that now we have Portugal, England is ours'.

57. Ibid., p.115.

58. Ibid., p.116

59. Fissel (2001), pp.139–42.

60. Bod. Lib. Ashmole MS 816, f.18.

61. Nolan (1997), pp.92–107.

62. Oppenheim, *A History of the Administration of the Royal Navy … 1509–1660* (1896), p.161.

63. Spence (1995).

Chapter Nine

GLORIANA: THE QUEEN AT WAR

1. Dietz, *English Government Finance* (1964), p.51.

2. SP12/156, ff.88–90.

3. Dietz, *English Government Finance* (1964), p.55.

4. By an unknown artist. Strong (1969), II, plate 199.

5. BL Harley MS 6798, art.18, f.87, which is a late sixteenth- or early seventeenth-century copy, endorsed 'Gathered by one that heard it and was commanded to utter it to the whole army the next day'. So its authenticity is not above question, *Elizabeth I: Collected Works*, p.326.

6. His father, Edmund Drake, was a shearman turned priest, of modest means. Francis was therefore illegitimate when he was born in 1540, and was brought up in the household of his kinsman, William Hawkins, a merchant of Plymouth. Kelsey (1998), pp.7–10.

7. As is clear from the 'Rainbow Portrait'. Strong (1977), p.50.

8. A.B. Grosart, ed., *The Works in Verse and Prose of Sir John Davies* (1869), p.207.

9. Bodleian Library, MS Rawlinson Poetical 85, f.1r. *Elizabeth I: Collected Works*, p.304.

10. Dietz, *English Government Finance* (1964), pp.97–100.

11. BL Lansdowne MS 52, ff.92–3. Kelsey (1998), pp.280–83.

12. Drake seems to have enjoyed a close personal relationship with the Portuguese pretender. Ibid. pp.233–4, 285–6.

13. BL Lansdowne MS 56, no.52, f.175. J.S. Corbett, *Papers Relating to the Navy during the Spanish War, 1585–1587*, (NRS, 1898), pp.105–6.

14. Kelsey (1998), p.292.

15. William Borough was later accused of mutiny for this desertion, but was not convicted. See Borough to the Lord Admiral, 5 June 1587. TNA SP 12/202, no.14. Corbett, *Papers*, pp.142–5.

16. Kelsey (1998), pp.281–2.

17. The costs at this point were running at £100,000 a month. Loades (1992), p.243.

18. Pierson (1989).

19. Ibid.

20. Martin and Parker (1988), pp.35–8.

21. Ibid., p.163.

22. For a full account of these engagements see ibid., pp.157–78.

23. Adams (1988), pp.173–96. Rodger (1997), p.268.

24. Martin and Parker (1988), p.187.

25. Ibid., p.193. J.K. Laughton, *State Papers Relating to the Defeat of the Spanish Armada* (1894), I, pp.344–50.

26. Martin and Parker (1988), pp.184–5.

27. TNA SP 12/216, no.3. Loades (1992), pp.253–4.

28. T[homas] D[eloney], *Three Ballads on the Armada Fight* (1588), *RSTC* 6557, 6558, 6565, reprinted in A.F. Pollard, *Tudor Tracts, 1532–1588* (1903), pp.485–502.

29. Thompson (1988), p.172.

30. R.B. Wernham, *The Expedition of Sir John Norris and Sir Francis Drake to Spain and Portugal, 1589* (NRS 1988), pp.xx–xxi.

31. Ibid., pp.83–88.

32. Ibid., pp.xxxvi, 107–30.

33. TNA SP 12/224, no.78. Loades (1992), p.257. R.B. Wernham, *The Expedition of Sir John Norris and Sir Francis Drake to Spain and Portugal, 1589* (NRS 1988), pp.179–81.

34. Loades (1992), p.257. R.B. Wernham, *The Expedition of Sir John Norris and Sir Francis Drake to Spain and Portugal, 1589* (NRS 1988), pp.lxiv–v.

35. Ibid., p.lvi.

36. Ibid., pp.290–91.

37. Kelsey (1998), pp.367–91.

38. Clowes (1897), pp.519–24. M. Oppenheim, ed., *The Naval Tracts of Sir William Monson* (5 vols., 1902–14), II, p.40.

39. Francis Seall, 'The Taking of the Madre de Dios, Anno. 1592' ed. C.L. Kingsford, *Naval Miscellany,* II (1912), pp.85–122.

40. Ibid., pp.96–7.

41. Ibid., pp.85–122.

42. Andrews (1964), particularly the appendix, pp.243–74.

43. Usherwood (1983), pp.15–25.

44. Ibid., pp.64–5.

45. BL Cotton MS Otho E.IX, f.313.

46. Lambeth Palace Codex 250. Usherwood (1983), pp.68–9.

47. Ibid., pp.84–6.

48. Clowes (1897), p.516.

49. The Queen, on the other hand, was elated. 'You have made me famous', she wrote, 'dreadful and renowned, not more for your victory than for your courage… Never was heard in so few days of so great a work achieved. Let the army know I care not so much for being a Queen as that I am sovereign of such subjects.' BL MS Otho E.IX, ff.335.

50. Ellis (1985), pp.306–7.

51. Smith (1986), pp.239–68.

52. Loades (2003), pp.262–3.

53. Nolan (1997), p.210.

54. Ibid., pp.191–3.

55. William Camden, *History of Elizabeth I* (1688 ed.), p.464.

56. Nolan (1997), pp.196–7.

57. Ibid., pp.210–11.

58. Jean Moreau, *Memoire du chronique Jean Moreau sur les guerres de la ligue en Bretagne,* ed. H. Waguet (1960), pp.202–4.

59. Nolan (1997), pp.218–32.

60. Ellis (1985), p.235.

61. Nolan (1997), pp.238–9.

62. Ellis (1985), pp.310–12.

EPILOGUE:
A CHANGING
SOCIETY

1. Henry clearly came to see the Royal Supremacy as a fundamental aspect of his honour, because it reflected the direct relationship that he claimed to have with God. His conflicts with the Pope and the Emperor thus became questions of conviction rather than politics.
2. James (1978).
3. Notably the Wellesbourne family of Buckinghamshire, who invented a fictitious son of Simon de Montfort (Wellesbourne de Montfort) to head their family tree. Stone (1965), p.24. Cecil's claim was almost certainly provoked by malicious rumours in Elizabeth's reign that Lord Burghley's grandfather had been an innkeeper. D. Loades, *The Cecils: Privilege and Power behind the Throne* (2007), p.13.
4. There were still a few baronies by prescription in the sixteenth century, but they did not entitle their holders to sit in the House of Lords. A writ of summons to parliament was the acid test of baronial status by 1485.
5. The Marquis of Dorset (Thomas Grey) was the Queen's half-brother, who had joined Henry in exile in 1483.
6. Grumitt (2009), pp.25–8.
7. Ibid.
8. Margaret's father, George, Duke of Clarence had also held the title of Salisbury in right of his wife, Isobel, the daughter and co-heir of Richard Neville, Earl of Salisbury and of Warwick. So this was a very 'lineage-conscious' creation. Henry Courtenay's mother had been Catherine, daughter of Edward IV.
9. BL Add. MS 46354, f.2. *Letters and Papers*, XVII, no.163.
10. Surrey was accused of quartering the arms of Edward the Confessor with his own, and this was interpreted as a claim to royal blood. He was also openly contemptuous of 'upstarts' such as the Seymours, whom the King had chosen to honour.
11. This was very noticeably the case with the Duke of Northumberland, who had no affinity to support him in the succession crisis of July 1553. Loades (1996), pp.262–4.
12. Loades (1991), pp.299–302.
13. A.R. Myers, *The Household of Edward IV*, (1959), pp.126–7.
14. BL Harleian MS 2252, f.147. Loades (1986), p.126. The poem continued 'But hunt and blow an horn, Leap over lakes and dykes, Set nothing by politics'.
15. G. Pettie, *The Civile Conversation of S. Guazzo*, sig.Av.
16. James (1978).
17. Ibid.
18. Hoyle (2001), p.415. By 1536 the aristocracy was consoling itself with the thought that only the 'rude commons' were capable of acts of outright rebellion.
19. Penry Williams, 'Government and Politics', in Trevor Herbert and Gareth Jones, *Tudor Wales* (1988), pp.134–162.
20. MacCaffrey (1969) pp.247–62.
21. Essex considered that the Queen's treatment of him after his return from Ireland was an infringement of his honour, for which he chose to blame the Secretary, Sir Robert Cecil. His rising was supported by a handful of 'swordsmen'. Smith (1986) pp.218–38.
22. A.P. McGowan, ed., *The Jacobean Commissions of Enquiry of 1608 and 1618* (NRS, 1971), pp.xiii–xxvii.

FURTHER READING

ADAMS, S., 'The battle that never was; the Downs and the armada campaign', in Rodriguez Salgado and Adams, ed., *England, Spain and the Gran Armada* (1988)

ADAMS, S., 'New light on the "Reformation" of John Hawkins; the Ellesmere naval survey of 1584', *English Historical Review*, 105 (1990), pp.96–111

ADAMS, S., *Leicester and the Court* (2002)

ALLMAND, C., *Henry V* (1992)

ALSOP, J.D., 'A regime at sea; the navy and the 1553 succession crisis', *Albion*, 24 (1992), pp.577–90

ANDREWS, K.R., *Elizabethan Privateering* (1964)

ANDREWS, K.R., *Drake's Voyages; a Reassessment of their Place in England's Maritime Expansion* (1967)

ANGLO, S., *Spectacle, Pageantry and Early Tudor Policy* (1969)

ARTHURSON, Ian, *The Warbeck Conspiracy, 1491–1499* (1994)

BARRIE, J., *War in Medieval Society; Social values and the Hundred Years War, 1337–99* (1974)

BENNETT, M.J., *Lambert Simnel and the Battle of Stoke* (1987)

BERNARD, G.W., *War, Taxation and Rebellion in Early Tudor England* (1986)

BERNARD, G.W., 'The Downfall of Sir Thomas Seymour', in Bernard, ed., *The Tudor Nobility* (1992)

BERNARD, G.W., *The King's Reformation* (2005)

BOYNTON, L.O., *The Elizabethan Militia, 1558–1638* (1967)

BUSH, M.L., *The Government Policy of Protector Somerset* (1975)

CARPENTER, E.F., *A House of Kings: Westminster Abbey* (1966)

CHRIMES, S.B., *Henry VII* (1972)

CLOWES, W. Laird, *The Royal Navy: a History* (1897)

COLVIN, H.M., *The History of the King's Works*, vol. IV (1982)

CONNELL SMITH, G., *The Forerunners of Drake* (1954)

CRUICKSHANK, C.G., *Elizabeth's Army* (1966)

CRUICKSHANK, C.G., *Henry VIII and the Invasion of France* (1990)

CURRIN, J.M., 'Henry VII and the Treaty of Redon (1489); Plantagenet ambitions and Early Tudor Foreign Policy', *History*, 81 (1996), pp.343–58

CURRIN, J.M., 'England's International Relations, 1485–1509; continuities amid change', in S. Doran and G. Richardson, *Tudor England and its Neighbours* (2005)

DAVIES, C.S.L., 'The Administration of the Royal Navy under Henry VIII; the origins of the Navy Board', *English Historical Review*, 80 (1965), pp.268–88

DAVIES, C.S.L., 'England and the French War', in J. Loach and R. Tittler, *The Mid-Tudor Polity* (1980)

DAWSON, J.E.A., *The Politics of Religion in the Age of Mary, Queen of Scots* (2002)

DIETZ, F.C., *English Government Finance, 1485–1558* (1964)

DIETZ, F.C., *English Public Finance, 1558–1641* (1964)

DORAN, Susan, *Monarchy and Matrimony; the Courtships of Elizabeth I* (1996)

DUFFY, E., *The Stripping of the Altars* (1992)

ELLIS, S.G., *Tudor Ireland* (1985)

ELLIS, S.G., *Tudor Frontiers and Noble Power* (1995)

ELTON, G.R., *The Tudor Constitution* (1982)

ELTON, G.R., *Thomas Cromwell* (1990)

FISSEL, M., *English Warfare, 1511–1642* (2001)

FRASER, Antonia, *Mary Queen of Scots* (1969)

FRIEL, Ian, *The Good Ship; ship building and technology in England, 1200–1520* (1995)

GLASGOW, T., 'The Navy in Philip and Mary's War', *Mariner's Mirror*, 53 (1967), pp.321–42

GLASGOW, T., 'The navy in the first undeclared Elizabethan war', *Mariner's Mirror*, 54 (1968), pp.23–37

GLASGOW, T., 'The maturing of naval administration, 1556–1564', *Mariner's Mirror*, 56 (1970), pp.3–26

GLASGOW, T., 'List of ships in the Royal Navy from 1539 to 1588', *Mariner's Mirror*, 56 (1970), pp.299–307

GLASGOW, T., 'Vice admiral Woodhouse and shipkeeping in the Tudor navy', *Mariner's Mirror*, 63 (1977), pp.253–63

GREENBLATT, S.J., *Sir Walter Raleigh; the Renaissance Man and his Roles* (1973)

GRUMMITT, D., *Henry VII, 1457–1509; the First Tudor King* (2009)

GUNN, S.J., 'The Duke of Suffolk's march on Paris in 1523', *English Historical Review*, 101 (1986), pp.596–634

GUNN, S.J., *Charles Brandon, Duke of Suffolk, 1484–1545* (1988)

GUNN, S.J., *Early Tudor Government* (1995)

GUNSON, W.N., 'Who was Sir Richard Hawkins?' *Mariner's Mirror*, 80 (1994), pp.72–3

HAMMER, P.E.J., ed., *Warfare in Early Modern Europe, 1450–1660* (2007)

HARBISON, E.H., *Rival Ambassadors at the Court of Queen Mary* (1940)

HOAK, D.E., 'The coronations of Edward VI, Mary I and Elizabeth I, and the transformation of the Tudor monarchy', in C.S. Knighton and R. Mortimer, *Westminster Abbey Reformed, 1540–1640* (2003)

HOOK, Judith, *The Sack of Rome, 1527* (1972)

HOYLE, R.W., ed., *The Military Survey of Gloucestershire, 1522* (1993)

HOYLE, R.W., *The Pilgrimage of Grace and the Politics of the 1530s* (2001)

IVES, E.W., *The Life and Death of Anne Boleyn* (2004)

JAMES, M.E., 'English Politics and the Concept of Honour', *Past and Present Supplement 3*, (1978)

JAMES, Susan, *Katheryn Parr* (1999)

JONES, M.K., *Bosworth 1485: the Psychology of a Battle* (2002)

JONES, N.L., *Faith by Statute* (1982)

JORDAN, W.K., *Edward VI: the Young King* (1968)

JORDAN, W.K., *Edward VI: the Threshold of Power* (1970)

KAMEN, H., *Philip of Spain* (1997)

KEEGAN, J., *A History of Warfare* (1993)

KEEN, Maurice, *Chivalry* (1984)

KELSEY, H., *Sir Francis Drake; the Queen's Pirate* (1998)

KELSEY, H., *Sir John Hawkins, Queen Elizabeth's Slave Trader* (2003)

KING, J.N., *Tudor Royal Iconography: Literature and Art in a time of Religious Crisis* (1989)

KING, J.N., 'Queen Elizabeth I: Representations of the Virgin Queen', *Renaissance Quarterly*, 43 (1990), pp.30–74

KNECHT, R.J., *Francis I* (1982)

LOACH, J., *Parliament and Crown in the Reign of Mary Tudor* (1986)

LOACH, J., *Edward VI* (1999)

LOADES, D., *The Tudor Court* (1986)

LOADES, D., *Mary Tudor; a life* (1989)

LOADES, D., *The Reign of Mary Tudor* (1991)

LOADES, D., *The Tudor Navy* (1992)

LOADES, D., *John Dudley, Duke of Northumberland* (1996)

LOADES, D., *Tudor Government* (1997)

LOADES, D., and C.S. Knighton, *The Anthony Roll of Henry VIII* (2000)

LOADES, D., *England's Maritime Empire* (2000)

LOADES, D., and C.S. Knighton, *Letters from the Mary Rose* (2002)

LOADES, D., *Elizabeth I* (2003)

LOADES, D., *Mary Tudor: the Tragical History of the first Queen of England* (2006)

LOADES, D., *Henry VIII: Court, Church and Conflict* (2007)

LOADES, D., and C.S. Knighton, 'Lord Lisle and the Invasion of Scotland, 1544' in *The Naval Miscellany*, VII (2008)

MACCAFFREY, W., *The Shaping of the Elizabethan Regime* (1969)

MACCULLOCH, D., *Suffolk under the Tudors* (1986)

MACCULLOCH, D., *Tudor Church Militant* (1999)

MARSHALL, R.K., *Mary of Guise* (1977)

MARTIN, C., and G. Parker, *The Spanish Armada* (1988)

MATTINGLY, Garrett, *Catherine of Aragon* (1963)

MILLER, G., *Tudor Mercenaries and Auxilliaries, 1485–1547* (1980)

MILLER, H., *Henry VIII and the English Nobility* (1986)

MURPHY, B., *Bastard Prince: Henry VIII's lost son* (2001)

NOLAN, J.S., *Sir John Norreys and the Elizabethan Military World* (1997)

OPPENHEIM, M., *A History of the Administration of the Royal Navy … 1509 to 1660* (1896)

OPPENHEIM, M., *Naval Accounts and Inventories of the Reign of Henry VII* (1896)

PARKER, G., *The Dutch Revolt* (1977)

PARRY, G.J.R., 'Inventing the Good Duke of Somerset', *Journal of Ecclesiastical History*, 40 (1989), pp.370–80

PEEBLES, R.L., 'The Many Faces of Sir Walter Raleigh', *History Today*, 48/3 (1998), pp.17–24

PIERCE, H., *Margaret Pole, Countess of Salisbury* (2003)

PIERSON, P., *Commander of the Armada: the Seventh Duke of Medina Sidonia* (1989)

POTTER, D.L., 'The Duc de Guise and the fall of Calais', *English Historical Review*, 98 (1983) pp.481–512

PUGH, T.B., 'Henry VII and the English Nobility' in Bernard, ed., *The Tudor Nobility* (1992)

READ, Conyers, *Mr. Secretary Walsingham and the Policy of Queen Elizabeth* (1925)

READ, Conyers, 'Queen Elizabeth's seizure of Alba's pay ships', *Journal of Modern History*, 5 (1933), pp.443–64

READ, Conyers, *Mr. Secretary Cecil and Queen Elizabeth* (1955)

REDWORTH, G., *In Defence of the Church Catholic: a Life of Stephen Gardiner* (1990)

REDWORTH, G., '"Matters Impertinent to women": Male and Female Monarchy under Philip and Mary', *English Historical Review*, 112 (1997), pp.597–613

RICHARDSON, W.C., *Mary Tudor: the White Queen* (1970)

RICHMOND, C., 'The war at Sea', in K. Fowler, ed., *The Hundred Years War* (1971)

RODGER, N.A.M., *The Safeguard of the Sea* (1997)

RODRIGUEZ- SALGADO, M.J., and Ian Friel, 'The Battle at Sea', in *Armada 1588–1988, An International Exhibition* (1988)

ROSS, Charles, *Richard III* (1981)

ROWSE, A.L., *Sir Richard Grenville of the Revenge* (1937)

RULE, Margaret, *The Mary Rose* (1982)

RUSSELL, F.W., *Kett's Rebellion in Norfolk* (1859)

RUSSELL, J.G., *The Field of Cloth of Gold* (1969)

SCARISBRICK, J.J., *Henry VIII* (1968)

SILKE, J.J., *Kinsale* (1970)

SMITH, L.B., *A Tudor Tragedy* (1961)

SMITH, L.B., *Treason in Tudor England: Politics and Paranoia* (1986)

SPENCE, R.T., *The Privateering Earl* (1995)

SPONT, A., *Letters and Papers relating to the War with France, 1512–13* (NRS 1897)

STONE, L., *The Crisis of the Aristocracy, 1558–1640* (1965)

STRICKLAND, M. and R. Hardy, *The Great Warbow* (2005)

STRONG, Sir Roy, *Tudor and Jacobean Portraits* (1969)

STRONG, Sir Roy, *The Cult of Elizabeth* (1977)

SUTHERLAND. N.M., *Princes, Politics and Religion, 1547–1589* (1984)

TAYLOR, E.G.R., *The Haven Finding Art: A History of Navigation* (1967)

THOMPSON, I.A.A., 'The Invincible Armada', in *Royal Armada* (1988)

THOMPSON, J.A.F., *The Later Lollards, 1414–1520* (1965)

TIGHE, W.J., 'The Gentlemen Pensioners, the Duke of Northumberland, and the attempted coup of July 1553', *Albion*, 19 (1987), pp.1–11

USHERWOOD, S. and E., *The Counter Armada, 1596* (1983)

WARNICKE, R., *The Marrying of Anne of Cleves* (2000)

WATERS, D.W., *The Art of Navigation in Elizabethan and Early Stuart Times* (1958)

WILLIAMS, Penry, *The Tudor Regime* (1979)

WOOD, A., *The 1549 Rebellions and the Making of Early Modern England* (2007)

WORMALD, J., *Mary Queen of Scots: A Study in Failure* (1988)

YOUNG, Alan, *Tudor and Jacobean Tournaments* (1987)

INDEX

Figures in **bold** refer to plate numbers.

K

Kett, Robert 106–7
Killigrew, Harry 129–30
Knox, John 145

L

Lane, Ralph 172
Le Havre 149–50, 155
Lee, Sir Henry 159
Legge, Robert 111
Leith 87–8, 102, 104, 155
Leo X, Pope 50, 52, 54, 63, 69, 76
Louis XII, King of France 27, 42, 45, 46, 48, 50, 52
Louise of Savoy, Queen Mother of France, 71
Lovel, Francis, Viscount 25
Luis, Dom, of Portugal 120
Luther, Martin 77–8

M

Madre de Dios capture of the 187–9
Malen, John 132–3
Manners, Henry, Earl of Rutland, 135
Mansell, Sir Rhys 86
Margaret of Anjou, Queen, 12, 12–13, 30
Margaret of Austria, Regent of the Low Countries, 67, 68
Margaret of Burgundy, 25
Mary, Queen of Scots 85, 105, 146, 148, 155, 157, 169–70, 220n1
Mary I, Queen **9, 10**, 115–16, 118–38, 139–40, 141, 150–1, 196, 199
Mary Rose, loss of the 93–4
Matilda, Empress 11
Maximilian, Holy Roman Emperor 49–50, 54
Medici, Catherine de, Queen Mother and Regent of France, 147, 159
Medway, the 51
Merlin 22

Montalembert, André de 104, 105
Montreuil 90, 91, 109
More, Sir Thomas, Lord Chancellor, 77
Morlaix 64, 65
Morton, John, Cardinal Archbishop of Canterbury, Lord Chancellor, 30, 208n55
Mountjoy, Charles, Lord 194–5, 203
Mulcaster, Richard 141

N

Navarre 45, 63
Neville, Anne, Queen 12
Neville, George, Lord Abergavenny 34
Neville, Richard, Earl of Warwick 15, 17, 32
Newcastle upon Tyne 87
Nieupoort 168
Noailles, Antoine de, French Ambassador, 125
Nombre de Dios 164
Norham Castle, siege of 28–9
Norris, Sir John 174, 186–7, 192–4, 199, 203
Norton, Richard 220n5

O

O'Neill, Hugh, Earl of Tyrone 194–5
Oppenheim, Michael 27
Osborne, John 96

P

Paget, William, Lord 119
Paimpol 192–3
Palmer, Henry 174–5
Parr, Catherine, Queen, 86, 213n20
Parr, William, Earl of Essex, Marquis of Northampton 73
Patten, William 101–3, 145
Paul III, Pope 80

PICTURE CREDITS

The publishers would like to thank the following for permission to reproduce their material. Every care has been taken to trace copyright holders, but we will be happy to rectify any omissions in future editions.

Credits by plate number

1 AKG-images/Sotheby's
2 Getty Images/The Bridgeman Art Library
3 TopFoto/HIP/The Board of Trustees of the Armouries
4 ©The British Library Board. All Rights Reserved, Cotton Augustus III, f.19
5 The National Archives E 36/12/32
6 ©The British Library Board. All Rights Reserved, Add. 22047
7 Dreamstime/Martin Garnham
8 The Bridgeman Art Library/Private Collection/© Philip Mould Ltd, London
9 The Bridgeman Art Library/© Isabella Stewart Gardner Museum, Boston, MA, USA
10 The National Archives KB 27/1185/2
11 AKG-images
12 The National Archives E 351/226/1
13 The National Archives MPF 1/6
14 The Bridgeman Art Library/Private Collection
15 TopFoto 16 Getty Images/Hulton Archive

ACKNOWLEDGEMENTS

IN THE COURSE of preparing this book I have incurred many debts of gratitude. To the numerous scholars who have trodden parts of this path before, and particularly to my colleague Dr Charles Knighton, who has done so much to enhance my knowledge of the Tudor navy. To the History Faculty of the University of Oxford, which has extended its hospitality to me, and to Catherine Bradley of the National Archives, who oversaw much of the writing. To my wife Judith for keeping me up to date with what happens online, and to the helpful staff of the Bodleian Library. I would also like to thank Sheila Knight of the National Archives for seeing the book through its final stages, as well as Slaney Begley for her editorial contributions, Ken Wilson for the sympathetic page and jacket design and Julia Ruxton, Kim Bishop and Alan Rutter for picture researching, proofreading and indexing the text. The errors and omissions remain my own responsibility.

DAVID LOADES
September 2009

Also from the National Archives by David Loades...

HENRY VIII
Court, church and conflict

FROM RENAISSANCE PRINCE to bloated monarch, Henry VIII dominated his country and court for almost 40 years. His reign changed the lives of nobles and commoners, priests and laymen, sending shock waves well beyond England's shores. Yet this clever and charismatic king survived rebellion, religious turmoil and the enmity of Catholic Europe, manipulating the most powerful—and ambitious—personalities of the age.

As intriguing as its subject, *Henry VIII* explores the king's volatile relations with courtiers, churchmen, advisers and wives. It shows how the larger-than-life ruler wielded his power—at court, in wars, in government, over his nobles, and in his ruthless, politically driven quest for an heir. David Loades draws on a wealth of knowledge of the Tudor period to reveal the man behind the monarch and the lasting legacy of England's most celebrated king.

ISBN 978 1 905615 42 1 (paperback)

THE CECILS
Privilege and power behind the throne

WILLIAM AND ROBERT CECIL were the most powerful statesmen
of the Elizabethan age. As privy councillors and diplomats, patrons
and spymasters they shaped events at the heart of history, from
the execution of Mary Queen of Scots and the aftermath of the
Armada to the unravelling of the Gunpowder Plot that threatened
James I's new regime. Outsiders to a perilous world of courtiers and
conspiracies, they nevertheless survived to secure Elizabeth's realm
and to establish James as her successor without rebellion or civil war.

In *The Cecils*, historian David Loades explores the compelling
public and private lives of father and son. He probes their often
volatile relationships with unsatisfactory children, royal favourites
and wayward monarchs, showing the remarkable range—and
limits—of their power and influence. He reveals how these strong
advocates of caution took great personal risks, and celebrated their
growing wealth in the great houses of Burghley, Theobalds and
Hatfield. The result is a fascinating insight into the successes and
failures of two extraordinary men.

ISBN 978 1 905615 55 1 (paperback)